BETHANY KEY

DARK PSYCHOLOGY AND MANIPULATION

2 Books In 1:

The Ultimate Guide to Mind Control, The art of Persuasion, Learn how to Influence People, Analyze Body Language , Gaslighting, Secrets how to Defend Yourself from Manipulators

THIS BOOK INCLUDES

BOOK 1:

DARK PSYCHOLOGY SECRETS AND
MANIPULATION TECHNIQUES:

Learn the art of how to analyze people, understand body language, read people. Discover methods for mind control and defending yourself from manipulators.

BOOK 2:

MANIPULATION AND MIND CONTROL:

The ultimate guide to learning how to recognize dark psychology techniques and use the secrets of emotional intelligence and influence to your advantage

DARK PSYCHOLOGY SECRETS AND MANIPULATION TECHNIQUES:

Table Of Contents

MANIPULATION AND MIND CONTROL:

Table Of Contents

BETHANY KEY

DARK PSYCHOLOGY SECRETS AND MANIPULATION TECHNIQUES:

Learn the art of how to analyze people, understand body language, read people. Discover methods for mind control and defending yourself from manipulators.

Introduction

People with some of the "Dark Triad" personality traits are fond of manipulating other people that may seem vulnerable to some extent. When a person manipulates another individual, they are focusing on fulfilling their selfish interests. If you are a vulnerable individual, you should focus on learning more about the "Dark Triad" traits.

In this book, you will also learn more about some of the deception tactics used by these individuals. By reading through this dark psychology handbook, you will learn more about the human mind and behavior. Also, you will get to learn more about how people have mastered the art of manipulating their colleagues for their benefit.

Dark psychology is about control and manipulation of the mind. It is said that we all have darknesswithin us as human beings.

After clarifying this otherwise broad subject, let us now attempt to familiarize ourselves with the various consequences of dark psychology. The victim and the perpetrator both feel the consequences of dark psychology.

With great power comes great responsibility, and as you learn to manipulate the minds of other people, you can also realize that you can influence and sway people—for better or for worse. You can convince someone else to do something that is naturally destructive or manipulative, or you can encourage them to do something that you know will make them happier, influencing them to act in ways that you know will help them.

Within this book, you will start to get a taste of exactly this; you will start to discover how dark psychology and manipulation exist. You will learn all about how manipulation is possible, how it works, and why it works the way it does, as well as the signs to note if someone else is attempting to manipulate you. This is essential information for you—you need to know what is going on so that you can guarantee that you can protect yourself. Manipulation itself is not inherently evil or problematic—it is the act of molding someone else to your liking. It is to shape them, much like how you can manipulate clay or other building materials. It does not have to be inherently dangerous or hurtful—though it certainly can be.

In this book, you will learn about why we are so vulnerable to dark psychology, diving into understanding that ultimately the way that people's minds work leaves them open.

You do not have to wait until you face manipulation before you start protecting yourself. It is wise to gain knowledge and use it to protect yourself from dark psychology. Purchasing this book is the first step towards being an individual who is aware of all the danger that lurks around. You need to protect yourself and your family from people who use dark psychology techniques to gain control.

Even if you have never heard about dark psychology, the book breaks down the topic in a simple way, making it easy for you to understand. The book focuses on key topics such as manipulation techniques and how they work. This book covers each of the topics discussed in detail, breaking the points to the most basic level so that it can be understood.

The book is not only based on the theoretical explanation of dark psychology, but it is the most practical guide you will come across. You will get to learn practical ways of avoiding manipulation. You will look at the practical ways of avoiding manipulative people and how to ensure that you stay safe. The actions you can take are clearly outlined to help you stand outside the manipulation window. This book will help you gain some kind of immunity against manipulation.

As you enjoy reading the book, keep in mind that you may also use manipulation yourself to grow in life. As much as dark psychology can be used to blackmail your life, you can also use it to blackmail other people. If you choose to use dark psychology to blackmail people and gain whatever you wish in life, you will be in a good place to experience success. As we delve into the details, follow keenly to pick out everything you need for your life and self-protection.

The following chapters will discuss everything that you need to know about manipulation and mind control. Do you want to make sure that you can get others to agree with what you like? Are you interested in getting a better lifestyle, getting people to purchase something, and so much more? If so, then this guidebook is so amazing, especially if you like to learn about manipulation and how it can help you out!

Getting what you want in this world is important. Often people will say no to you,but if you know how to manipulate and persuade, you can easily get people to always say yes.

Mind control is the last resort for dealing with people who won't do what you want.

Chapter 1:

What is Dark Psychology?

WHAT IS DARK PSYCHOLOGY

Dark psychology refers to the study of the psychological nature of human beings to prey on one another. Psychology shows that all human beings tend to prey on one another to harm for self-gain. This is something that has manifested among humans since time immemorial. This behavior does not only affect humans, but also affects other animals. Other animals tend to intentionally want to hurt each other without specific reasons. The difference between other animals and humans is that, in most cases, humans use dark psychology for personal gain. According to *Psychology Today*, at least 99.9% of the instances where human beings try to harm others are motivated by personal gain. However, there is a small percentage of human beings that may intend to harm others for unknown reasons.

The study of these human tendencies opens your mind to the reality of the world. You should understand the techniques that dark psychologists use and how they approach the subject if you wish to be free from manipulation. One of the most dangerous dark psychology approaches is the use of NLP.

WHO USES DARK PSYCHOLOGY TO INFLUENCE PEOPLE?

You might be thinking that you do not have to learn dark psychology because you do not have the intention to control people. While this might be true, it is important to learn dark psychology. In reality, we do not learn dark psychology so that we can control people. We only learn dark psychology so that we may protect ourselves from manipulative individuals.

Even if you do not learn dark psychology, you will still encounter dark people. Although all human beings are dark to some extent, some have an extreme level of evil in their system. Some individuals are constantly looking for another person to hurt. You must protect yourself from those individuals by being able to read their thoughts and intentions even before they start talking to you.

There are several groups of people who thrive in using dark psychology to control others.

You need to protect yourself from them. Some of the people that use dark psychology include coworkers, politicians and romantic partners.

COMPETITORS AT THE WORKPLACE

You might be thinking that there is a special group of people who use dark psychology techniques. The reality is that all people are dark. If you are keen, you should have noticed that even your mother might use dark psychology to control your life. The most common causes of dark psychology occur in the workplace. This is because there is a motivation to succeed. Since all people have a desire to succeed in whatever they do, they will do whatever it takes to gain control at the workplace. You must be very careful at your workplace if you hold a high position. In most cases, dark psychologists target high positions. Dark psychologists know that if they can get in your mind and extract information through techniques such as NLP, they might find a strong reason to control your life. One thing to learn is to hide any information related to your wishes. Unless you can hide any relevant information about your personality, you may end up suffering in the hands of manipulators.

POLITICAL LEADERS

Another group of individuals who use dark psychology are political leaders. Politicians will do whatever they need to gain power and influence.

One of the biggest motives for dark psychology is having influence. If a person wants to control your life, they will strive to gain power and influence. Political leaders learn the art of mass control by using dark psychology techniques such as brainwashing and persuasion.

When they learn about your weaknesses, they can use those weaknesses against you. They use dark psychology to discredit their opponents and use manipulation to control the voters.

CONTROLLING RELATIONSHIP PARTNERS

The other group of people that thrives in using dark psychology involves controlling partners. Some individuals only feel comfortable if they are the heads of their relationships. They work hard to see that they take charge of the relationship. If you happen to be in a relationship with a person who loves to be in control, you should be very careful. Such people will do everything to ensure that they control every aspect of the relationship. A controlling relationship partner does not give you the freedom to make choices. They will use techniques such as NLP to learn about your personality and try and control your actions. If a person can study and master your ways, it is easy for that person to control your life. Dark psychologists use NLP to capture your thoughts. They first understand your way of operating and way of life, and then they use it directly against you.

COMPOSITION OF DARK PSYCHOLOGY

Dark Psychology includes everything that helps make us who we are related to our evil side. This proverbial cancer is present in all societies, all faiths, and all of human existence. From the time we are born to the moment of death, there is an aspectwithin us that some have named immoral and others have categorized as unlawful, deviant and psychopathic. Dark Psychology brings a third philosophical concept which gives a different view to these behaviors as compared to religious dogmas and ideas of modern social science.

Some individuals commit these same actions in Dark Psychology, and do so for power, money, romantic love, vengeance, or any other recognized intent. Without a target, they commit those horrendous acts. In simple words, its ends don't justify its means. There are individuals who defy and wound othersfor the sake of doing so. That potential lies within each of us. The area which I explore is a possibility to harm someone without cause, justification or intent. Dark Psychology implies that this dark potentiality is extremely complicated and even harder to describe.

Dark Psychology implies that we all have the ability for predator behaviors, and this capability has the full right to our thoughts, feelings and experiences. We all have this capability, as you will learn throughout this book, but only some of us act upon it. At one time or another, we all had feelings and thoughts about intending to behave painfully. We have all had thoughts that we want to seriously damage others without kindness. If you're truthful with yourself, you'll have to agree that you've had ideas and feltlike you wanted to do heinous deeds.

Because of the fact we perceive ourselves to be some kind of virtuous species, one would want to assume that these feelings and thoughts would not emerge. Sadly, all of us have these ideas, and thankfully never practiced them. Dark Psychology suggests that there are individuals who have similar ideas, emotions and experiences but operate upon them in a meticulously planned or impulsive fashion. The important distinction is that they respond upon them, whereas others have merely short-lived thoughts and emotions to do so.

Dark Psychology claims that this type of predator is intentional and has a certain logical, purpose-oriented motive. Religious belief, philosophy, psychology and other belief systems have been cogent in their ways to explain Dark Psychology. It is true that almost all human behavior connected to evil actions is purposeful and purpose-oriented, though Dark Psychology implies that there is a region where purposeful behavior and purpose-oriented motivation appear to become vague. There is a spectrum of maltreatment of Dark Psychology varying from opinions to pure deranged deviance, with no evident reasoning or purpose. This spectrum, Dark

Continuum, allows the Dark Psychology philosophy to be conceived.

Dark Psychology identifies that aspect of the human psyche or basic human status that enables unethical behavior and can even help persuade it. Some of the features of this change in behavior are the absence of apparently reasonable motivation, its universality, as well as its lack of clarity in many instances. This basic human condition is assumed by Dark Psychology to be different or an outgrowth of evolution. Let's dig at those very simple evolutionary tenets. First, consider that we evolved from many other animals and are the shining beacon of all animal life at present. Our frontal lobe enabled us to become the entity at the peak. Now let us presume that being alpha predators doesn't exempt us from our animal impulses and aggressive behavior.

Chapter 2:

Dark Psychology Traits

MACHIAVELLIANISM

This method traces the roots of Machiavelli, the renowned political philosopher. Machiavelli's well-known work on influence and political power,' The Prince,' shares with the rest of the world his version of ideas, principles and tactics that have preserved the purpose of a kind of design for those who could seek influence throughout history. Based on this, we then wonder what this Machiavellian individual is and how he is doing. What puts this specific strategy on the map is essentially the manipulator's ability to concentrate only on his interests at all moments, the exercise of cruel strength and cruelty, the knowledge of the significance of picture, and the perception and surface appearance. So, the ramifications and implications that they generally have are well understood and evaluated as to how they might affect their life if they do that in a certain manner.You can simply define a Machiavellian person, as their discourse often revolves around something like, "How does this help me and how does this outcome impact my public reputation?"Machiavellian people do what they do personally, whilst at the same moment being able to preserve the highest government picture without being the wiser. Perhaps one of the greatest examples of such a person is the former US president Bill Clinton. While in office, he succumbed to his sexual wishes time and again while at the same moment maintaining anadmiration for him. This is truly a benefit over the majority of the same lifestyle leaders, but it is spoiled by the general public. Another instance is President Barrack Obama and George W. Bush in the political arena. During his time in office, Barrack Obama developed his love for peace and capitalized on it, while Bush strengthened his picture as that of a man always having war on his mind. Obama manipulated the masses to build a public perception that even evil bush had tried to serve his one purpose. This is despite the reality that the two presidents were as militant as the next.

For many people who do not meet the clinical definition of Machiavellianism, their government figures usually reflect their real private self. Everyone shapes theirimage and behavior in public a bit, but in general, most people's outward image is nothing more than a polished portrait of who they are. They often have a good idea of what they are really and the person they often portrayin the public eye. Perhaps the finest instance is that of serial killers. Often the best have escaped the grip of the law because their outer picture is the farthest away from their morbid fascination. The most popular instance is that of the famous serial killer Ted Bundy. According to those who knew him, he was a beautiful guy. He was also very eloquent and just showed that nobody thought that he had a single poor bone in his body. This allowed him to kill up to 30 females before he was finally captured.

Examples of such a difference between intent and appearance in less extreme fields than serial killing can be discovered. There are numerous stories of company leaders who succeed by ruthlessly cutting employment and making profits as much as possible. Concerning Machiavellianism, the very best of these managers can get people to understand that they are compelled or even compassionate! Such rulers are almost role models for those who only want to serve their wishes, and at the same time appear to be "a person of the people." Another characteristic of Machiavellian men is a willingness to exploit people. Let us look at an instance to understand this well. A newcomer to a specific office that has such Machiavellian characteristics would see each colleague, boss or team member as a resource or part of a puzzle to use and use. The Machiavellian would not see other people as fellow humans, but would see a series of strategic threats and weaknesses to manage, exploit or neutralize. This is an important part of why Machiavellians are so aware of how they are. They know that this outward image is the key to efficiently exercise effect and exploit everyone they come across.

Another feature of the Machiavellians is the instillation of fear into their surroundings. This stems directly from "The Prince," who urges people to be both fearedand loved at the same time. If this is not possible, the book states that those who are feared are easier to love. At the same time, the concept of loveand fearis linked directly to the Machiavellian trait of separating public and private perception. The perfect Machiavellian can inspire fear and obedience in people who genuinely pretend to feel higher love than fear.

PSYCHOPATHY

It would be very hard to tell you in black and white what psychopathy is, but the fundamental definition of psychopathy , or instead of a psychopath , is that specific person who has a psychological disorder. When most people hear these people mentioned, the first picture they often get is that they look old, with a machete and a mask, like John Wayne Gacy. But their identity's truth is far from that. It is most probable that they will be very beautiful strangers who win over their victims by havingjust the correct amount of charm before they ultimately ruin or end their life. Surprisingly, several trials, experiments and observations have shown that many of these people are at the helm of the globe of the company. Most individuals are starting to see psychopathy as more of an issue for the entire community that the psychopaths themselves have. They are generally programmed to survive in any sector in which they choose to go. This is primarily due to their indifferent opinions about the ordinary human sense of love, empathy and so forth.

In all respects, it is essential to understand how this group of peoplemanifest themselves to detect them at an early stage and to protect them from themselves . Charm is one of the most common conducts of a psychopath. This charm should be understood to be superficial rather than deep, true charm. If you think of a genuinely charming person from your lifetime, you likely recognize that they have favorable features that support external behavioral displays. However, if a person truly shows a charming personality as an expression of goodness, theyshould not be labeled a psychopath. Psychopaths can demonstrate all external charm signs like physical attraction, apparent warmth and an interest in others. The inner motivation behind these outer flags is why they are so red. Psychopaths see the charmas a portion of an equation. The manipulator often asks himself whether it gives the victim a certain emotion to feel in a specific euphoric manner, and also whether the outcome is advantageous or beneficial. They are calculative individuals who are addicted to ordinary human emotions. Lying is another feature that distinguishes psychopaths. All of us lie in our daily lives. This doesn't imply we are all psychopaths necessarily. However, when combined with other features, it can indicate a psychopathic personality. Lying is as natural for a psychopath as breathing is for most people who are psychologically healthy. A psychopath can present reality convincingly at a certain moment as whatever it needs to be. Furthermore, psychopaths do not show outward signs of lying because they have no emotional attachment or feelings of disgust, guilt or excitement about their lies. For psychopaths, lying is just "doing what's needed right now."

An absence of impulse control is another signature element of psychopathy. Most people have procedures and internal controls that prevent them from acting rapidly. These prevention mechanisms are missing for a psychopath. If a psychopath sees an opportunity to take advantage of, it happenswithout hesitation or a second thought. This may involve killing someone they want to kill, rape someone, or steal something they want to steal. This cruel impulsiveness is what makes psychopaths some of the most effective people in fields such as the military and business. The automatic implementation of a crucial action is one of many characteristic non-psychopaths do not have, and this lack is harmful to lives.

The absence of remorse is another feature that distinguishes psychopaths from non-psychopaths. Many people who have committed an atrocity, such as murder, feelprofoundly guilty of what they have done and take their own livesdue to these feelings. Psychopaths don't choose to be remorseful— they can't do it physically. Asking a psychopath to feel remorse is like asking a deaf person to listen to music. The absence of guilt is strongly linked to a lack of remorse. Usually, people feel guilty when they break a certain moral standard they value themselves. Since psychopaths don't think properly or incorrectly, they just think helpful or unnecessary; their guilt is a foreign concept. The closest to a psychopath's guilt or remorse is regret that it has not conducted its psychopathic deeds following its elevated norms.

NARCISSISM

If you ask someone who they believe a narcissus is, I can bet that the most probable response to get is "a person who just enjoys themself". This is in the right line, but not precise enough, especially when narcissism is grasped by a dark triad lens. You can have self-love without being a narcissist. So, what are some distinctions in the Dark Triad spectrum between an extremely self-esteemed person and someone narcissistic? Someone who meets the medical diagnostic criteria for narcissism, so much so that they are considered psychological disorders, can show a range of the following features continually. They are generally prisoners of the inflated sense of self-worth, which manifests itself in many ways. This means that they see their life as the most significant and unique thing that ever happened. Often this conduct represents their self-worth.

Narcissists are likely to be extremely self-absorbed, so much as to see their lives as unique and ones of the most significant in history. In their minds, narcissists are not only special— they are superior. They are better individuals, better than "ordinary" individuals. They are better. Your conduct represents your feelings of self-worth. Oneof the common external manifestations of narcissism is being unable to tolerate criticism or dissent in any way. The need to be flattered is comparable to that which must be agreed upon. Narcissists need on-going praise, support and gratitude, and tend to organize their lives in a way that offers them constant access to other people who fulfill this need.

After looking at the foundation of this special ghost theme of dark psychology, let us now dive into how the dark triad manifests themselves in the conduct of different people.

The fantasies of one'scomplete strength and high feeling of significance are twoof the most common features in almost all narcissists. Most of these people are to blame for the continual praise they have received as kids while speaking about these fantasies. As adults, these people will still require love from all over because they have fostered the impression that their colleagues are the most important.

The inflationary sense of self-worth experienced by narcissists internally also has implications for their external reality. This usually shows in two aspects–consent and praise, or criticism and hatred of dismissal. Lobbying and consensus are like oxygen for the narcissistic ego while criticism and dissent are like poison. Picture an inherited dictator to understand how narcissism looks when it comes to its logical conclusion. Such persons ask for the worship of those over whom they have power, the construction of a monument and complete obedience and appreciation. Any act of disagreement or disagreement shall soon and brutally be punished. North Korea would be an optimal modern example of the extreme expression of narcissism. The leaders of that nation ask for reverence as Gods and torture anyone who even dares to express an opinion or idea which is not completely following the official state doctrine.

Chapter 3:

What is Emotional Manipulation? & Types of Emotional Manipulation

E motional manipulators use mind games to take power. The ultimate objective is to use the ability to control the other person. A healthy relationship is established on confidence, understanding and mutual respect.

It is true of intimate as well as professional relationships. Sometimes people try to exploit certain aspects of a relationship so they can profit in some way. There can be visible signs of emotional manipulation. They are often difficult to identify, especially when they do happen to you.

How are Emotional Manipulation Tactics in Dark Psychology Used?

None of us want to be the target of manipulation, but, quite often, it happens. We may not be exposed to someone directly in Dark Psychology. Still, daily we face dark psychology tactics with average, everyday people like you and I. Such strategies are often used in advertisements, web ads, sales techniques and even the actions of our bosses. If you have children (especially teenagers), you will most likely experience these strategies as your kids play with behaviors to get what they want and try autonomy for themselves. The people you trust and love often use covert manipulation and dark persuasion. Here are some of the techniques that ordinary, everyday people use most frequently.

SHOWING LOVE

Best wishes, companionship or buttering someone up to make a request.

FALSIFYING

Untruths, distortion, partial truths, false tales

LOVE DENIAL

Holding back on attention and affection

WITHDRAWAL

Avoiding people or silent treatment

RESTRICTION OF CHOICE

Giving those choices that separate you from the option that nobody wants to make

Reverse Psychology

Saying one thing to a person or doing something to inspire them to do the opposite; it is what you want.

Semantic Manipulation

Using terms meant to have a shared or collective sense, but later the manipulator tells you that theyhavea different definition and interpretation of the conversation. Words are important and influential. By knowing these, you will manage to tackle being manipulated. These are to remind us all how easy it is to use those tactics to get what we want.

They Maintain Home Court Advantage

Whether it's your real home or just a favorite coffee shop, being in your home turf can be inspiring. If the other individuals often insist on meeting within their domain, they might be attempting to create a power imbalance. They claim to own that space, which leaves you at a disadvantage.

For example: "Come when you can to my office. I'm too late to walk to you." "You know how far. I'm on a drive. Coming over tonight."

They Come Close Very Quickly

In the typical get-to-know-you process, emotional manipulators could skip a few steps. They "share" their most profound flaws and secrets. Nevertheless, what they are doing is trying to make you feel different so that you can share your secrets. Later on, they can use those sensitivities against you. For instance: "I feel like we just communicate on an intense level. That's never happened before." "I've never had someone like you share their dream with me. We are truly meant to be together in this."

THEY LET YOU SHARE YOUR SECRETS FIRST

With some business relationships, this is a popular tactic, but it can also happen in personal ones. If a person wants to establish control, theyshould ask questions of sampling so you can share your thoughts and concerns early on. They can then use your answers to influence your choices, with their secret plan in mind.

For instance: "Gosh, I've never heard good things about that firm. What have you been experiencing?" "Alright, you're going just to have to tell me why you're crazy about me again."

THEY TWIST THE FACTS

Emotional manipulators are masters of manipulating reality to confuse you with lies, fibs, or misstatements. They can exaggerate incidents, so they appear more vulnerable. They may also underestimate their role in a dispute to gain support for you. For instance: "I asked a question about the project, and she came to me, screaming how I've never done anything to help her, but you know I do, right?" "I cried and didn't sleep a lot all night."

THEY INVOLVE YOU IN INTELLECTUAL BULLYING

When you ask a question, someone overwhelms you with numbers, jargon, or evidence, and you may experience emotional manipulation. Some of them presume to be the expert, and their "knowledge" is imposed upon you. That is particularly common in circumstances of financesor sales.

For example: "You are new to this, so I wouldn't expect you to understand." "I know it's a lot of numbers for you, so I'm going to go through it slowly again."

THEY INVOLVE YOU IN BUREAUCRATIC BULLYING

Additionally, emotional manipulators in the business setting can try to weigh you down with paperwork, red tape, procedures, or anything that might get in your way. It is a distinct possibility when you express accountability or ask questions that call into question their shortcomings or weaknesses. For example: "This will be way too hard for you. I would just quit now and save the effort." "You have no idea what a nightmare you are making for yourself.

THEY MAKE YOU FEEL SORRY IF YOU ASK ANY QUESTIONS

When you ask questions or offer some advice, an emotional manipulator may respond aggressively or try to draw you into an argument. This technique lets them manipulate your choices and influence your decisions. They can also use the situation to make you feel guilty for voicing your concernsin the first place. For instance: "I don't understand why you just don't trust me." "You know I'm just an emotional person. I can't help but always want to know where you are."

THEY ALWAYS PREFER TO DISCUSS THEIR ISSUES

If you are having a bad day, an emotional manipulator can seize the opportunity to raise their questions.

The goal is to invalidate what you are experiencing. This is so you are forced to concentrate on manipulators and put your emotional energy on their issues. For instance: "Do you think this is bad? You do not need to deal with a cube-mate who is chatting on the phoneall the time." "Be glad you've got a brother. All my life I felt lonely."

THEY ACT AS A MARTYR

Someone who manipulates the emotions of people enthusiastically wants to help with something, but then changes and drags their feet or looks for ways to avoid agreeing to it. They may act like it ends up being a huge burden, and they will try to exploit your emotions to get out of it.

For example: "I know this is something you need from me. That's just a lot, and I'm already exhausted." "This is more difficult than it looks. When you told me, I don't think you knew that.'

WHEN THEY SAY SOMETHING RUDE, THEY BEHAVE AS THEY WERE JOKING

Critical comments can be interpreted as sarcasm or irony. They can claim they're saying something in jest when it's planting a seed of doubt that they seek to do.

For instance: "Geez, you look exhausted!" Well, if some of you were to get up and walk around your office, you wouldn't be out of breath so quickly."

THEY NEVER TAKE RESPONSIBILITY OF THEIR MISTAKES

Emotional manipulators will never be held responsible for their errors. Nonetheless, they will try to find a way to make you feel bad about all this, from astruggle to a failed project. You might end up apologizing, even if they are the ones to blame. For example: "I just did it because I love you so much." "If you hadn't been to the awards program for your kid, you could have finished the project in the right direction."

They Take the Energy Out of the Hall

Manipulators have a way to go into a room and drag along with them a dark cloud. They want the attention and focus on them, and they want to make sure that everyone in the room notices they are upset, unhappy, or unsatisfied in some way. People tend to try to please the manipulator or "feel good" to support them. They may inquire, "Are you OK? Is there anything wrong?" It is just the opening to feed the compassion and energy of others that the manipulator needs. A sensitive person will feel exhausted and off-balance when they are in the room with a manipulator.

They Always Criticize You

Without the notion of jest or sarcasm, emotional manipulators may reject or weaken you. Their comments are meant to chip away at your self-esteem. They're supposed to mock you and marginalize you. The manipulator also expresses his weaknesses. For example: "Don't you think that suit is somewhat provocative for a meeting with a client? I suppose that's one way to get the wallet." " Everything you do is eat.

They Use Your Feelings Against You

If you're angry, somebody who manipulates you might try to make you feel guilty about your feelings. They may accuse you of being irrational, or of not having invested sufficiently.

They Are Passive Aggressive

Emotional manipulators also attempt to threaten others with aggressive language, overt threats,or absolute rage. Especially when they see that you are uncomfortable with conflict, they'll use it to manipulate you quickly and get their way.

SPECIFIC TYPES OF EMOTIONAL MANIPULATION

Within these major categories of emotional manipulation techniques, psychologists have also identified a wide range of more subtle variations that we all likely encounter daily. These techniques include:

LYING

Dark Triad personalities, particularly psychopaths, are highly skilled at lying and cheating, so often we may not detect their intent until it is too late. Beware of those who have demonstrated a pattern of dishonesty.

LYING BY OMISSION

Lying by omission is a little more subtle. The predator may not say anything untrue, but may withhold necessary information to cause you to fail.

DENIAL

Often the damage from emotional manipulation is inflicted after the fact. When you confront someone with evidence of their dishonesty and abuse, their refusal to admit wrongdoing can cause even greater psychological harm.

RATIONALIZATION

The increase in popular news media has led to the growth of public relations and marketing firms who produce "spin" to deflect criticism in both political and corporate environments. Rationalization is a form of spin, in which a manipulator explains away their abuse.

MINIMIZATION

Like rationalization, a minimization is a form of denial in which the predator understates the seriousness of their offense.

SELECTIVE ATTENTION OR INATTENTION

Manipulators will pick and choose which parts of an argument or debate should be considered so that only their views are represented.

DIVERSION

Manipulators often resist giving straight answers to questions, particularly when they are confronted by their victims.

Instead, they will divert the conversation to some other topic or change the subject altogether.

EVASION

More serious than a diversion, a manipulative person confronted with his or her guilt will often completely evade responsibility by using long rambling responses filled with so-called "weasel words," like "most people would say," "according to my sources," or other phrases that falsely legitimize their excuses.

COVERT INTIMIDATION

Many manipulative people will make implied threats to discourage further inquiries or resolution.

GUILT-TRIPPING

A true form of emotional manipulation, a manipulator will exploit the integrity and conscientiousness of the victim by accusing them of being too selfish, too irresponsible, or not caring enough.

SHAMING

Although shaming can be used to bring about social change when large corporations or governments advance abusive or discriminatory policies, manipulators may attempt to intimidate their victims by using sharp criticism, sarcastic comments, or insults to make them feel bad.

BLAMING THE VICTIM

This tactic has become increasingly common. When a victim accuses a predator of abuse, the predator will attempt to turn it around by creating a scenario in which the victim alone is responsible for the harm that came to them. The predator may also try to accuse the victim of being the aggressor by complaining about the violation.

PLAYING THE VICTIM

Using the tactic opposite to blaming the victim, the predator will lure a conscientious person into a trap by pretending to have been grievously wounded and cultivating feelings of sympathy. The real plan, however, is to take advantage of the caring nature of the conscientious person by toying with their emotions.

PLAYING THE SERVANT

This tactic is common in environments marked by a strict, well-established chain of command, like the military. Predators become skilled at manipulating this system by creating a persona of suffering and nobility, in which their bad actions are justified as duty, obedience and honor.

SEDUCTION

This technique does not always have to involve sexual conquest or intimacy.

Emotional predators may use flattery and charm to convince people to do their bidding, and they often look for people with low self-esteem.

PROJECTION

This term is used in psychotherapy. Predators who use this technique will look for victims to use as scapegoats.

When a manipulator does something wrong and is confronted, they will "project" their guilt onto the victim to make the victim look like the responsible party.

FEIGNING INNOCENCE

This technique can be used as part of a denial strategy. Under questioning, the manipulator will "play innocent" by pretending that any violation was unintentional, or that they were not the party who committed the violation.

A skilled manipulator who lacks morality and empathy can be very successful at planting the seed of doubt.

FEIGNING CONFUSION

This technique can also be used as part of a denial strategy. Under questioning, the manipulator will "play dumb" or pretend to be confused about the central point of the conflict or dispute.

By creating confusion, the manipulator hopes to damage the confidence of their victim.

PEER PRESSURE

By using claims, whether true or not, that the victim's friends, associates or "everyone else" is doing something, the manipulator will put pressure on theirvictim to change their behavior or attitude.

CATEGORIES OF EMOTIONALLY MANIPULATIVE BEHAVIOR

Understanding the basic dynamics of manipulative and abusive relationships is important. Each of these general types of relationships may be characterized by specific types of behavior. Psychologists have identified many specific techniques of behavior modification commonly employed by emotional manipulators. Some of these techniques include:

POSITIVE REINFORCEMENT

This technique was identified by the behavioral psychologist B.F. Skinner, whose theory of operant conditioning resulted from his experiments with small animals placed in cages. In his experiment to prove the theory of positive reinforcement, he used cages equipped with two levers—one lever did nothing, while the other produced a food pellet whenever the small animal pushed it. Soon, the animals learned through positive reinforcement which lever to push to get their reward.

Emotional manipulators employ positive reinforcement in their strategies by using techniques such as praise, false and superficial demonstrations of emotions such as charm and sympathy, excessive rewards including gifts, money, approval and attention and other outward demonstrations of emotion meant to make the victim feel good.

NEGATIVE REINFORCEMENT

The other part of Skinner's experiment proved the effectiveness of negative reinforcement. For this part of his experiment, small animals were again placed in cages, which were again equipped with two levers. This time, the cages were charged with a mild voltage of electricity that caused slight discomfort to the animals that were placed in them. Once inside the cages, the animals would press one of the two levers. One of the levers did not produce any results, while the other stopped the electrical current, relieving the discomfort. Soon, the animals learned to press the lever that lessened their pain.

Emotional manipulators employ negative reinforcement in their strategies by using techniques such as removing someone from a difficult situation or relieving them of the responsibility to complete a previously agreed job or task in exchange for some type of favor.

INTERMITTENT REINFORCEMENT

Intermittent reinforcement can be either positive or negative and is used to create doubt, fear or uncertainty. An emotional manipulator may "train" their victim by imposing inconsistent reward and punishment mechanisms to lessen the victim's sense of confidence, control and autonomy.

For example, in a romantic relationship, the predator may condition the victim to wear certain clothing, listen to certain music, eat certain types of food and work at a certain type of job. As the victim in this relationship gains confidence, the predator may begin to discourage their victim, who will be caught off guard. As the victim scrambles to respond, the manipulator may again change tactics.

PUNISHMENT

Punishment is a very basic form of emotional manipulation that may involve an entire range of psychologically and emotionally negative and damaging behavior, such as threats, yelling, nagging, complaining, intimidation, insults, guilt and other forms of emotional blackmail. Skilled predators may find a way to incorporate this abusive and controlling behavior into the relationship over time so that the victim will develop a tolerance for abuse.

Traumatic one-trial learning

This technique is related to the use of punishments, but rather than being a feature of a long-term relationship, these punishmentsinvolve discrete episodes in which the manipulator uses verbal abuse, demonstrations of anger and other forms of dominance and intimidation to discourage the victim from certain types of behavior.

Chapter 4:

How to Secretly Analyze People and Understand Body Language

HOW TO READ AND ANALYZE PEOPLE

The best way of escaping dark psychologists is being able to spot them and run away in advance. You should be in a position to determine the behavior and actions of a person and run away from a dark person before they get access to your life. If you allow a dark person into your life, it can become nearly impossible for you to get out of that relationship.

Given that you are trying to understand the character of every person you interact with, you must learn how to read people. Once you are in a position to read a person, you can separate the good people from the evil ones. In this section, we will be looking at the available techniques for reading people. First, hereare the general techniques you will need to read people.

CREATE A BASELINE

You cannot understand anyone if you do not have a reference point. If you want to spot a person who has a certain personality or mental disorder, you should have a baseline. Although people behave differently, there should be basic factors that ring a bell when you meet a new person. Setting a baseline entails putting in place measures or factors of consideration that will determine your interactions.

LOOK FOR DEVIATIONS

After setting a baseline, look for all deviations from that baseline. For instance, you know that when you meet a new person, you will first greet and exchange a few pleasantries. A deviation would be a case where you are meeting a person for the first time, and they want to hug you so tightly as if you have known each other for ages. When you have a baseline, you understand how humans behave in certain situations. You are open to observing any behaviors that are outside the norm. When you are meeting a new person, you can easily observe how they talk about themselves and spot a self-absorbed person.

NOTICE CLUSTERS OF GESTURES

Clusters of gestures include activities or actions that a person does over and over. When you are meeting a new person, you expect that they are unique in a certain way. For you to spot their uniqueness, you have to observe their actions. A person who is unique in a certain way may do certain actions over and over again. When you have a person who does something specific repeatedly, or they do a certain action in a specific way, you should be able to note it down. Noting down clusters of gestures will help you draw clues about a person and their personality.

COMPARE AND CONTRAST

The other way of understanding a person's personality is comparison. If you are meeting someone, you may choose to compare their actions to another person. If you know a person who suffers from a certain mental disorder, you can try comparing their actions. This is especially important if you feel that something is off. If you look at a person and realize that they do not act in a normal way, you may try comparing their actions to other people. A comparison will let you know if a person is slightly off the radar.

LOOK INTO THE MIRROR

Looking into the mirror simply means comparing a person's actions to your own. Ask yourself what you would do if you were in the same position. For instance, if you are meeting a new person in your life and they keep talking about something specific, you could examine yourself and try to gauge your actions if you were in their shoes. If you deem yourself a normal person, the actions of the people you meet should not be very far off. A person should not act as if they are new to this world. If you come across a person who seems too new to your world, you have to give them special attention. Try to find out why a specific person is behaving in a certain way.

IDENTIFY THE STRONG VOICE

Every time you interact with a new person, there will be a voice from within that will speak to you about their personality. Pay attention to your sixth sense and try to observe the personality of the person you are getting to know.

BODY LANGUAGE

Body language is an important aspect that can help us analyze people. The gestures that a person makes when they are having a conversation say a lot. If you are a keen person, you may be able to extract a lot of information from a person's body language. NLP experts rely on body language to extract important data. The information can be obtained through posture, the position of arms and other aspects of the body during communication. Those are some of the most important aspects of body language to consider in a conversation.

When you try to know more about theirgoal and how they view the world, body language will be crucial. Too many times we get caught in the words that someone else tells us, and we won't concentrate on the other indications they also give us. There is so much that can be disclosed by these body language clues, and it makes a large difference in how effective you are in understanding and working with your goals.

Body language will refer to some of the nonverbal signals we use to interact with others. These nonverbal signals will take up much of the interaction we communicate every day. From the movement of our body to our facial expressions and everything in between, things we don't say can still share a ton of information during the process. Indeed, 60 to 65% of our interaction could be accounted for by body language and other nonverbal communications. So how do we learn to read this language to our advantage? Let's begin by learning more about the various indications of body language, and how we can read this for our benefit. First off, we have the facial expressions.

Thinkabout how much data someone can convey by the expression on their face. A smile is a nice way to show happiness or consent. A frown can imply the other way around. In some instances, facial expressions can show our real emotions about a scenario. While an individual may say they'reokay, the way theylook like when theysay this might talk otherwise. There are many feelings on our facial expressions, including:

1. Contempt

2. Desire

3. Excitement

4. Confusion

5. Fear

The expression that appears on the person's face helps us to determine if we trust and think anything of what the person says. In reality, one research discovered that the most credible of all facial expressions will be a small eyebrow raise and a slight smile. This is an expression that in many instances shows us trust and friendliness.

The other type of body language cues will have to be the mouth. Mouth expressions and motions can be another vital component of body language reading. For instance, if you notice someone else chewing on theirbottom lip, it may show that there are feelings of insecurity, fear and worry. The individual can cover theirmouth to be polite when theycough, but sometimes to the other person's disapproval. Also,smiling will be one of the best signals of corporeal language, but the smile and what it says about a person can be evaluated differently. Some of the stuff you can care about when reading someone else's mouth movements include;

PAY ATTENTION TO THE POSITION OF THE ARMS

People wrap their arms around their chest and lean back to show authority. In a sittingposition, a person may cross their legs and spread their arms around a chair to show superiority. It is important to read such signs. If you do not know how to interpret the meaning of gestures such as the position or movement of the arms among others, you may never be able to influence people. You must look at the position of a person's arms and be able to tell if a person wants attention. People also use the positions of the arms to demand respect.

OBSERVE THE EYES

It is difficult for most people to keep eye contact when they are telling lies. If you want to further understand the person you are talking to, you must pay attention to their eye movements. A person is paying the most attention when their eyes are focused on you. Do not keep talking to someone who is paying attention to their phone or is busy with something else. You should aim to have the full attention of the audience to ensure that the message arrives home.

PAY ATTENTION TO PROXIMITY

The level of the relationship and the type of conversation determine the distance between you and the other person. In a professional conversation, there must be a safe distance between the two individuals. There is less contact, and every word is explained with clarity. However, in a personal conversation, people talk much closer to each other. The privacy levels of a discussion also determine the proximity.

WATCH THE HEAD MOVEMENTS

The head plays an important role in body language. Nodding of the head is a traditional sign of approval. Some people will not talk much, but will keep nodding their heads during a conversation. You must ensure that the person you are talking to is listening. One of the ways to gauge their attention is by looking at their heads. However, it is not a must that a person nods their head if they are paying attention. Some people just listen without having to nod.

PAY ATTENTION TO THE LEGS AND STANDING POSTURE

The feet and the standing posture play an important role in interpreting the attention that a person is paying. You can tell if a person is paying attention just by looking at their feet. You can also tell if a person is comfortable with the conversation. If a person feels uncomfortable, they will keep moving their feet anxiously. A person can have serene eyes, but their feet may tell a different story.

LOOK OUT FOR HAND SIGNALS

Hands can also be used to pass around a lot of information. For instance, if someone is frustrated, they may throw their hands in the air. This is a show of arrogance or frustration. You must be able to read and interpret hand signals. Some arguments cannot be explained by words alone. In such cases, people use hands to try and explain their points.

PURSED LIPS

If you see your goal tightened up, it's a sign of distrust, disagreement and disgust.

LIP BITING

This is when you bite your lower lip, usually when you are stressed, anxious or distressed.

MOUTH COVER

Any moment someone wishes to conceal one of their emotional responses, they can cover their mouths to assist.

TURNED UP OR DOWN

Even a slight shift in your mouth can be a subtle indication of how you feel right now. When your mouth turns up, it's a sign that you are hopeful or glad. It could be a grimace, disagreement, and even sorrow when the mouth turns down.

ANOTHER AREA TO OBSERVE AS BODY LANGUAGE CUE IS GESTURES

Gestures can be a very evident, direct sign of body language to be careful about. Waiving, pointing and fingering can be common and easy to understand gestures. Some may even be cultural. Some of the most popular gestures and the significances that come with them include:

A CLUNG FIST

In most cases, this will show anger, but sometimes it can also imply solidarity.

Thumbs up or down : This is used as a sign of approval and disapproval.

The "all correct" gesture: This one will assist others to say you're fine in the United States. But it is seen in some other cultures as a vulgar gesture.

The next thing we have to do is look at the arms and legs of the individual you talk to. These can be useful if a lot of information is to be transmitted nonverbally. Crossing the weapons will often be a defensive maneuver. Crossing the legs away from another individual will also show a person's discomfort or dislike.

Other subtle signals, including the large expansion of the arms, can sometimes help us to seem bigger and more comfortable while maintaining the arms close to the body. When you try to measure your body language a little, be careful about some of the following signals that your legs and arms will transmit to you from the target:

CROSSED ARMS

This will give you a signal that they're closed, safe, and defensive. As a manipulator, you need to uncross the arms of the targetto make themfeel comfortable.

STANDING WITH YOUR HANDS ON YOUR HIPS

This can be a good sign that the person is ready and controlled. This will sometimes be a sign of aggression.

CLAMPING THE HANDS SO THAT THEY'RE BEHIND THE BACK

This will be a sign that your goal is angry, anxious or boring. You have to look at some of the other signals that come first.

TAPPING FINGERS OR FIDGETING QUICKLY

The other person is frustrated, impatient, and even bored.

CROSSED LEGS

This is a good indication that someone feels closed or needs some privacy.

POSTURE IS ANOTHER THING YOU SHOULD LOOK AT

The way we hold our bodies will also be a significant component of body language. Posture refers to the way we hold our bodies and to a person's general physical shape. Posture can give a wealth of data on how someone feels and also suggests that a person's features are submissive, open or confident.

For instance, if you sit directly, it can show that an individual is concentrated and is attempting to look at what is going on. Sitting down with the body to the side, will show that someone is indifferent or boredmost of the time. Looking at your goal will assist you to understand whether theyare interested in what you do or say, or if you need to move on to find a different destination.

Whenever you attempt to read some of theirbody language, tryand find out some signals that your goal's position is attempting to tell you. Some of them are:

OPEN POSTURE

This includes keeping the body's trunk exposed and open.

CLOSED POSTURE

This one will require hiding the body's trunk and hitting the legs and arms. This posture will be more indicative of anxiety, discomfort, and depression in the target.

Chapter 5:

Techniques to Manipulate and Influence Anyone

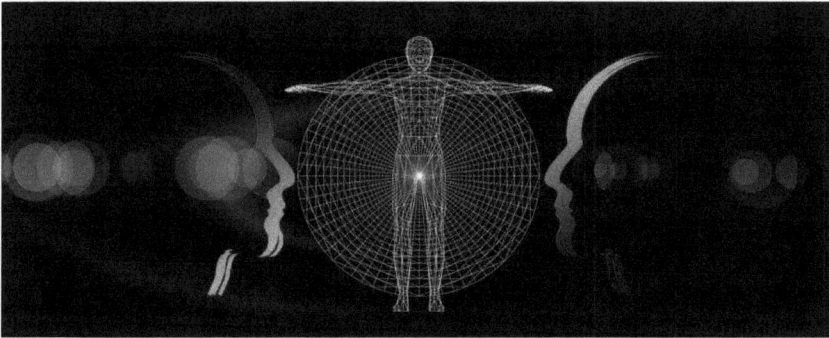

anipulation is, in essence, the art of deception. And, as it is an art, it is teachable—and something which you can learn to master.

COMMON MANIPULATION TECHNIQUES THAT WORK

Manipulation techniques can be nice to work with because they will allow you to determine how you would like to request something from your target or another person. Since you already know what you want to request from that person, the only answer now is to determine how to make that request. You can do so easily by following the guides below for three of the best manipulation requests that exist. Let's take a look at a few of the best manipulation techniques that you can use to manipulate anyone that you want.

KNOWING WHEN THEY ARE READY

Before you can get started with manipulating anyone, you must know when they are ready. You can't just get started with manipulating them without laying some groundwork, orif you just jump into your plan without knowing that person. With basic manipulation, you will often need to start out using small requests on some level to get your target saying yes often—once they are in the habit of saying yes regularly, you can get them to say yes with the big request.

STARTING SMALL

The first technique that we will take a look at is the idea of starting small. With this one, first you are going to need to consider the personality type of the individual you are working with. This ensures that you ask the questions in the right way, and that you are sure to ask the escalating requests throughout the conversation in the right manner. What you request, and the way that you request it will depend on the personality type, so let's divide them up and see how you can do this method with each personality.

THE LOGIC-DRIVEN

For the personality type that is more logic-driven, you will be working to persuade the target with lots of facts. If you become too vague, and you don't find the right kinds of facts, you will turn them off from you, and they will beless likely to say yes to the request at all. The request will come in when you ask them to trust your facts. Some of the ways that you will choose to word the request to the logic-driven person would include:

I read one time that this was the best couch that you can purchase on the market today. I'd have to say, I agree. Do you?

I feel like I've heard that this car is the fastest in the world. Have you heard about that?

I give back what I borrow every time, and I feel like I'm a reliable person, don't you agree?

THE EGO-DRIVEN

For the personality type that is driven by ego, you will need to go through and change things up, and you will need to make sure that you appeal to the ego or the idea that the person needs to be seen as the best person in the room. You can then go through and manufacture your requests to appeal to this need by using words that will talk about how that product or that request will make them look, and how it will make them appear to other people at the same time.

When you are working on your requests to your ego-driven target, you will need to make sure that you are always worried about appearances and some of the ways that the target would like to appear to other people. Some of the ways that you could word your request to an ego-driven person would include:

I am so grateful for the help I got. (Friends name) is amazing for helping me out, don't you agree?

This could make your living room look like something straight out of a design magazine. Who doesn't want to have the fanciest furniture?

Many celebrities drive this car. It commands the road. Can you imagine all of the heads turning to see you drive by in this car?

THE EMOTION-DRIVEN

Now we need to take a look at how to work with the emotion-driven individual. When it comes to these kinds of people, you need to make sure that your requests can appeal to their feelings. You want to make sure that you are using the types of words that talk about how they will feel about certain things, and then you need to take it a bit further and get them to affirm those feelings by agreeing with you. Some of the wording that you can use when you are working with the smaller requests would sound something like this:

I feel like I am a reliable person, and that I have always been honest and caring to those who are willing to help me out. Don't you think so?

This couch is made from a material that will continue to be soft for years. No matter how much time you sit on it or how much you use it, it will stay cozy and soft. I just love the idea that it will stay this cozy forever, don't you?

This luxurious car has the nicest feeling leather seats out of any car I've ever sat in. Plus, they have heat warmers with three settings to ensure that you will be comfortable, no matter what. Wouldn't you love that?

Since you will word these in a way that has a lot of feelings init, you are easily appealing to the emotional drive of the person you are targeting. There are also some logic-driven words inside it, so if this is the secondary personality of your target, then that is taken care of.

BLACKMAIL

The purpose of utilizing this sort ofintimidation is relying further on the subject's emotions. In regular blackmail, the target has a danger to cope with, often involving physical damage to themselves or anyone they love. For theemotional coercion, the manipulator must strive to evoke feelings powerful enough to motivate the victim to action. Although the target may believe they are supporting out of their goodwill, the trickster has managed to ensure they are having the assistance and drawing out the emotions whenever required.

Blackmail is the first strategy that a trickster would use. Blackmail is deemed to be an act that involves irrational threats to make a certain benefit or cause a loss to the target unless the manipulator's demand is met. It can also be described as the act of intimidation including threats of arrest , threats of taking properties or money from the subject, or threats of physical damage to the subject.

PUTTING DOWN THE OTHER PERSON

The manipulator has other choices should they decide to persuade their target to help achieve the ultimate objective. One method that does have quite a bit of success is when the manipulator can put his subject down. For most situations where the manipulator uses verbal skills to bring a target down, they may face a strong risk of having the subject feel as though they have been exposed to a personal assault. When the subject feels that they are being targeted, they would bristle and not be able to support the manipulator in the manner they like. We will be more careful with the procedure to find a way to do so without creating or ringing alarm bells.

LYING

No matter what the manipulator's ultimate purpose is, lying is something they are a specialist at and can do all the time to obtain everything they want. There are many various types of lies that the manipulator will employ to help them reach their final objectives. Some are spreading full lies while othersare omitting portions of the facts from their targets. If the manipulator lies, it's because they realize that the lie willtravel far moreeasily that the reality would. Telling anyone the reality could render them unable to support the manipulator out and that would go against their plans entirely. Alternatively, the manipulator would say a lie and persuade the target to do something for them because it's too late to correct the problem by the time the subject found out about the lie. The manipulator may even want to withhold some of the facts of the lies they say. They willrevealsome of the reality in this approach, but they will leave out other unsavory details, sincethat could impede the progress being made. These types of lies can be just as hazardous as telling what the reality of the story is, and what the lie is becomes increasingly difficult. It's important to understand that when you're dealing with the manipulator— anything they say to you can be a lie. It's not a safe decision to believe what the manipulator does, because they're only attempting to manipulate and exploit their targets to accomplish their end objective. The manipulator can do and say whatever imaginable, including lies, to get what they want, and they won't feel bad for it. Because as soon as they get what they want, they're not concerned about whether it impacts the target.

CREATING A HALLUCINATION

The manipulator will not only lie but also be an expert in the creation of illusions and be more successful in achieving their ultimate target. They must try to construct a vision they like, and then persuade the target that this image is a reality; whether it matters to the manipulator or not. To achieve so, the manipulator must put up the facts required to make the argument that functions against their objective. The manipulator must plant the theories and the proof into the subject's head to launch the deception. If these theories are in motion, the manipulator would be willing to step aside for a few days to encourage the abuse to take place in the minds of the targets during that time. By this point, the manipulator would have had more opportunities to get the subject to go through with the plan. Manipulation is a type of mind control that the subject has trouble resisting. Except for brainwashing and hypnosis mentioned in the preceding paragraphs, deception may occur in daily life, and in certain cases, it may occur without any awareness or influence of the subject.

ISOLATION

We are a very social species—we always want to work to foster relationships with other people. This is the natural order of humans in general; we just want to make sure that we can interact with each other, and that requires us to make concessions sometimes. We know this, and we usually will have no problems sometimes compromising to keep those groups. However, social groups also represent protection and power. When you are in a group of people that all care about you, they will be on the lookout for anything that might harm you. They will do what they can to protect you because they want to keep you safe.

CRITICISM

You will commonly see manipulators wielding criticism to control people as well. No one likes to feel criticized—it makes them feel like they have been treated poorly or like they are unappreciated. Think about the last time that you felt criticized—it probably felt awful. You probably did something that you hoped would be appreciated, only to find that in reality the other person was annoyed or told you that you weren't good enough.

With criticism, you find that you are stuck feeling like you are never good enough. You might do one thing that your manipulator wants from you, only to realize that theyhavesuddenly changed the goalposts and now want even more from you. Think of it this way— imagine that your partner has requested that you make sure that you cook dinner and have it done at 6:00 exactly every single day. You are busy, but you find a way to make it happen, knowing that it matters to your partner, and so you do it. You make sure that dinner is made at exactly 6 in the evening the next day when theywalk in the door... And theyarestill not satisfied.

IMPOSE AN UNREASONABLE REQUEST, THEN PRESENT A REASONABLE ONE

This is a technique that has proven to be very effective, and many manipulators often use it. It is also shockingly simple. Whenever a person wants to manipulate someone, they come up with a request that is not reasonable. The other person will reject the unreasonable request and, in that instance, a reasonable request is presented. The new request should be appealing to the individual who is being targeted. The best example to use in such a case is when an employee may not accept a permanent request to arrive early at work, but they will voluntarily accept a request whereby they are supposed to arrive at work early over a specific period to handle various urgent duties. The employee will prefer engaging in a short-term request, since it is less cumbersome when compared to the long-term request.

INSPIRE FEAR, THEN ENSURE THAT THE VICTIM HAS A SENSE OF RELIEF

A manipulator may have chosen their victims carefully, based on who is the most vulnerable. In this case, a manipulative person will make sure that a victim's worst fears have come to life. In the process, they will then focus on ensuring that these fears are relieved, and the victim will be happy enough to give them what they want. This kind of manipulation is dangerous, and you should reach out to people who can help to keep you safe from an abusive dynamic like this.

An example of how this kind of behavior might begin – assume that you have a car. Your friend might try to shock you by telling you that the car was producing some funny noises and that the engine might be dead. At that juncture, you will be in fear. After that, they inform you that they realized the strange noise was being produced by the radio. You are relieved. Since you are relieved, your friend may go ahead and ask for another favor, such as – they want to borrow the car again.

ENSURE THAT A PERSON FEELS GUILTY

A manipulator may try to get what they want by invoking guilt in another person. For starters, they might carry out an evaluation and learn more about how to make someone feel guilty, by making that person feel bad for a variety of reasons.

If the manipulator is targeting their parents, for example, they would showcase that it's their parents' fault that they are the way they are at that moment.

If they are invoking some form of guilt among one of their friends, they may make sure that they have enlightened their friend about the number of times that they have been let down by them.

BRIBE A PERSON

When a manipulative person is after something, they may issue a bribe. In such an instance, they do not have to use tactics such as blackmail to get what they want. A reward may be given but in the form of a bribe. The manipulator will learn more about your needs, but will try to hide the fact that they are issuing a bribe.

PRETEND THAT YOU ARE THE VICTIM

When a manipulative person pretends that they are a victim, they will attract some sympathy. This is a commonly used method for some people, who "play" the victim any chance they get. They usually make sure that they don't overdo the act in an attempt to get what they are looking for at the end of it all. Victims always appear helpless, and that means that the target will appear vulnerable as they offer to help them. They will pretend to be dumb, although they know what they are doing. They may pretend to be pathetic and helpless, but will get more desperate and even enraged if you realize and don't give in to this type of emotional manipulation. You need to try to discern who is a real victim and who is manipulating you.

USE LOGIC

Logic is important in some of the days to day activities that you engage in. Always ensure that you have come up with a list of reasons as to why you would benefit from the things that you are asking for from someone. A manipulative person will always present their case, calmly and rationally, but they will make sure to display some emotions to get what they want at the end of it all.

MAINTAIN THE CHARACTER

Depending on the method that has been used, a manipulator will try to make sure that they have displayed some emotions that could relate to their current scenario. They may appear worried or even upset, depending on the matter at hand.

PEER PRESSURE

Peer pressure is incredibly powerful—we all have this inherent need to be liked, and peer pressure allows for that to be exploited and controlled. When it comes to peer pressure, you will find that people are far more likely to agree to something that they don't want to do when they realize that their peers are doing itas well. This is a common form of persuasion in general—you make it clear to someone that other people in their demographic are doing something, and they begin to feel like that is what is expected of them, making them more likely to give in, whether they want to or not.

FEAR OF ALIENATION

Similarly to peer pressure, fear of alienation can also be manipulated easily. Typically, when you first meet the manipulator, you will find that you have met a person that appears to be kind, fun and someone that you like or want to hang around. You start to think that theyare probably great—after all, look at everything that they are doing? A common tactic is to make use of what is known as love-bombing—the tactic in which an individual tries to win your affections and loyalty through making you feel loved and special in hopes of manipulating those feelings later on. Your manipulator might have taken you out to special dinners or showered you with lavish gifts.

REPETITION

Repetition is highly powerful, especially as persuasion. It works quite simply—when you make it a point to repeat something to someone enough times, they will naturally start to believe it, especially if you are slow and subtle about how you bring it up and how you use the information that you are providing. In particular, you are likely to see that people will make it a point to use repetition to push new ideas into someone else's mind. Now, you might think that this is silly—can't you just resist and tell yourself that something is false?

FATIGUE

When you are tired, you are naturally more suggestible. This is because your brain just isn't working as efficiently as it should be. When you are tired, it is difficult to continue to police yourself over time; you are more likely to just give in to what is being said to you so that you can move on. Your brain simply wants to get to sleep.

It has been shown in studies that at the point of being awake for just 21 hours, you are already more susceptible to persuasive measures, such as repetition. This is commonly utilized during brainwashing, and perhaps the most widely known through the use of manipulating cults. When forming cults, especially those malignant ones that push harmful ideas, the cult leaders work to indoctrinate their followers, often through forms of physical impairment, such as being sleep deprived. The more sleep deprived that you are, the more likely that you are to absorb and accept the message.

FORMING NEW IDENTITIES

Another common form of manipulation is the act of forming new identities, typically through processes such as mind control. The idea here is that manipulators want to find a way to re-define you. They want to sculpt you, to manipulate you into exactly what they want, and they want to make sure that you are as obedient and useful as possible. Now, it is socially unacceptable to physically beat you into submission or to torture someone into fearing the manipulator enough to listen to everything that is ordered. Because of that, they typically go for tactics that are not as likely to be prosecuted as crimes. Though just as nefarious, mental warfare and emotional abuse don't leave physical, visible signs that something has happened, meaning that they can be used effectively without there ever being any evidence of abuse occurring in the first place.

DECEPTION

Finally, when you look at common manipulation tactics, you will see deception.

Chapter 6:

How A Manipulator Makes You Feel

FEELING CONFUSED

Manipulation is confusing for just about anyone. It is hard to go from thinking that someone in your life loved and supported you, but is now hurting you without any sort of confusion. Frequently, you feel like your world has been turned upside down, especially with those different tendencies and tactics that were likely thrown your way. If you were ever the victim of gaslighting, you probably doubt yourself. You probably feel like you are to blame or that you made your partner like this. You probably feel like you are hurting or like you don't know up from down anymore. Rest assured, this is typical in these situations, and you are not alone. However, you should make it a point to change. Don't let yourself fall for these habits long-term. Let this be the red flag that you need to see that the manipulation is there.

QUESTIONING YOURSELF

You may feel like you can't trust yourself when you are trying to recall an event. This is especially true if you are constantly gaslit into believing whatever it is that the manipulator insists is the case. You find that it is easier to question yourself, to blame yourself for what is happening than to accept that the fault lies with the manipulator. You then ask if you had everything to do with everything that ever happened to you—you point out how, ultimately, you must have been at fault just by what happened and because your manipulator has said that much.

FEELING ANXIOUS OR HYPERVIGILANT

Being manipulated is traumatic, especially when it comes from someone that you loved or trusted. It is so easy for you to feel like you are unable to trust others after this; you will probably feel like you were wrong once before, so you have to be on guard for this so that it doesn't happen again in the future. This is not something that anyone can fault you for; of course, you are worried about being victimized again. However, if you are not careful, you can have some worse effects.

FEELING ASHAMED OR GUILTY

No one wants to admit that they were made a victim. It is almost discouraged in this day and age, especially because most people who have never been there before are so quick to ask you why you would possibly put yourself in that position in the first place. They are all so quick to ask why you would seek out someone like an abuser or a manipulator, despite not realizing that most of them wear highly attractive masks. They don't get that, ultimately, the manipulator doesn't get other people to stick around them through being abusive or manipulative the first time they meet the other person. It takes time to build up to that level. They are great at playing the long game. Especially in relationship settings, you will find that manipulators will work hard to be perfect at first. They want to build that emotional attachment before they start to turn on their victim, and often the victim is left entirely blindsided to what just happened—they didn't realize that would happen, nor did they have any way of knowing.

THEY MAKE YOU FEEL INSECURE

No matter if the manipulator is a family member, a partner, a friend, or a coworker; you will notice that when you are around them, you will always feel insecure. They will leave you constantly feeling insecure no matter what you do, and that can be a huge problem. It is also a huge red flag, especially if before meeting that person, you were always completely comfortable with yourself.

THEY MAKE YOU FEEL PRESSURED

Manipulators love to make you feel pressured—they will lay it on regularly, because they have little interest in actually pursuing anything meaningful with you. All they care about is getting you to cater to their whims, and if that means that they need to lay on the pressure, they are perfectly happy doing so.

THEY MAKE YOU FEEL CRAZY

Manipulators tend to use a tactic called gaslighting. We will be going into this in more depth later, but essentially, it is a tactic in which the manipulator will tell you that things are not how you perceive them. Theirgoal is to leave you feeling like you can't trust yourself or your perception of reality; theywant you to doubt that you are recalling what is happening so that theycan take complete advantage of you.

BECOMING PASSIVE OR SUBMISSIVE

When you are constantly being manipulated, especially with passive-aggressive or otherwise hurtful methods, you will probably find that you become passive. The longer that you are in with a manipulator or an abuser, the easier it becomes to simply give in. It is so much easier to just give in, to let your partner or manipulator have their way than it is to try to fight it or defend yourself. You find that it is so much easier than you don't even bother trying anymore.

Alternatively, you may learn that your needs are associated with pain or discomfort. You learn that your partner or manipulator will not be particularly sympathetic to you when you need something, and in fact may berate or belittle you for having those needs in the first place. This is especially true with narcissists, who only want you around for them. It becomes so bad to try to get your way or get what you need that you eventually just stop trying. You become afraid or ashamed of the needs that you have, and you sit back quietly, waiting for your manipulator to tell you what to do next.

Taking action effectively becomes associated with pain, and because of this, passivity becomes the default coping mechanism. It is hard to act if you worry about what will happen next if you do, and you decide that at least you know what the current pain or discomfort is—thisis better than the unknown that you will be exposed to if you try to vocalize your needs at all.

FEELING LIKE YOU ARE ON EGGSHELLS

Similarly, you may find that you constantly feel like you are on eggshells. Your partner may constantly snap without any sort of warning. You may discover that your partner is not stable or reliable, and it is so much easier to just try to walk around them and their problems than it is to try to do what you want. It is easier to keep the peace by trying not to set off the other person.

However, this is problematic; you are always working in anticipation of being hurt. This usually carries over outside of that one context as well, and you very quickly find that you are constantly worrying about how you will be perceived and what you can do to avoid running into further problems. You will, in other contexts, attempt to avoid setting other people off as well, becoming a people pleaser. However, unfortunately, this just sets you up for more abuse and manipulation in the future. Remember, this people-pleasing attitude was one of those that were a big red flag that many manipulators look for to control their targets.

FEELING NUMB

The longer that you spend in a relationship or around someone that never seems to care for your feelings and what you need, the more likely that you are to just give up on feeling in the first place. After all, emotions become dangerous weapons against you; with those emotions that you have, you only feel worse over time. You feel hopeless as the manipulation continues; you may not even really react much to the criticism anymore when it happens more and more.

SEEKING APPROVAL

When you are constantly being torn down in your relationships, you often get to a point in which you are constantly seeking approval from others. You effectively make all of your value being able to get that approval from other people, and the less of that you get from others, the worse you end up feeling.

Effectively, because you are so used to being belittled, made the problem and even potentially blamed for what is happening to you and the interactions that you have, you start trying to do everything you can to just please everyone in your area. This is your coping mechanism for the manipulation and rejection—if you are constantly exceeding expectations, can anyone criticize you? If you are constantly doing what you must, can anyone get back at you or hurt you or fault you for it?

RESENTMENT

Resentment is how all of your negative emotions surrounding the entire situation are bottled up so that they can be purged. However, it is difficult to do this constructively. Resentment, while it serves its purpose of making you want to leave your current situation so that you can be in a better one, is also quite unhealthy to harbor, especially if it is toward yourself. You may start to resent yourself for not seeing the signs sooner or not being strong enough to leave the situation. You might resent your manipulator for being the way that they are. You might resent friends and family for not warning you of the red flags. It is important that, if you are resentful, you learn to process this the right way.

DEVELOPING DEPRESSION OR ANXIETY

Some people become depressed or anxious after they have been manipulated or abused. It is easy to believe the lies that you were told to keep you down when they were repeated so much. It becomes easy to tell yourself that, really, you are worthless for letting the situation get so bad, or that it is your fault, and you deserved what happened to you. The more depressed that you get, however, the less likely it is that you are going to seek help or try to escape.

You may feel like you are worthless, or that you are too stressed out or anxious to do anything. You might withdraw and give up entirely, not seeing the value in trying any longer when nothing ever changes from your perspective. It becomes easier to just remain in the situation and resign to your fate, even though there is help out there and no one deserves to live in constant stress.

Anxiety can be debilitating. It can lie to you and tell you that there is no escape. It can make you feel like things will only get worse if you try to do anything to defend yourself or to leave or make your situation better. Remember, anxiety is only there to lie to you. It isn't your friend. It isn't there to help you, and it is there to keep you back.

SELF-SABOTAGING

When you are suffering in a manipulative situation, you may decide that there is no point in trying anymore. You may find that you simply give up because there is no point anyway. You acknowledge that your manipulator will never change, and because of that, you stop trying. However, is this the right option for you? Think about it—instead of making it a point to walk away from the situation; you have chosen to make yourself stuck in it longer.

When it comes right down to it, you have two options—you can stay, or you can go. However, no one can make you stay in a manipulative or abusive situation without your consent, whether you believe it or not. This is how manipulators get people in the first place—they make them want to stay. They make them feel like they need to stick around or that things will be better if they do, whether through threats or through constantly oscillating between manipulating and hurting the victim and showering them with love.

ISOLATION

Did you notice you don't splurge time with friends and family anymore? A toxic friend will expect your undivided attention and make you feel guilty if they feel they don't give you enough of themselves.

For example, John, a toxic person, gets to control your entire time, to the large extent that he blurts out because he notices on social sites that you are trying to hang out with other fellows and friends — and also without him. You realize then that you spend almost all of your leisure time with that kind of individual and have completely overlooked how your other mates are doing. This is not nice.

ALWAYS MAKING YOU GUESS ABOUT THEM

One day they'll be delightful and then another day you'll wonder what you have done to get them upset. There is often nothing evident that will justify the shift in attitude-you know that there is something wrong. They may be prickly, cold, sad, cranky or cold, and if you question them ifthere's something not right, the response is likely to be 'nothing' – but they'll just give you enough to make you realize that something is there. The 'just enough' could be a shuddering gasp, an eyebrow raised, a chilly shoulder. You may find yourself trying to make justifications for them when it happens or doing anything you could to keep them happy. See why that's working for them?

Quit trying to make them happy. Toxic people have long since figured out decent humans would go to exceptional lenghtsto keep the individuals they valuehappy. If your efforts to satisfy don't succeed, or if they don't last for long, then it's time to give up. Step back and return once the attitude has changed. You aren't accountable for the emotions of someone else. If you have executed anything to hurt someone unknowingly, ask, discuss this and apologize if need be. You don't have to conjecture at any cost.

DO NOT OWN THEIR FEELINGS

They will behave as if the emotions are yours, instead of possessing their own emotions. It is termed projection, as when they project their thoughts and feelings on you. For instance, you might have been accused of being upset with somebody who is frustrated but can't be held accountable for it. It could be as dramatic as, "Are you alright with me?"Or a little more straight forward, "What's the reason for being mad at me?" or, "Whyhave you been down all day?"You will find yourself explaining and securing yourself and often that's going to happen constantly – because it has nothing to do with you. Be clear about what is about you and what is about them. If you feel like you are defending yourself far more times previously against baseless accusations or unfitting questions, you might be projected onto that one. You don't have to clarify, validate, or fight to protect yourself or cope with an allegation that was misfired. Bear that in mind.

MAKES YOU PROVE YOURSELF TO THEM

They will place you in a situation where you'll have to pick among them and some other thing regularly – and you will always feel inclined to pick them. Poisonous people would wait till you have an involvement; therefore the drama would then emerge. 'If you ever really cared for me, you'd be skipping your exercise lesson and spending quality time with me.' The problem with this is that enough is never enough. Several events are deadly-unless it is lifeor death, it's likely to be waiting.

ALWAYS TRYING TO MAKE YOU FEEL LOW

They're trying to pursue excuses why the interesting news is not perfect. Examples are: For a promotion – 'Money is not so great for the type of work you will do.' For a vacation on the beach – 'Well, weather will be hot. Do you think you would like to go?' On becoming a Universe Queen– 'Well you know the Universe isn't that big, and I am sure that you're not going to have breaks.' don't let someone discourage you or reduce you to their size. You do not need their authorization anyway – and for that matteranybody else's.

Chapter 7:

Types of Manipulators

DIFFERENT MANIPULATIVE PERSONALITIES

Manipulators have perfected the art of trickery. They may seem reasonable and genuine, but often it's just a cover; it's a way of drawing you in and pulling you into a connection before they reveal their hidden colors.

Manipulators are not invested in you, but use you as a tool that helps them to acquire charge and therefore you are a reluctant member. As you'll acknowledge, they have many ways to do this. They often end up taking what you say or do and wiggle it around so that what you've said and done will hardly be recognizable to you. They'll try to mislead you, and perhaps even make you feel like you're crazy. They stretch the facts, and if it helps their end they may succumb to lying.

DECEITFUL PERSONALITIES

The victim role can be portrayed by dishonest men, making you appear to be the one who created a crisis they began but never accepted accountability for. They can act as passive-aggressive or pleasant for one minute and stand off the next, keeping you speculating and prey on your fears and worries. Often, they do make you nervous. Also, they can be highly violent and brutal, resorting to character insults and criticism, savaged in their quest to get what they want. They are bullying and threatening, and will not let go till they wear you down.

Manipulators possess the following traits, so when one catches your eye, you'll know what to look out for. Knowing these underlying concepts of operation can help safeguard you from getting drawn into a deceitful relation. Staying vigilant, staying connected with what you know is true about yourself, and anticipating what is to come will allow you to prevent a dispute and preserve your dignity.

1. Manipulative individuals often lack understanding of how they involve someone to construct those situations, or they genuinely feel that their method of coping with a problem is the right option as it ensures their desires are being fulfilled and it's all that counts. Inevitably, all the circumstances and partnerships are for them and it just doesn't matter what others say, hear and want:

2. Controllers, bullies and men who are manipulators are not challenging themselves. They aren't asking themselves whether they are the problem. They always conclude others are the problem.

3. A manipulator shuns accountability for his actions by accusing others of triggering them. It is not because dishonest men do not recognize what responsibility is. They do; a dishonest person finds nothing immoral with failing to accept accountability for their acts, even though they force you to take responsibility for yours. They can eventually seek to get you to assume accountability for fulfilling their needs, leaving no place to satisfy yours.

4. Manipulators do not understand borders. They are ruthless in pursuing whatever they want and have little consideration as to who gets caught along the way.

5. They're not worried about crowding into space — physically, mentally, socially, or religiously. They have no understanding or just don't care about what private space and individuality mean. They can be compared to parasites-this is mostly an appropriate relationship in the natural environment. However, in individual interaction feeding off others at their cost is depleting, draining, diminishing and demeaning.

6. Manipulative people prey on our sensibilities, interpersonal sensitivity and, in particular, conscience.

They know they will have a decent chance to draw you into a friendship because you're loving, sensitive, compassionate and of course, you want to support them. Atfirst, they will care for your goodwill and generosity, always thanking you for the amazing individual that you are. But over time, praise for these attributes will be lessened since you are being used to serve someone who doesn't truly care for you. They just really care what you can offer them.

7. Never spend your energy attempting to justify who you are to those who are dedicated to misunderstanding you. When someone doesn't see you, don't sit around wondering until they do. You don't have to make it your task to make them appreciate and understand you — they are not interested in you as an individual.

8. If you'd like a simple means of identifying manipulators from emphatic individuals, pay close attention to how they talk toothers concerning you. Frequently, they discuss you behind your back the same way they speak about someone else to you. They are masters of "triangulation"—creating situations and complexities that facilitate suspense, competition and envy - promoting and fostering disharmony.

9. Describe individuals by their acts and you'll never be deceived by their sayings. Always keep in mind that what an individual says and does are two very distinct aspects. Watch somebody else carefully, without finding excuses for them – usually what you're seeing is what you get.

10. Investigate what you understand regularly. We don't do this sufficiently. As life progresses, our perceptions and opinions may change, and we need to understand how these shifting ideas impact us. If we're not sure what we

understand, it's all too easy to let somebody else who is sure that their views are right — not just for them but for you as well — to try to influence your thought process.

11. If an individual makes as much exertion to be a nice person as they do to pretend to be one, they might even be a good person in reality.

12. This is an important truth - Our initial contact and perspective of someone heavily color our growing connection with them. If we grasped from the outset that an individual is not who they appear to be and is only hiding behind a facade of what appears to be culturally acceptable behavior, then maybe we would be more cautious about getting involved.

If it comes to manipulating human beings, there is no stronger tool than lies.since you know people live through ideologies and values can be twisted. The only thing that matters is the ability to exploit ideologies.

TRAITS OF MANIPULATORS

Remember, not every manipulator will have all of these traits. Some will have a few of them while others will possess the vast majority. Despite this, each of these traits should have alarm bells ringing if you approach someone exhibiting behaviors consistent with them.

If you see someone engaging in these sorts of actions, you should always stop to reevaluate your relationship and the situations in which they have occurred, as there is always the possibility that you have been victimized by a manipulator.

LACKING EMPATHY OR REMORSE

Perhaps the most important trait of master manipulators is their ability to not feel remorse for their actions. Sincethey lack empathy, one of the most important traits for regulating behaviors into effective, productive actions that benefit the survival of the group, these master manipulators see no problems with their actions, allowing them to engage in all of the manipulation and abuse they please without ever feeling bad about it.

LACKING MORALS

Whether the individual has chosen to disengage from their sense of morality or simply never had a sense of morality to begin with, those who are not concerned about things as petty and abstract as morals are far more willing to utilize behaviors that would be seen as a moral grey area simply because they do not feel constrained by such an arbitrary concept. Why bother with morals if they do not feel guilty anyway?

SEE PEOPLE AS TOOLS

Oftentimes, manipulators fail to acknowledge the value in human life, instead focusing on the utility of a person rather than the inherent value. The utility is how much use a person or an object has. When a person is more concerned with the utility of people rather than the value of that person as a genuine human beingworthy of respect, they are more likely to resort to manipulation simply because manipulation will get the desiredresults.

SPITEFUL MOTIVATIONS

Sometimes, although this can oftentimes seem quite counterintuitive, the manipulator will do certain things and engage in certain acts that are self-harming out of spite. If theyfeel wronged, theywill twist the situation around to force theirpoint, even if doing so will hurt themin the process. Theysee themselfas collateral damage and accept the cost simply to watch the other person suffer in some way to try to coerce them back into obedience.

EGOTISTICAL

Manipulators typically have an ego so inflated that it is a wonder they manage to walk around at all. They are frequently so focused on themselves that they struggle to recognize how their actions hurt those around them.

They will use other people to make sure they can continue to feed their ego and achieve whatever it is they want simply because they believe they are more important than those around them.

These individuals ultimately care more about their selfish gain than the feelings of others, and because of that, they are even willing to go to lengths such as manipulating or coercing others to get their desired results.

ENTITLED

Those who manipulate others typically do so because they are entitled-they believe that they are entitled to a certain result during a certain timeline, and they have no qualms about pushing that timeline forward with manipulation if necessary.

Through manipulating others, they can get what they want, and because they were entitled to that particular result anyway, they see no harm in doing so.

This again goes back to Machiavellianism-the people are seen as tools rather than as whole people capable of thought and feeling. The manipulator may believe that theydeserve to be catered to, so theywill force the point with those around them. If theybelieve theydeserve to get a new job, theywill apply and will have no qualms about lying during the interview to be hired.

SUPERIORITY COMPLEX

Oftentimes the manipulator, through years of experience getting their way repeatedly, will end up believing that they are superior to others. Whether due to a personality disorder that causes these beliefs of superiority or because they have justified them throughout their experience of getting their way, the manipulator believes they are better than everyone else.

SADISTIC

Sometimes, manipulators simply enjoy hurting others. These are people who will manipulate just for the experience of hurting other people to get their way.

They will see hurting other people as a game-if someone else gives them the power to hurt them, then they can utilize that to their advantage, and it also allows for the manipulator to feed their ego.

SELFISH

Manipulators, more often than not, are doing so because they are being selfishly opportunistic. They see an opportunity to manipulate someone else and they decide to run with it to ensure they get what they want simply because they want it.

They want to ensure that they get the best result for them above all others, and they will do whatever it takes to ensure it happens. The manipulative behaviors can be justified to the manipulator, so long as they have benefitted in some way.

Chapter 8:

Favorite Victims of Manipulators

WHY ARE WE VULNERABLE TO DARK PSYCHOLOGY?

Now, let's begin—first, we will take a close look at dark psychology itself. Dark psychology is defined as the study of the dark personality types that exist in the dark triad of personality types. There are dark people in this world—predators, monsters in human clothing, who would like nothing more than to sink their teeth into their prey. They target similar people, which is why once you have found yourself in a manipulative relationship, you will probably find that it happens again and again. This is not necessarily your fault— manipulators typically take what makes us the best versions of ourselves and turn it into something that they can use to control us. They find ways to influence and control you that are different than the ones you could have ever imagined, and as a direct result, you find yourself caught off guard, unaware and falling into every trap.

We are, for the most part, quite susceptible to manipulation, despite the assertion that we are better than that. Even though you may assert to yourself that you are above petty control tactics that will keep you down, that is not the case at all. You must be willing to see how you can better interact with yourself and with those around you if you want to be able to control yourself. Within this chapter, we will explore those vulnerabilities, but first, we must take a look at the definition of manipulation itself. From there, we will address the most common red flags—the signs that you are currently being manipulated, as well as what manipulation and dark psychology can do to you.

WHO IS MORE VULNERABLE TO MANIPULATORS?

Manipulators are often retired people who have a macabre idea of howpeople generally function. The primary type of links with others is to use them for their private benefit. Who can then be said to be these manipulators' preferred victims? Manipulators are often attracted to two individual sets. The first group is those who want a certain degree of love and those in relationships. Love is universal. Love is universal. Love is universal. Love is universal. It is a primordial emotion instinctively desired. We are conceived as human beings for love.

We love and feel loved. We love. We enjoy it. We enjoy it. Nobody is so glad as a person or a woman in love who understands they are loved in return. Some individuals work for procreation together. Some individuals are squatting about denying social pressure. Some even encourage the association of strong families. The primary reason for friendships, however, is love. Having said that, things can easily be degraded to the point where love is used as a chip to negotiate for more authority over another individual. And here are some dark psychological aspects. You heard the phrase "use what you're meant to be getting," which says, "this kind of thinking goes hand-in-hand in the company world." But manipulation is called in relation. Let me take this example: A lady understands that she is sexually attractive and irresistible to her partner. Over time, he is scheduled to do the job his partner refused to do on sexual grounds. This is a seemingly harmless situation. But dark psychology is used here if you look carefully. The fella was manipulated for sex, albeit voluntarily. She understood the power and performed to get what she wanted. The nice thing is that in this situation everyone is pleased. Sincethe female receives a precious contribution from her partner, and the guy receives the sex that he wants from a lady he likes. But things are not always mutually helpful when it comes to dark psychology. This can get dark for the victim. Let's look at another couple. Look at thiscouple. I'd call this fresh couple Dave and Maya.

He starts to collect tiny information about her, such as her selection of apparel, make-up and hair, and of course, makes snide comments on her love weight. This impacts her confidence and when she brings her friends together, she utilizes flimsy occurrences to demonstrate and reinforce her fictitious theory. These tiny seeds of doubt develop and develop into a coin that splits Maya and her friends further. Because of her newly discovered absence of trust, she thinks Dave is the only one whoreally cares forand accepts her. This makes Dave want to do everything he can to put her where he wishes her to be, precisely. . . Under his thumb and his completecommand. In both cases, we see instances where relationships that should be between the two involved individuals, through manipulation and deception, become a way of fulfilling a partner's desires. Both relations started with good intentions, and although the final results of the former were satisfactory for both parties, it was the opposite in the latter story.

The difference is that all of the victims have done what they have done for their partners. Our desire to be loved can, therefore, render us susceptible. It can be manipulated and used for the benefit of others. The other group of people forwhom manipulators tend to have an affinity is those people with powerful religious convictions. These excessively religious individuals generally pursue their doctrines without issue. No matter which faith you practice, it is a fact that our faith sometimes creates a blind spot that distorts reality and leads us to decide that we would likely not have been in our own right and appropriate state of mind. But before we get into what, let's see why. When I talked about vulnerability in the past section, I said that what makes us human makes us susceptible to machinations of dark psychology. Some individuals see these impacts as evident as others. Even the oldest civilization precedes our faith in gods.

Man has always seen his presence as a tiny aspect of the universal system of things, so we think there are more and more divine forces. Looking logically at things, it produced sense because it helped our minds cope with the unexplained things around us. You see a lovely flower and wonder how it can exist so exquisite and sensitive. . . Without thought or pattern. We look at the big expanse of the sky and wonder what lies beyond it. Will it go forever? Or is it just tapping into an infinite end?

When you hear the strong grumbling of the waterfall or the sound of a thundering blow, even with the advancement and understanding we have, we are still terrified by fear. At that moment, you decide to allow fear to make you dumb or to simplify the scenario by placing it in a higher sovereign being. Some of the braver individuals decided to explain science to themselves. Staying along the same lines of thinking, if someone we love dies, we must face our mortality. Our sadness is compounded by issues of life and death. Is the trip here over or does it continue into the afterlife? This was a powerful motivation behind the views of today. The fear and consideration provided to living after this life have resulted in many individuals creating the "correct decisions" here, so that life, will hopefully proceed when death arrives. It is our way to manipulate the outcome, as it has been shown because the alternativeis so horrible. Some bring our afterlife fear to manipulate us for what they want. If we keep this afterlife hypothesis so high, you can imagine how we treat individuals who are deemed the mouthpieces of afterlife-controlled deities. Pastors, imams, elders and all the other rulers of religion are so reverent that God's words are seen as words.

These religious leaders are usually meant to apply sound moral principles and to behave in the best interests of their respective offices. If not to encourage the values of faith that they pretend to represent, at least for some other purpose. However, this is not always the case, as we know it. Many religious rulers abuse their roles and impact by deceiving their members to make choices that serve their selfish agenda exclusively. The common practice is that, whatever the story they tell is, the name of the main god twists the words drawn from the religious manual into something new that will help to manipulate people successfully. Many were swindled, physically harmed and even committed atrocious crimes. Another way is claiming that these fake rulers have a vision or spiritual insight into the need for the victim.

They are creating a complicated tale that is a mixture of lies tied up with confidence, and the primary purpose is to extort the victim only for cash, favor or authority. Some victims are compelled to split more cash than ever before. In some instances, impressive youthful victims in occult situations are brainwashed in fear. However, such situations do not only end in religious buildings. Some individuals are not religious, but want to be spiritually accessible. These persons are false psychics and media who pretend to be powerful with the Netherworld. Again, our attachment to the dead and our concern forwhat happens after death clouds our decisions and opens our doors to individuals who manipulate the scenario for their benefit. They use the same trick of fake religious rulers in deception and lies to manipulate their victims. Victims have to psychically read their horoscopes and palms ten minutes for years to maintain their commitments, altered realities and false expectations. They are spending tens of thousands and thousands of dollars on the search to find the elusive "truth." Think again because your faith is embedded in a legible and factual science.

When a crisis occurs, individuals return to their confidence. Naturally, a scientist turns to science. Some individuals who have weakened their health look for unconventional medicine to survive the disease. Since they realize the best of conventional medicine has failed, they turn to outsiders who say they have the answer in their experimental medicine,but the resultsare never achieved. Unfortunately, these processes are too dangerous, too expensive and often uninsured. But every penny is worth a slim life chance, and the fraudulent people take advantage of this. And this isn't just in crisis. You have discovered excellent alternatives to issues such as weight loss and so on. You claim that your recent nutritional fad, pill or technology can transform us through untested and verified scientific theories. Many individuals buy this pledge of conversion based on data especially manipulated for extortion.

The primary distinction between religious rulers and such fake science providers is that they use science to swindle their victims rather than a deity. And unfortunately, most individuals do not know how badly they are impacted until it is too late. As far as faith is concerned, they use it as the dark key for their deepest requirements. Theyuse asacred thing to manipulate your process of thinking. And sometimes the sacredness doesn't matter. They view it as a kind of gold mine, as long as it is essential to you. And for me or anyone, there's no bettertime than when this person is experiencing a crisis. This is because you're at your weakest and the most important time of crisis is when individuals understand how to manage stuff for their good.

EMPATH

The empaths will be individuals who can be deeply sensitive and will discover that they can tune in to others' energy and emotions. They can quickly deal with the feelings of those around them and turn them into their own. This can be a big challenge sometimes, if your boundaries aren't that strongbecause you can absorb the stress and pain of others. However, if you can carefully select the people around you and be careful with your energy, you may find that you attract those with a lot of happiness and joy. You can also absorb these positive emotions in your life.

With dark psychology, your goal is to be able to find people with more positive emotions and use them to your advantage. This doesn't have to be a bad thing. But if you want to get the control and power you want, you may find that you absorb this type of energy at the cost of harming another person. It will take some time to explore this and how it will work later.

Many times those who use dark psychology like to work with empaths because they can take any negativity, regret and more on their actions and pour it on the other person. An empath will often take on all that, guilt and shame, without even really knowing why. The person who made the dead will feel better because he has been able to discharge the empath, and the empath will suffer.

As an empath, you must first make sure that you have created some healthy limits for yourself. You don't want to go through this process and then find out that someone else is taking advantage of the fact that you are empathetic yourself. But since you already know that the empathy you want to work with is an emotional sponge and you can set limits so that certain emotions bounce off you, you will be able to use it to your advantage.

STRANGERS AND NEW ACQUAINTANCES

As social beings, we always learn and meet new people. But not everyone you meet is authentic. They could plot to manipulate you in various ways. Meeting new people is severe enough, but adding potential risks further complicates things. Most of the people you meet won't be out to pick you up. Occasionally you may run into a bad actor. Someone with a superficial charm can present themselfas a friendly person, but be fierce towards indie. Strangers pose a significant risk to your interpersonal relationships. It is, in fact, the opposite scenario: you have nothing to make a psychological profile disappear. In that case, the best solution is to keep your head still, but also do your research on who this person is. Closed strangers (closed body posture, a secret about themselves) can be suspicious. On the other hand, they may simply be shy or suffer from social anxiety.

VULNERABILITIES TRAITS

Now you, like most other people, probably think that you are a pretty steady person. You probably believe that you are not likely to be swayed or taken advantage of too easily. However, most people believe this—most people believe that they are likely to resist manipulation. They don't realize when they do have vulnerabilities, leaving them wide open to exploitation, and manipulators with malicious intent typically can sniff out the reason behind the actions with ease. They can identify those vulnerabilities, and take complete advantage of them so easily that you never even realize or suspect it, and that is where they get their power. Manipulators all tend to go for very similar people, and they typically have very predictable vulnerabilities. Let's look at some of the most common.

THE NEED TO PLEASE

Perhaps the easiest victims of manipulation are those that feel a constant need to please. They are constantly driven forward by this need to make people around them happy. Often, these people are quite naïve; they believe that it is the case that they are only good for making sure that those around them are pleased. Usually, they fear conflict and find that it is vastly easier to give in to conflict than it is to figure out how to avoid the problem entirely through giving in to whatever everyone around them wants.

THE NEED FOR APPROVAL

Similarly, some people feel that they must earn the approval of others—they find that they only have any real value when other people believe that they are okay or that other people are accepting them. Their self-esteem is typically drawn entirely by making sure that other people are willing and able to please them, so they find that approval is the only way that they can feel good about themselves.

THE FEAR OF NEGATIVE EMOTIONS

When it comes to negative emotions, some people become phobic of them—they are terrified of running into these negative associations with other people and want to do their best to figure out how to avoid triggering negative feelings from other people. They want to make sure that they can avoid being the target of disapproval, frustration or anger, so they will give in to whatever the manipulators request of them in hopes of being able to do better.

AN INABILITY TO BE ASSERTIVE

Some people are simply what is known colloquially as doormats—they are too weak to say no to other people, usually for any number of reasons on this list. Itmay bethat they need approval, they are afraid of negativity, or any other reason. No matter the reason for their lack of assertiveness, however, they are easy targets for manipulators and are typically favored for that reason.

WEAK OR NO PERSONAL BOUNDARIES

Similarly, people who struggle with asserting and maintaining their boundaries tend to find that they struggle to protect themselves from manipulation. Boundaries, as you will come to find over time, are perhaps the biggest threatsof all time to manipulators. When someone has strong personal boundaries, they can keep themselves separate from the wills of other people. They can prevent themselves from falling victim to the ways that people tend to treat them because they will not allow things to get bad enough to let them be victimized in the first place. When those boundaries are missing, however, the manipulator has the perfect storm to simply steamroll over the victim to take control.

LOW SELF-RELIANCE

Self-reliance is something that everyone needs and yet is so hard to maintain. If you do not feel like you can rely on yourself, there is a good chance that you will find yourself taken advantage of. Feeling like you cannot trust yourself, that you are always wrong when you do something, is perhaps one of the best ways for you to end up the victim of a manipulator at some point.

A NATURAL NAÏVETÉ

When the target is naturally too naïve to understand what is happening around them or is likely to constantly give the other

93

person the benefit of the doubt, they will end up victimized. The common belief behind this is that he or she would not do something nefarious, so why would anyone else? It is so easy to take advantage of people who always want to see the best in someone else.

BEING OVERLY CONSCIENTIOUS

Similarly, some people always want to give those around them the benefit of the doubt. When something goes wrong, they assume that it was unintentional. They assume that when someone does something to them, they can justify it somehow, saying that the manipulator probably didn't mean it, or that it was probably an accident. They are so quick to try to see the side of the manipulator that they unintentionally throw themselves under the bus.

LACKING SELF-CONFIDENCE

People lacking in self-confidence are too quick to let themselves talk themselves out of believing what is happening. They will readily tell themselves that they must have been at fault because they are *always* at fault. Their beliefs that they can never do anything right typically make them very easy for manipulators to take advantage of.

SUBMISSIVE PERSONALITY TYPE

Some people have what is known as a submissive personality. They naturally give other people what they want, and they are quick to let themselves depend on other people to make all of the decisions and choose out everything that will happen. They are so dependent upon the other person that they often end up exploited and manipulated, even though they really should have been able to avoid the problem in the first place.

Chapter 9:

What is Persuasion?

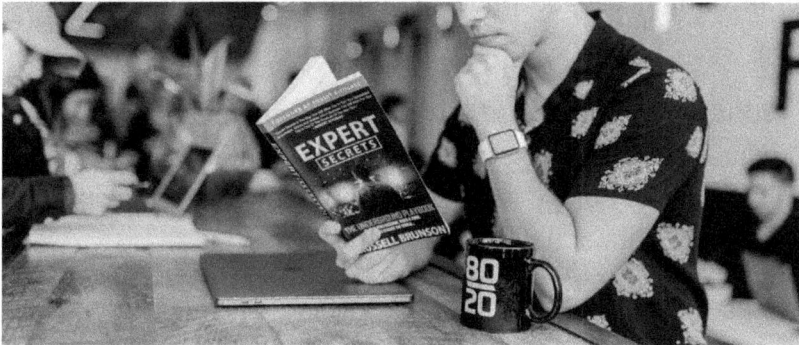

THE ART OF PERSUASION

The power of persuasion means nothing more than using mental abilities to form words and feelings used to convince other people to do things they may or may not want to do.

Some people are better able to persuade than other people. And some people are easier to persuade than other people.

People who are at a low point in their lives are easy prey for others who might try to persuade them to do something they might not usually do.

The first step in persuasion involves the idea of reciprocating. If a person does something nice for someone else, then the receiving person usually feels the need to do something good in return.

If someone helps their elderly neighbor carry in the groceries from the car, that neighbor might feel obligated to bake homemade cookies for that person. A coworker who helps complete a project is more likely to receive assistance when it is needed. Many people do nice things for others all the time without expecting anything in return.

The person who does nice things for people and then mentions some little favor that can be done in return maybe someone to watch closely.

Nonprofit organizations use this tactic to gain more contributions to their causes. They will often send some little trinket or gift to prompt people to donate large sums of money, or even just to donate where they might not have originally.

The idea behind this is that the person opening the letter has received a little gift for no reason, so they might feel obligated to give something in return.

Some people are automatically tempted to follow authority. People in positions of authority can command blind respect to their authority simply by acting a certain way or putting on a uniform.

The problem with this is that authority figures, or those that look like authority figures, can cause some people to do extraordinary things they would not normally do had a person in a position of authority not been the one asking. And it is not simply held to people in uniform. People who carry themselves a certain way or speak a certain way can give the impression that they are something they are not.

For someone or something to be considered a credible authority, they must be familiar and people must have trust in the person or organization. Someone who knows all there is to know about a subject is considered an expert and is more likely to be trusted than someone who has limited knowledge of the subject. But the information must also make sense to the people hearing it.

If there is not some semblance of accuracy and intelligence, then the authority figure loses credibility. Even the person who is acknowledged as an expert will lack persuasive abilities if they are seen as not being trustworthy.

The worst part of the power that goes along with persuasion is that things that are scarce or hard to get are seen as much more valuable. People value diamonds because they are expensive and beautiful.

If they were merely pretty stones, they would not be as interesting. Inconsistent rewards are a lot more interesting than consistent rewards. If a cookie falls every time a person rings a bell, then they are less likely to spend a lot of time ringing the bell because they know the cookie reward will always appear.

If, however, the cookie only appears sometimes, people will spend much more time ringing the bell, just in case this is the time the cookie will fall.

There are ways to improve the power of persuasion. Just like any other trait, it can be made stronger by following a few strategies and by regular practice.

Persuasion is a powerful tool in the game of life. Persuasive people know that they have amazing power, and they know how to use it correctly. They know how to listen and hear what other people have to say. They are very good at making a connection with other people, and this makes them seem even more honest and friendly.

They make others feel that they are knowledgeable and can offer a certain sense of satisfaction. They also know when to momentarily retreat and regroup. They are not pushy. They are persuasive.

Did you know that your body speaks more eloquently than words? Body language is at work constantly whether you are aware of it or not.

When you want to master the art of persuasion, you need not only understand (and read accurately) body language, but also learn to use it to drive your point home.

Body language is a mix of hand and facial gestures, posture and overall appearance.

Using these to your advantage you can get people to do what you want without them realizing that you are controlling the outcome of the discussion.

WHY PEOPLE ARE PERSUASIVE

What makes a person convincing? Why are they persuasive, and you aren't? This is the answer we're going to pursue in this e-book, but I'm telling you now, there is no single, short answer to that question.

What makes this persuasive influence so difficult to pin down an elusive is precisely this almost mosaic quality it has. It's the result, the perfect merger of several important aspects that you wouldn't normally attribute to such an influence.

These aspects of their being don't only affect them, but affect us as well. That's the fascination around it. It's all psychological; it's an overwhelming and sometimes unintentional psychological influence on the people around them.

Confidence is the absolute most important aspect when it comes to persuasion. There's no doubt it's been scientifically proven that it's easier to persuade people when you're confident. That's because it's just assumed you're an authority on the topic and they'll listen to you, because they have no knowledge or experience, but you seem to have both.

It's also crucial to understand that humans are doubtful creatures. We're not very confident and we don't believe in our abilities or even experience, so when someone comes along and appears to be confident and to know more, we follow them like a herd of dim sheep.

Persuasion is just as much about the impression you leave upon people as it is about your actual skill. Like many other times in life, appearances are more "real" than actual reality, because it's all other people will ever know about you. It doesn't matter if deep inside, you're insecure or you don't think you know what you're doing.

On the outside, you're this dazzling, confident creature that can persuade anyone into anything because you've mastered all the important contributing factors: confidence, eye contact, body language, manner of speaking, tone, facial expressions, as well as your general demeanor.

CONFIDENCE

How do you think so many scammers make a living? No, that sketchy guy selling you snake oil isn't a doctor, but he speaks like he is one, so people believe him and throw money at him, genuinely believing he will solve their problems.

Now, I'm not advocating that you try to trick people, but I am telling you that you need to work on your confidence. You'll notice that every single person you find convincing has some sort of authoritative stance. It's like their presence demands attention and respect.

EYE CONTACT

Eye contact is a classic, natural display of dominance. It's a technique that's even present in the animal kingdom, and if a lion doesn't intimidate you, I don't know who does. Indeed, the goal isn't to intimidate. Eye contact can do that very effectively.

BODY LANGUAGE

Do you know how often people underestimate body language, or just ignore it outright? I don't know why, because body language is an amazing tool for persuasion. People are always advised to display open body language, like facing your audience, making sure not to keep your arms crossed against your chest, keeping your palms open, and all sorts of little tips that we'll discuss at length later.

What you maybe haven't heard is that to be effectively persuasive, you also need to take note of and use the body language of the person you're talking to.

MANNER OF SPEAKING

Your choice of words is overwhelmingly important when attempting to convince someone because it must be very deliberate. There's a clear strategy behind verbal persuasion, and it relies on appealing to the person's emotions.

The way you speak and what you say are both equally important because, even though your message may be perfect, if the delivery is lacking, it won't do much good. We've already established that speaking with authority is half the battle, but you also have to speak the right words, to win it.

TONE

Continuing on the idea that the way you say things is vastly important, let's talk about tone and why it matters. I lied when I said tone and message are equally important: tone weighs much more on a person's impression.

If someone has a very somber voice, a serious, measured tone, and an equally severe facial expression, it almost doesn't matter what they're saying – you will assume it's grave and important; the actual words or what they mean matters less. A joke told with a serious tone isn't funny at all.

FACIAL EXPRESSIONS

The facial expression goes hand in hand with body language and eye contact and is similarly important to tonality. Creating the impression that you mean what you say involves your face, because it will be the very first to betray you or, on the contrary, help you enforce your message.

GENERAL DEMEANOR

Now, a lot of different aspects of your being can fall under "demeanor". In a way, it's a sum of everything we've discussed so far – body language, facial expression, tone, etc. General demeanor is one of the main things you need to master, and it has one major rule: mirror the demeanor of the person you're trying to persuade.

WHAT YOU CAN OBTAIN THROUGH PERSUASION

Persuasion is a very powerful and very valuable skill that not everyone has, but that everyone should have. It comes in handy throughout your life in virtually any aspect of your existence, from sweet-talking your way into free movie tickets to convincing your boss you deserve a raise.

YOUR RELATIONSHIP WITH YOUR SPOUSE

Far from being unfair or manipulative, having the ability to convince your significant other can improve your relationship, because you have fewer fights about your disagreements and lack of compromise. Now you can use all that extra time and energy implementing your superior decisions.

YOUR RELATIONSHIP WITH YOUR KIDS

Having the persuasion skills and indisputable power and authority to convince your kids to do what you tell them to is as close to magic as you can get. If you don't believe me, try it!

YOUR RELATIONSHIP WITH YOUR FRIENDS

We all have that one friend who always makes terrible life choices, and no one can get through to them and steer them towards the right path…except you, that is. If you have influence and persuasion skills, don't keep them for yourself. Use them for good, not evil.

GET PAID WHAT YOU DESERVE

Negotiating falls under persuasion so really absolutely everyone should have this skill. No matter if you're haggling at the market or discussing a higher salary, you need to have the ability to convince your 'opponent' that you deserve this, and you should have it.

It's mostly applicable in the workplace, where – let's be real – no boss will ever willingly part with their money and hand it over to you. So, it's your job to convince them to do it. You've earned it, you deserve it, and it's rightfully yours. You have to ask for it, but you have to knowhow, and persuasive skills help with that.

EARN THE TRUST AND RESPECT OF YOUR BOSS

You can accomplish that by becoming their go-to person. Offer your bright ideas, come up with solutions to problems the company is facing, persuade them to implement your suggestions and that they're the contribution the company needs right now. In time, you will reap the rewards when your boss comes to consult with you first.

BE A GOOD LEADER TO YOUR COLLEAGUES

Your persuasive abilities will prove to be invaluable to a position like this if you want people to respect you, your work and your ideas. It should be obvious for everyone that your way is the right way and there will be minimal dissent if you have the necessary influence over them.

GET OUT OF PAYING TICKETS

Legally, a ticket is a mandatory consequence of breaking the law in some way, by speeding, failing to wear your seatbelt, talking on your cell while driving, etc. Practically, however…a ticket can be a negotiation, as long as you have the necessary skills.

GET INTO COVETED CLUBS OR RESTAURANTS

If you're persuasive enough, you can influence any menial gatekeeper and convince them to just let you through without needing to jump through fiery hoops or grease the well-meaning palms of anyone. Talk about some sweet perks!

GET IMPORTANT INFORMATION

If you can talk well enough, you can convince anyone to tell you anything. Gossip from your friend, preferred customer sales dates from sales attendants, where they keep the extra free peanuts from the flight attendant…you get the idea. Sweet talk yourself into perks and valuable info.

HOW TO PERSUADE PEOPLE

The ability to influence someone during a conversation and make a decision is necessary to become one of the most important people in the world today. This ability is useful in business negotiations and everyday life.

In general, the impact on people is not so obvious. The basic idea is that people's behavior is often guided by their subconscious simple desires. And to achieve your goals, you need to understand the simple desires of people, and then make your interlocutor passionately wish for something.

It should be noted that to influence people you should NOT try to impose or force them to make a hasty decision. It may seem incredible, but the person that wants to reach mutually beneficial cooperation becomes a huge advantage compared to those that are trying to impose something on others.

If you are willing to put yourself in the shoes of another person from whom you want to get something and understand their thoughts, then you do not have to worry about your relationship with the person.

The secret lies in the ability to help the self-affirmation of the interlocutor. It is necessary to make sure that your companion looks decent in theirown eyes. First things first, six basic principles will affect any of your interlocutors.

To achieve their goals, people often use the influence of psychology, which helps to manipulate a person.

Even in ancient times, it can be seen that priests ruled the people, instilling in them that religion is harsh and everyone will be punished if they cannot follow the established rules and practices. Psychological influence strongly acts on the subconscious, causing the victim to be influenced to be led by a skilled manipulator.

If you want to succeed and learn how to manage people, these words of the great American entrepreneur should be your credo. You will grow your personality only when you are in close cooperation with the community.

From childhood, we develop the basic patterns of behavior and outlook, produced by the long historical, biological and mental development of humankind.

To have influence and control over another person, it is required that you know their personality and behavioral traits. Most importantly, learn how to use this knowledge to master the specific methods and techniques of influence and control the behavior of the other, based on his outlook, character, personality type and other important psychological features.

If you want to learn how to manage people, secret techniques in this article will let you know not only the theoretical aspect of the question but also allow the use of this knowledge in real life.

This method of direct influence on the psyche, whose essence consists of the introduction of the narrowed state of consciousness, makes it easy to control someone else's suggestion and management.

The ability to manage people, primarily, is to combine the knowledge of human psychology and their characteristics. They help to change their behavior so that this change will cause the desired reaction in others.

Try to be more observant while communicating; it will help you better understand the individual psychological characteristics of the interlocutor. Based on this knowledge, try using the following methods and techniques that will help you manage people correctly and efficiently.

To learn how to manipulate people, you must know how it feels to be on both sides. After all, you need to understand the feelings and emotions experienced by each side. This section of the learning process will be much more efficient!

Just focus on the moral side of the issue. If you are ashamed to receive from people that are important to you, do not accept selfish purposes - better close and do not hurt their highly moral consciousness of the information received.

HYPNOSIS

There are many misconceptions regarding the practice of hypnosis. Many people maintain the idea that hypnosis is a powerful mind-control technique that leaves the victim vulnerable to be controlled by another person.

This notion is driven by the numerous hypnosis stage instancesthat are common in shows and movies these days. In such instances, you will likely observe the hypnotist swinging a pendulum, often a watch, a few times before the face of the person to be hypnotized while mumbling some things.

Within a short moment, the hypnotized person will enter into a state of trance, and it is then that the hypnotist causes themto do absurd things, like forget their name or a number, which they do. This state remains until the person is 'released' from the hypnotic state by theirhypnotizer.

107

This is usually done by a simple command such as, "You may now remember your name." To the surprise of the audience, the hypnotized person goes back to theiroriginal state.

If this is what you perceive hypnosis to be, then you are wrong. It is, in fact, quite far from the truth. In reality, at no time does the hypnotist have power over the hypnotized. The hypnotized person remains well in control of his actions throughout the entire process. According to the American Psychological Association, a leading authority on all matters psychological, the definition of hypnosis is, "a cooperative interaction in which the participant responds to the suggestions of the hypnotist."

From this definition, it is clear that the hypnotist, contrary to what many people perceive them to be, is merely a conduit to something rather than the cause of it.

In truth, when someone is hypnotized, the person attains an altered state of mind that is characterized by heightened awareness and extreme body relaxation.

Research shows that people who attain such altered states of mind are more open to suggestions and that is where hypnotherapy gains its power from. When someone has achieved this state of heightened awareness and extreme relaxation, hypnotherapists can then go on to issue suggestions, to which the hypnotized will be very receptive, and that are meant to take effect even after the hypnosis is over and done with.

The probability or intensity of being hypnotized varies from one person to the next. Some people are considered to be highly hypnotizable.

This category is usually made of people who are highly sensitive and creative. Creativity is required because during the process of hypnosis one is required to 'picture' various things and scenarios as guided by the hypnotist. As such, children and young adults make up the bulk of this category of people. In total, highly hypnotizable people make up to between 5 and 10 percent of the population.

The next category of people, with regards to their ability to be hypnotized, makes up the bulk of the total population, at around 70 to 80 percent.

This group falls somewhere around the center of the scale. Their ability to be hypnotized is considered medium, and they are averagely receptive to hypnotic suggestions. These are people whose sensitivity and creativity levels are considered average, and thus the average score on their ability to be hypnotized.

The last category of people is minimally receptive or unreceptive to hypnosis.

This group is characteristically made up of very insensitive people who are not very creative. Psychopaths make up the bulk of this group. Insensitivity and a lack of creativity is a recipe for lack of hypnotic capacity because it means that this group of people neither trust their hypnotists nor do they have the capacity to imagine scenarios as suggested by their hypnotists. In total, those who lack hypnotic capacity make up to between 5 and 10 percent of the total population.

DARK NLP

NLP is a lot like a User Manual for the brain, to help you communicate the goals and desires of the unconscious mind to the conscious self. Imagine you are in a foreign country and craving chicken wings, so you go to a restaurant to order the same, but when the food shows up, it ends up being liver stew because of a failed communication.

Humans often fail to recognize and acknowledge their unconscious thoughts and desires because a lot of it gets lost in translation to the conscious self. NLP enthusiasts often exclaim: "The conscious mind is the goal setter, and the unconscious mind is the goal-getter".

The idea being that your unconscious mind wants you to achieve everything that you desire, but if your conscious mind fails to receive the message, you will never set the goal to achieve those dreams.

NLP was developed using excellent therapists and communicators who had achieved great success as role models. It's a set of tools and techniques to help your master communicate, both with yourself and others.

NLP is the study of the human mind combining thoughts and actions with perception to fulfill their deepest desires. Our mind employs complex neural networks to process information and uses language or auditory signals to give it meaning, while storing these signals in patterns to generate and store new memories.

We can voluntarily use and apply certain tools and techniques to alter our thoughts and actions in achieving our goals. These techniques can be perceptual, behavioral and communicative and used to control our mind as well as that of others.

One of the central ideas of NLP is that our conscious mind has a bias towards a specific sensory system called the "Preferred Representational System (PRS)". Phrases like "I hear you" or "Sounds good" signal an auditory PRS, whereas phrases like "I see you" may signal a visual PRS.

A certified therapist can identify a person's PRS and model their treatment around it. This therapeutic framework often involves rapport building, goal setting and information gathering among other activities.

NLP is increasingly used by individuals to promote self-enhancement, such as self-reflection and confidence, as well as for social skill development, primarily communication.

NLP therapy or training can be delivered in the form of language and sensory-based interventions, using behavior modification techniques customized for individuals to better their social communication and improved confidence and self-awareness.

NLP therapists or trainers strive to make their client understand that their view and perception of the world is directly associated with how they operate in it, and the first step toward a better future is a keen understanding of their conscious self and contact with their unconscious mind.

It is paramount to first analyze and subsequently change our thoughts and behaviors that are counterproductive and block our success and healing. NLP has been successfully used in the treatment of various mental health conditions like anxiety, phobias, stress and even post-traumatic stress disorder.

An increasing number of practitioners are commercially applying NLP to promise improved productivity and achievement of work-oriented goals that ultimately lead to job progression.

Based on how our mind processes information or perceives the external world, it generates an internal "NLP map" of what is going on outside. This internal map is created based on the feedback provided by our sense organs, like the pictures we take in, sounds we hear, the taste in our mouth, sensations we feel on our skin and what we can smell.

However, with this massive influx of information, our mind selectively deletes and generalizes a ton of information. This selection is unique to every person and is determined by what our mind deems relevant to our situation.

As a result, we often miss out on a whole lot of information that can be immediately noticed by someone else right off the bat, and we end up with a tiny and skewed version of what is occurring. For example, take a moment and process this statement: "Person A killed person B", now depending on our circumstances and experiences we will all have our version of that story.

Some might think "a man killed a woman", or "a lion killed a man" or "a terrorist killed a baby" or "John Doe killed Kennedy" and so on.

Now, there's a method to this madness, whatever story you come up with, realize there is a way you got to that story which was driven by our own life experience.

Our mind creates an internal map of the situation at hand, and then we compare that map with other internal maps from our past that we have stored in our mind. Every person has their own internal "library" based on what is important or relevant to them by their personality.

Did you ever feel that once your conscious mind makes you aware of what you want to do or gain, suddenly the universe seems to be propping up signs that could help you find your way to get what you want? For example, one day you wake up thinking I need to take my family on a vacation.

You go on with your day the same way as you have been for days or weeks, but you suddenly notice a poster on an exciting trip to Florida on your way to work, that you later learn from your coworker has been up for over a month now. You suddenly see that, close to that same Starbucks you visit every day, there is a big travel agency that you had never paid attention to.

When browsing the Internet, you will suddenly see travel ads all over your Facebook or ads from Airbnb popping up on your

YouTube videos. Now all these may come across as coincidences, but the matter of the fact is those things or signs had been there all along, but your mind deleted that information or perception because they were not relevant to you.

So, as your conscious mind starts connecting the dots between your wishes and the reality of the world, you start picking up on new information that may have already been in plain sight, but you are only tuned into now.

Your personality profile also plays a major role in what information your mind chooses to exclude and what is processed. People who are more focused on security are constantly assessing their situation to determine whether it's safe for themor not.

On the other hand, people who are more freedom-oriented tend to think of their situation in terms of options and limitations with no focus on safety at all.

Your personality determines how you update your mental library and ultimately the meaning you add to these internal maps. For example, a kid looking at a roller coaster is thinking only about the fun of traveling through open space in a cool looking ride and given the opportunity will easily and fearlessly jump on the ride, because theirpersonality is not security-oriented.

BRAINWASHING

Brainwashing has already been briefly touched upon during the topic about mind control, but it is so important and relevant to dark psychology and manipulation, it deserves its segment of the book. When you think of someone who has been brainwashed, the result is someone who is mindlessly obedient, oftentimes out of fear. They may have been kept prisoner for so long that they became obedient just to survive, or maybe they were beaten into submission. No matter the cause of the obedience, the results of brainwashing are undeniable—they create someone who is effectively under someone else's control.

Initially used in the 1950s by Edward Hunter, brainwashing was used to refer to American soldiers that were Chinese war prisoners. Upon release, many different American soldiers declared that they were against Western thoughts and were converting to a communist belief system, which of course triggered everyone to fear that the Chinese had developed a legitimate form of mind control. In reality, however, those techniques far predated the Chinese and their usage of it in the '50s.

Brainwashing refers to thought reform—it involves several different techniques that, over time, sway a person to change their very thoughts, feelings, behaviors, and core beliefs. They change so much that they have essentially lost their ability to make free choices—they become obedient. The techniques that cause the change can vary greatly, but as a general rule, when brainwashing has occurred, it is typically combined with some sort of danger and threat, with force frequently used.

Brainwashing has several different steps, despite being a somewhat simple concept. To brainwash someone, at least in the way that it was done to those soldiers who were studied carefully and extensively, there are twelve different steps. Each of these culminates to create a changed person.

Assault on the individual's identity

This challenges a person's identity. People are frequently beaten when answering their questions about their own identities and immediately contradicted afterward. For example, if asked their name, they may answer, get beaten, and then told a new name. They quickly develop doubt about who they are as people.

Guilt

The person being brainwashed is then exposed to massive amounts of guilt, being forced to believe that he or she deserves the treatment being given. It is incredibly important here to make the person feel as if everything is their fault, or if something does not work out just right, then it is on them, and they must feel guilty.

Self-betrayal

This stage involves the brainwashed individual being systematically forced to denounce everything they held dear -friends, family, religion, culture and anything else. It essentially culminates in destroying the identity of the person being brainwashed.

Breaking the individual

Eventually, the person being brainwashed recognizes that there is no escape. Without the hope of escape and returning to life, the individual is consumed by fear and the fear of being destroyed, rendering them unable to reason and oftentimes desiring death as quickly as possible.

Leniency

At this stage, when the prisoner or brainwashed individual is sure he or she will break, someone offers a tiny beacon of kindness. The tiniest of leniencies here creates a new hope. This is paired with the manipulator insisting that if the person does as requested, then everything can be put behind them, and the prisoner is willing to do so to escape destruction.

Compelling to confess

At this point, the prisoner likely feels a need to confess all sorts of perceived crimes—the point is to cleanse the sense of self to allow for progression. The captor of course encourages this.

Channeling guilt

The prisoners then begin to feel guilty for his or her very sense of self rather than for the crimes. Everything, involving their beliefs, their family and their likes becomes a cause for guilt. As they are accepting the viewpoint of their captors, they become guiltier over themselves.

Progress

The more they begin to accept the captors' perspectives and beliefs, the more they are welcomed into society and treated as humans, encouraging them to continue on their path.

Final confession

At this point, prisoners are given one last confession—they are speaking as the new selves that were created by the process and given the chance to clean themselves of their past identity.

Rebirth

Now, the prisoners are recognized as humans once more. They are rewarded for good behavior while punished if they do anything reminiscent of their past lives.

Release

With the process complete, the prisoners are released into the real world, where they are given their rights as humans, but always faced with scrutiny for their new identity, or their old identity, and they are questioned.

Ultimately, the effects of brainwashing can be quite dramatic—an entirely new person can be created over a relatively short period. This personality is taken as a defense mechanism, happening solely to cling to any form of survival possible to be sure the individual continues to live. By protecting themselves, victims of brainwashing became precisely what those around them desired them to be out of necessity. They knew that the only way out would be through pretending to be someone they were not, even if doing so was denying and rejecting who they were fundamentally as people.

The people are suddenly entirely new entities, much to the shock of those around them, but ultimately, this can be changed. Brainwashing is relatively simple to correct—as soon as people are out of danger, the effects of the brainwashing start to let up, little by little. While of course, there will be plenty of necessary intervention, therapy and other treatments, the process can be undone.

DECEPTION

Deception means the act— huge or small, toxic, or kind— of motivating followers to accept data that is not true. Lying is a popular type of deception — the statement of something identified to be false with the intention of deceiving.

Though most people are usually honest, there are times when even those who adhere to honesty participate in deception. Research suggests the typical citizen lies multiple times each day. Some of such lies are major ("I've never betrayed you!") but more frequently than not, they are tiny white lies ("That suit looks perfectly fine") employed to escape awkward circumstances or to protect the sentiments of someone.

Trust is the foundation stone of all types of social life, from the love story and parental involvement to government. This is often compromised by deceit. Since truth is so necessary for human company, which focuses on a common vision of reality, most individuals have the general assumption that everyone else is sincere in their connectivity and dealings. Many traditions have strict societal prohibitions against deception.

Several forms of deception may occur. There are 5 specific forms of deceit discovered, according to the Interpersonal Deception Theory. Some of these have been demonstrated in other aspects of mind control, showing that some overlap can occur. The 5 major types of deception usually involve:

Lies

This is where the operator makes up information or offers data that is opposite to what the reality is. This information will be presented to the target as fast and the target will see it as the reality. It may be risky because the subject is not likely to know that they are being given fake facts; if the target realized the facts were inaccurate, they would certainly not speak to the operator and there would be no deceit.

Equivocations

This is where the agent renders comments which are inconsistent, vague or conditional. This is executed to lead the target into confusion and not to know what's happening. It could also help the operator to save face when the target returns later and wants to accuse them of misinformation.

Concealments

This is one of the most prevalent forms of deceit used. Conceals are when the operator omits data useful or relevant to the setting, or they purposely engage in any conduct that would hide the information relevant to the target for that specific context. The operator may not have lied explicitly to the issue, but they would have assumed that the crucial knowledge that is required will never reach the target.

Exaggeration

This is where the agent overestimates an aspect that twists the facts a little, to transform the narrative the way they want. While the operator may not be telling lies directly to the target, they are trying to do the complete opposite of the method of exaggeration in that the operator will understate or lessen elements of reality. They'll tell the target that an incident isn't that big a deal when it could be the factor that defines whether the target gets to graduate or gets a very nice raise. The operator will be ready to look back later saying how they didn't even realize how big of a deal it was, letting them look good and the target looks just about petty if they whine. These are all just a few of the kinds of deception that could be found. The operator of the deception will use any method available to them to reach their ultimate goal, much like what happens in the other types of mind control. If they can accomplish their target using another approach against the target, then they can do so and the above list is not unique in any way. The deceit operator will be very harmful as the target may not be able to recognize what the reality is and what is an act of manipulation; the operator may be so experienced at what they are doing that it would be nearly difficult to decide what is the reality and what is not.

Chapter 10:

How to Identify Dark Triad Traits

To identify the Dark Triad traits, psychologists need to measure different personality types. In 2010, Dr. Peter Jonason developed and published a rating scale known as the Dirty Dozen: A Concise Measure of the Dark Triad with Gregory Webster, a professional psychologist. The rating scale comprises a 12-item methodology, and it comes in handy when measuring the dark traits. Psychologists normally ask people to rate themselves using the following questions:● I tend to lack remorse.

● I have used flattery to get my way.

● I tend to want others to pay attention to me.

● I tend to want others to admire me.

● I tend to exploit others toward my own ends.

● I tend to seek prestige or status.

- I tend to expect special favors from others.

- I tend to be cynical.

- I have used deceit or lied to get my way.

- I tend to manipulate others to get my way.

- I tend not to be too concerned with morality or the morality of my actions.

- I tend to be callous or insensitive.

At a basic level, a person can be rated from one to seven, although the rating scale has twelve questions. The possible score is from 12 to 84. A higher score indicates that a person may possess some of the Dark Triad traits.

How to Spot a Fellow Manipulator

While manipulating others might be gainful to you, being manipulated by someone else is not. It is for this reason that it is just as important to know how to spot a manipulator as it is to know how to manipulate.

Some people are simply born manipulators blessed with the gift of the gab, and these natural-born manipulators all seem to share some common traits as described by psychiatrist Abigail Brenner.

They are incapable of true altruism

Manipulative people hardly, if ever, do something out of the goodness of their hearts—there is usually an ulterior motive. For example, a manipulative person might buy you lunch today, and while you'd think that they were simply being generous, the aforementioned manipulative person would be planning to ask you to work one of their shifts tomorrow.

They're Big Talkers, but That is Where It Ends

Manipulators do not usually follow up with their grandiose speeches or ideas with actual action. They build these incredible castles in the sky to draw you in, without the intention of ever acting on any of the commitments or promises they might make. For example, your boss may continually hint at a promotion before every big project they assign to you, but has no intention to promote you—they're simply trying to manipulate you into giving 110% to a project in the hope of furthering your career.

They Are Not Empathetic

Manipulators either choose not to empathize with others or are simply incapable of empathy. You might spot a manipulator in this way, for example, when your company is undergoing downsizing. Under normal circumstances, even the employees who are not being laid off will feel sad and sorry for their colleagues who are losing their jobs, but a manipulator may be smug, or perhaps entirely apathetic, about their colleagues' misfortune.

They Will Misuse Even the Smallest Kindness You Might Show Them

If you give manipulators an inch, they take a mile. Manipulators take advantage of people; it is simply what they do—and there's no easier way for them to do this than if you have already opened the door to their abuse by doing them a favor or by being kind to them. An example of this might be if you brought your coworker coffee for the morning meeting one day, and suddenly, this is what is expected of you—and now this coworker gets upset when they arrive at the meeting and their cup of coffee is not already waiting for them. This coworker might be a manipulator.

THEY LIKE TO PLAY THE BLAME GAME

Manipulators don't want to accept responsibility for their wrongdoings, so they attempt to assign the blame to someone else— even if it means ruining that person's career, relationships or friendships. An example of this might be that one coworker who made a blunder on a project they had been working on, but when confronted blamed the team leader for their failure or incompetence—resulting in their team leader losing their job. A manipulator would happily sacrifice somebody else's career in this way.

THEY DO NOT HAVE BOUNDARIES. AT ALL.

Manipulators usually do not understand or do not care about, the social contract prescribing the rules of etiquette to which the rest of us subscribe. A manipulator might ask you questions that are just a little too personal, or might call you about a work-related matter at an unreasonable hour, or might show up at your house unexpectedly. They don't understand, or don't care about, the concept of being "rude."

THEY ARE UNWILLING TO COMPROMISE

It's their way or the highway. Manipulators insist on things being done exactly as they expect them to be done. Whether this is due to a need to insist on having authority or whether this is an inborn defect is unknown. And when they do not get their way, the resulting outburst is often incredibly aggressive and explosive. For this reason, people are often wary of going against a manipulator, which is why so many of them allegedly end up in higher management positions.

They think that they are important. Very important

Psychopaths tend to have a grandiose sense of self, and often think of themselves as the center of the universe. As a result of this inflated ego, psychopaths often demand special or superior treatment. They expect to be treated like the royalty they believe themselves to be—and all hell breaks loose when their incredibly high standards are not met.

They are incapable of feeling guilt or remorse

Psychopaths do not have a conscience. They can contemplate things which would make others rile back in disgust, gagging at the very thought. Psychopaths are often born with an underdeveloped or maldeveloped frontal lobe, impacting their ability to feel empathy or understand what is morally right or morally wrong. As a result of this, they are often capable of acts of incredible cruelty.

They are master manipulators

Here, you can refer back to the common traits of manipulators listed above. Psychopaths are fantastically talented at guilt-tripping others and equally gifted at flattery and seduction. You might find yourself unknowingly or unwittingly obeying a psychopath's every command due to their ability to manipulate.

They are incredibly charming

This slots into the flattery and seduction mentioned above. Psychopaths are very good at getting people to be "on their team." They smile and joke their way into the lives of the people around you, and these people are often unable to see the psychopath for what they truly are. A psychopath will have the entire neighborhood wrapped around their finger in no time. They might even get elected for office.

THEY ARE ALSO INCREDIBLY RUTHLESS

You will know if you have crossed a psychopath in some way as they are likely to reciprocate through small (or large) acts of revenge. They are also more than happy to turn those who are nearest and dearest to you against you if they feel that you have wronged them in some way. A psychopath usually dispenses their justice, usually with disastrous effects.

THEY VIOLATE THE RIGHTS OF OTHERS

An example of this would be the case of Robert Maxwell, the incredibly wealthy publishing giant who, after his death, was found to have stolen millions by defrauding the pension funds of thousands of innocent people.

THEY ENGAGE IN SOCIALLY IRRESPONSIBLE BEHAVIOR LIKE BINGE DRINKING, ADDICTION TO NARCOTICS, PROMISCUOUS SEXUAL ACTIVITY, OR OTHER CRIMINAL ACTIVITIES

An example of a psychopath engaging in socially irresponsible (or rather, reprehensible) behavior is Ted Bundy, the infamous serial killer and promising law student who confessed to murdering 30 women in his spare time.

THEY ARE FREQUENTLY IN TROUBLE WITH THE LAW

This happens as a natural consequence of socially irresponsible behavior and violating the rights of others. Psychopaths are not always caught red-handed for murder, thoughsometimes these transgressions are as small as not believing that the speed limit applies to them, thus amassing a small mountain of fines.

THEY LIKE TO HURT OTHERS AND ARE OFTEN SADISTS

An example of this is Ilse Koch, the wife of a Nazi secret service member, who would walk around naked in a Jewish concentration camp and had any man who so much as dared to glance at her shot on the spot.

AN INABILITY TO, OR APATHY TOWARD, UNDERSTANDING RIGHT FROM WRONG

Psychopaths either do not care about doing the right thing or do not know that they are doing the wrong thing. An example of this is the "angel of mercy" stereotype found within the study of criminology. Offenders who fall under this stereotype commit murders with the belief that they are doing the victim a favor by euthanizing them.

THE NEED TO FIX AND HEAL THOSE AROUND THEM

Those who are easy to manipulate are always on the lookout for someone down on their luck to help out of the gutter. The reason this makes them easy to manipulate is that absolutely anybody can pretend to be going through a hard time, and in doing so win the loyalty and trust of the aforementioned person.

THEY USE STATISTICS CONSTANTLY TO OVERWHELM YOU

You may find that the manipulator will constantly, in an argument, inundate you with statistics that may or may not be accurate or in context to try to force you to give in. They do this in all sorts of different ways in hopes of keeping control of you. After all, you can't argue with logic and numbers, can you? The manipulator will take advantage of the fact that most people won't stop to consider correlation vs. causation.

THEY ARE PASSIVE-AGGRESSIVE

Typically, manipulators will lay on the passive-aggressive attitudes if they think that you won't give them what they want. They will hope that the pressure will make you cave; they rely on making you feel bad or undermined so that they will get what they need or want from you. They have no qualms with taking advantage of you, and this is one of the easiest ways that they can do so.

THEY MAKE YOU FEEL JUDGED OR CRITICIZED

Manipulators will also lay on the judgment or criticism in hopes of making you feel more likely to give them what they want. They know that if they can make you feel like they are constantly judging you, you are far more likely to bow to their demands just because you will often be sensitive to that. No one likes feeling judged, after all, and that means that most manipulators have a very easy built-in weapon that they can take advantage of to control other people.

THEY INSIST THAT YOU SPEAK FIRST

If you find that the other person always wants you to speak first, just to criticize and tear apart everything that you say, they are probably trying to manipulate you. It is a method that works to make you feel dragged down or like you can't voice your complaints or disagreements. When this happens, you will find that you are constantly at the mercy of the other person and may even stop trying to justify yourself and what you have done out of fear of being torn down again and again. It becomes easier just not to share your thoughts or opinions at all.

THEY GET LOUD OR AGGRESSIVE IF YOU DON'T GIVE THEM THEIR WAY

Typically, you will find that manipulators will very quickly shift over to yelling or being aggressive if they are not getting their way.

They will feel like they have no choice but to escalate further if that is what it will take to get you to obey. Typical manipulators will start with the least amount of force possible as they escalate, trying to get you to do whatever it is that they want. There are typically no real qualms about having to get louder or more aggressive if that is what it will take. They will suddenly go from 0 to intimidatingly aggressive in the blink of an eye, leaving you confused, hurting and wondering what happened.

THEY PRESSURE YOU TO ACT QUICKLY

You may find that your manipulator will also constantly weigh on you to make decisions quickly. The pressure is there to serve one simple purpose: Decisions made in times of heightened emotion are typically not as good as those that you can make when you have the time to mull over a decision. You might find that you get time limits to manipulate you or to get you to obey quicker than you intend to. They will set arbitrary limits in hopes of making you feel like you have to rush and, therefore, not think thingsover in a very responsible manner. As a direct result, they get to have some degree of influence over the decision that you make.

THEY INSIST ON MEETING IN PERSON TO ARGUE

Finally, you will probably notice that all of the arguments or confrontations that you have are in person—and on the other person's terms. The manipulator wants that home-field advantage—they want to take you somewhere that you are not completely comfortable in so that they can take advantage of what is going on. They want to be able to essentially belittle you into their decision or to get you to give in to them, so they make it a point to bring you somewhere that they are comfortable, and you are not. Furthermore, they usually are masters at using body language to intimidate and dominate over their victims, and that requires them to be in your general presence to be effective.

THEY TRY TO DECEIVE.

We all value truth and accountability, but tricksters either conceal the truth or try to show you just one version of the story. Consider, for example, the boss or worker who deliberately circulates unverified rumors and gossip for a tactical advantage.

Tactic: Don't trust everything you listen to. Instead, focus the judgments on well-known facts, and pose questions when specifics are not obvious.

WHEN YOU ARE HAPPY, THEY REAP THE BENEFITS OF IT.

Frequently, when we're in a particularly positive mood, we're inclined to say yes to anything or hop on prospects that look great at the time (but we didn't think through that). Manipulators know how to manipulate certain moods.

Tactic: Strive to make your optimistic feelings more conscious; almost as muchas your hurtful feelings. When making choices, aim to find a balance.

THEY'RE PLAYING ON WORRY.

To scare you into action, a trickster will misrepresent facts and overemphasize particular points.

Tactic: Beware of remarks that imply that you lack the courage or try to instill a fear of falling out. Before taking any action ensure you have the full picture of the problem.

THEY ARE PUSHING FOR AN ADVANTAGE IN THE HOME COURT.

A deceptive person can demand that you meet and engage in a physical space where more power and influence can be exerted.

These men may try to negotiate in an environment where they feel control and familiarity like their workplace, house, or some other place where you may feel less secure.

Tactic: An invitation to do so in a neutral environment if you need to talk. To help you get your bearings if you have to meet the individual on his or her property, ask for a drink, and engage in small talk at the arrival.

THEY USE RECIPROCITY TO THEIR ADVANTAGE.

Manipulators understand it's harder to say no if they do you a favor — so they may try to impress you, cheese you up, or say yes to little favors... and afterward ask for massive ones.

Tactic: Offering brings more delight than receiving of course.

But knowing your limitations is also important. And don't be scared to say no if need be.

THEY SHOW PESSIMISTIC EMOTIONS.

In an attempt to control your feelings, a few people purposely raise their voice or use powerful body language to show they're angry.

Tactic: Practice the timeout. If someone's exhibiting deep feelings, pause for a moment to respond. In certain situations, you might also take a few minutes to move away.

THEY ASK PLENTY OF QUESTIONS.

Talking about ourselves is simple. Manipulators realize this and take advantage of it by posing questions with a secret agenda — discovering secret vulnerabilities or knowledge that they can exploit for their gain.

Tactic: Of course, in anyone who intends to get to understand you effectively you should not suspect false motives. But watch out for those who inquire only questions — whereas refusing to disclose the same details about themselves.

THEY OFFER YOU AN INCREDIBLY LIMITED AMOUNT OF TIME FOR ACTION.

A person may try and force you within a very unreasonable amount of time to make a decision. By so doing, before you even have time to consider the implications, theytryto persuade you into making a decision.

Tactic: Don't give in to excessive demands. When your partner fails to give you more time, then you're better off heading for something you need in another place.

THEY TRY TO TALK FAST.

Manipulators may often talk at a quicker speed or use different terminology and phrases to try to gain benefits.

Tactic: Don't be scared to ask people to describe their statements or ask specific questions. You could also repeat their argument in your phrases or request them to mention an example — letting you reclaim control of the narrative.

THEY'RE DEALING WITH YOU USING THE SILENT TREATMENT.

By intentionally failing to respond to your acceptable calls, texts, emails or other queries, the manipulator presupposes power by having you wait and intends to put doubt and confusion in your mind. The silent treatment is a head game where secrecy is used as a power.

Tactic: Give your partner a time limit after you have tried communication to a fair extent. In cases where solutions are not accessible, it might be appropriate to provide a frank conversation about his or her contact style.

HARDLY CRUEL.

Help accelerate somebody's objectives to get them to provide you a favor. It's a bit measured, but it's straight out of Zig Ziglar: If you help plenty of other people gain what they want, you'll get everything you want in life.

TRICKY.

To get clients to purchase your item, use an alternative item. Attempting to get people to purchase a more costly version of the product? A third alternative is introduced — one that is the same price, but less powerful.

Based on the context, thismight be malicious.

Start concentrating on what your trading partner is obtaining, not losing. Looks reasonable, but if you hide that you are offering a crap deal to somebody, I hope you're doing something else to address your karma.

Perhaps a little manipulative...

Modify the environment to get individuals to perform less selfishly. Asking favors in a social situation rather than a corporate setting helps make people more willing to behave like a buddy than a competitor.

HYPOCRITICAL.

Show a picture of the eyes to encourage people to act appropriately. When we see the eyes, we think that we are being monitored, so we believe like everything we do is being observed and evaluated.

MANIPULATIVE.

Imitate the body language of the people to make them admire you. Research suggests that if you replicate their body language, people are more prone to subconsciously relating with you. And this makes them more inclined to perform what you would like.

BEING ATTRACTED TO INSECURITIES.

Use nouns rather than words to encourage people to alter their habits. When people hear nouns, they think of their self-identity. They think of actions when they notice verbs.

SCHEMING AND FALLACY.

Ask people for help because they're sick of someone asking them to comply." Similar to a couple of other suggestions on the list, they're more inclined to accept as people are stressed down. Car dealers use this tactic — that is why it's so hard to just turn up and get a quote.

DECEPTIVE.

Speak fast to get a rival to comply with you. Overpower people with your pace, and bring them down. Sometimes they'll agree since they can't digest what you're saying — and don't want to acknowledge it.

TERRORIZING.

Instill fear in people to make them give you what you need. That is the essence of most marketing— making people scared of something, and then offering them the antidote. That doesn't make them any less evil. It is very successful though.

THEY ASSUME IT'S THE CORRECT APPROACH.

This is anyone who is hell-bound to exploit another human, no matter what would hold their ground. They appear to be very outspoken about how the only thing that will function is their strategy to a specific problem or issue and they need everybody to get on the same page.

VERY EVIL.

Confuse others to cooperate with your order. Individuals don't like to accept that they don't grasp something, so they comply. The example cited is to interpret the cost of something in pennies, instead of in dollars, since processing takes longer.

There are many explanations for this; specifically, they need to manipulate people to handle the situation and control what people see to stay in control.

If they're telling lies about something or attempting to cover up something, the best way is to be in power to make sure they're not discovered.

Manipulative people "really assume that their way of dealing with situations is the only way to do so because it implies their requirements are satisfied, and that's all that is crucial."

You may have an iconic manipulator on your shoulders if you feel like you're attempting to deal with someone who never provides you an inch even though you give them a mile.

THEIR RELATIONSHIP CROSSES LINES.

Manipulators can do whatever they can to make you feel small and incapable of their affection and care.

They will cross boundaries that make you doubt your integrity and you will wind up thinking like your relationship's collapse is your own.

People that are dishonest, insecure and have a weak sense of self continue to break personal limits on many occasions. If you inform them not to do anything, you can bet your area that the very next opportunity they get they will take it. However, it is not because they're terrible people. This is because, no matter what, they needto be the person in control.

It's like having to manage a kid who isn't going to stop throwing hissy fits because they want sweets in the shop.

BLAMING YOU FOR THEIR ISSUES.

Take into account how many times you walkaway from a discussion with them feeling terrible about yourself or being guilty about making their scenario worse when you are interacting with someone you believe might be trying to exploit you.

This is identified as "gaslighting," in which trickery is used to get people to question themselves and what they have done wrong.

You may feel a sense of regret or defensiveness if you're being gaslighted – like you've done something bad. This is what I call "the blame of the manipulator" because "they are not taking responsibility."

In case you are trying to deal with a trickster, both of these accusations will be accurate. Manipulators have the means to skirt blame and point fingers at others.

They'll accuse you and other individuals ofeverything from why they're not earning enough money with their work to the reason they couldn't get Saturday night's concert tickets.

When it comes to making sure that they don't bear any responsibility for their own lives, they are professional artists.

CODEPENDENCY DEVELOPMENT

Codependency is purely a psychological game that is anchored on the fact that the manipulator needs you in their life. Because the manipulator wants to get something from you, they must make sure that you deem the relationship beneficial. If a manipulator wants to get your money or your influence, they will draw you close and make you feel that you need each other in the relationship. They will create an ideal situation where you cannot live or survive without each other. Through continuous use of lies and creating scenes, the manipulator will find a way of making you believe that the relationship is important for both of you. While this tactic may work, sooner or later the victim may realize that they are being used. If you are in any relationship where you feel that you cannot live without the other person, chances are that you are being manipulated. The reality is that life cannot be built around a single person. You should be able to survive in any part of the world without the fear of lacking anything just because of a single person.

ISOLATION

Isolation is a tactic that manipulators use to take the victim to a place where they do not have any help. In dark psychology, a person cannot completely manipulate you in public. It is difficult for a person to control your life and take full advantage of you if you have friends around. For this reason, most manipulators isolate the victim. Unfortunately, most victims never notice when that isolation is happening. The manipulator will tell you that you are being targeted by other people. Manipulators create conflict between the victim and their friends and family. Often, such conflicts lead to the rupture of relationships. If you are in a relationship where you have been forced to break your connection with friends or family, you should run away as quickly as possible. No one should ever come in between you and your family or friends. Even if you are in love, you must make sure you maintain old relationships.

TAKING YOU ON A GUILT TRIP

The other obvious sign of manipulation is when a person keeps taking you on guilt trips. A guilt trip involves a situation where a person makes you feel guilty even if you did not do anything wrong. Manipulators will use guilt trips to get whatever they want. A manipulative person knows that you will do anything if you feel guilty. It is common for people to repair their mistakes by pleasing the person they have offended. If a person keeps taking you on guilt trips, they are looking for favors. Such favors are only a way of taking advantage of you and this is the clearest form of manipulation that you can experience.

ATTACK ON SELF-ESTEEM

A manipulative person aims to ensure that you doubt yourself. A manipulative person will attack your self-esteem in every way possible to make you feel as if you are not worthy. If you are in any relationship where the other party keeps throwing insults your way, you need to examine the relationship. Manipulative individuals attack a person's self-esteem by using verbal abuse, demeaning words and mind control tactics. You need to keep a clear mind at all times if you wish to stand against manipulators. You can use your strong stand to silence the manipulators and ensure that you protect your emotions from being affected by the insults. If you allow the manipulator to affect your emotions, they may end up taking full control of your life.

SETTING UP TRAPS

Other manipulators use traps to take you on guilt trips. For instance, someone may ask you a question for the sole purpose of trying to trap you. If a person asks you a question where any answer you may give is controversial, the chances are that they are trying to set a trap for you so that they can manipulate you.

MANIPULATORS ARE CROSSING LINES TO HAVE THEIR WAY.

If you don't have limits right away, then for a manipulative individual you might be a perfect candidate.

Unfortunately, manipulative people sometimes claim victimhood and prey on caring caregivers with weak (or no) limits.

LOOKS LIKE YOU'RE SPEAKING TO A WALL OF BRICKS.

Deceptive people are tough and swift in their reasoning. It's a form of protection, but it's still a weapon they use to take charge of the situation. If you turn to someone you believe you are being manipulated by and you try to have a conversation with them, they will shut down. Deceptive people tend to participate in the "playing stupid game":

By claiming that theydon'trealize what you need or what you won't want themto do, the deceiver passive-aggressively convinces you to take on theirduty and convinces you to break a sweat. They would also transform the topic on you to make you sound like a poor guy in the first place for even raising the issue. They're just going to sit there feeling arrogant and be blunt with you, doing something like, "yup, all right, good, nice, mmhmm." It's distracting, which makes you sound like you're not making them understand.

THEY'RE PLAYING ON YOUR FEELINGS.

Manipulators are clever and subtle, and they will operate a scenario or a task with a level of pride that can leave you feeling icky. They not only undermine individuals' right next to them but also tend to feel ashamed regarding your feelings. They have a sneaky way to make you feel terrible when you're feeling sad. If you're annoyed, a manipulative individual may attempt to make you feel guilty for your emotions.

THEIR WORDS AND ACTIONS DON'T MATCH.

The easiest way to know if someone is tryingto manipulate you or is generally a deceptive person is to watch their actions. If they're saying one thing and doing another, they're likely trying to hide stuff or not being true to their commitment. You can judge individuals by their acts to detect dishonest people so you can never be tricked by their expressions. Remember, every time there are non-identical things regarding what a person tells and does.

Chapter 11:

How to Manage People With Dark Triad Traits

MANAGING PEOPLE WITH DARK TRIAD TRAITS

If you usually exhibit the Dark Triad traits, you may be wondering whether there is something that you can do about it. The answer to how the Dark Triad traits can be managed is quite complex. Experienced psychologists can weigh in on the matter. For starters, when looking into different personality types, you will notice that there are many gradations. A person's behavior can change daily. As a manager, you will have to look into ways that you can address some of the associated negative behaviors so that you can ensure that your team works in harmony, and their productivity levels will also be good.

Given that there are plenty of people out there trying to manipulate your life and control your life choices, you must learn how to spot manipulation. You should be able to tell whether a person is trying to control your actions and thinking process. Most manipulators are very cunning. They will not show their intentions outwardly. When a manipulative person comes to you, they come with the best intentions. They try to show you that they care and that they can't hurt you. This is the reason why you have to pay more attention to subconscious cues during conversations. People do not always mean what they say.

HOW TO ESCAPE MANIPULATION

Understanding that manipulation is real and accepting the fact that manipulators are out there to hurt you is the first step to being able to escape the long hands of manipulation. Manipulation is a very complex subject and understanding manipulators will help you escape manipulation. Here is a simple step by step guide on how to escape manipulation.

STUDY YOUR RELATIONSHIPS USING NLP

Do not just look at your relationships from the outside. You need to look at all the relationships you have from an internal perspective. From that internal perspective, look at any relationship and try to spot the subconscious motive of your relationship partner. You cannot escape a manipulative relationship if you do not know their motives. This first step should help you categorize your relationship as either manipulative or non-manipulative. You can use the characteristics mentioned above to observe your relationships and try to determine which ones are manipulative. Look at all types of relationships, including romantic, friendships and even family relationships. There are many cases where parents or siblings manipulate one another. Take your time to monitor all relationships while comparing them to the factors above. Compare your relationships to the signs of manipulation above. If you realize that your relationship shows more than three signs of manipulation, you need to move to the next step.

REBUILD YOUR RELATIONSHIPS

If it is true that you are in a manipulative relationship, then there are high chances that you have been isolated. Only a few manipulators will try to take control of your mind without isolation. In most cases, you are isolated and forced to break relationships with friends and family. If it is true that you are in a manipulative relationship, you must first rebuild those broken relationships. Since the relationships are with close people, including friends and family, you can approach several old friends and try mending fences. You may also try to explain to them that you are under a manipulative relationship.

However, if you are still at the early stages of the relationship, you should stop isolation. If you realize that a person is trying to separate you from the people you have known for a long time, you should stop them. One of the best ways to stop manipulation is to ensure that you always have friends and family around. Have a person you can share your secrets with. Try to explain to these people the things that are happening in your life. If you keep your relationship open, you will enjoy a fulfilling relationship that is not manipulative in any way.

FIND HELP FROM OLD FRIENDS AND FAMILY

Once you have rebuilt your old relationships, find help from those people. There are many reasons you will be needing these people in your life. If you are already in an advanced relationship, the chances are that the manipulative individual has taken control of your social and financial life. Manipulative individuals will lower your self-esteem and reduce you to nothing. They will take your money and sabotage your success so that they may control your life. If you wish to get out of such relationships, you will need financial help and social support. Unless you have someone who can support you in your quest to escape manipulation, you may easily find yourself walking straight back into the same relationship. For this reason, it is important to bring old friends and family on board. Talk to those people and try making them understand your current situation.

CUT COMMUNICATION AND MOVE OUT

If you are living with a manipulative person under the same roof, you have to move out. Given that you have support in all areas of your life, you are now in a position to move out of the relationship and start rebuilding your life. Ensure that you cut all forms of communication between you and the other party. If you continue communicating, the other person may pull you back into the relationship and may cause you to lose track of your decision. Most people try moving out of manipulative relationships and end up being pulled back. If you are not careful, you might be pulled back into the same relationship that you were trying to escape.

PSYCHOLOGICAL WARFARE: DON'T BE MANIPULATED-GAINING MANIPULATION SKILLS

When it comes to manipulation, the manipulator will always focus on getting what they want, using various forms of trickery. Many people believe that manipulation is immoral. Since psychological manipulators use various deception techniques, we will look into each of these tactics and offer a suitable solution on how people can defend themselves in case of any eventuality.

TAKE AN ACTING CLASS

When it comes to manipulation, it is good to learn more about how to master emotions while making sure that other people can become receptive, whenever you tend to become emotional. To learn more about expressing yourself using various techniques that play on people's emotions, it is good to enroll in an acting class. While in an acting class, it will be possible to gain some powers of persuasion. Always focus on the main goal, which involves understanding the methods of manipulating people, so you can protect yourself.

ENROLL IN A PUBLIC SPEAKING CLASS

The acting classes are meant to make sure that you can master your emotions and how you display them. The main reason why enrolling for a debate class is advisable is because you will be able to learn more about convincing other people ofyour argument. You will learn more about how to organize your thoughts. Additionally, a public speaking class will also enlighten you about how to sound convincing. A manipulative person will use these skills to influence the actions of others by convincing them to do what they want.

COME UP WITH SIMILARITIES

Manipulators always make sure that they have learned more about the body language of their target victims. They also look into the intonation patterns of their victims before they can proceed with the manipulation process. Eventually, the manipulators will come up with persuasive methods, and they will also appear calm. Watch out for this type of behavior.

BEING CHARISMATIC

Charismatic individuals often have a way of getting what they want. When understanding how charming people can manipulate others, you will have to ensure that you have worked on your charisma. Not everyone who is charismatic is manipulative, so pay attention to understand who is sincere and who is misleading you. You should also be able to smile, and your body language should showcase that you are approachable, so that people feel they can easily approach you and talk to you. You must also be able to initiate a conversation with any individual, regardless of various factors, such as age. Some of the techniques that you can utilize to become charismatic include:

• Ensuring that people feel special. The best way to achieve this is by maintaining eye contact while conversing with a person. Make sure that you have also initiated a discussion about how they feel and the interests that they have. Always show the other person that you care and you want to learn more about them. An insincere charismatic person will pretend to care about the other person, even when they don't.

• Always maintain high levels of confidence. Charismatic people are always passionate about everything that they do. It is also advisable to have confidence in yourself.

LEARN FROM THE MASTERS

If you have a friend who happens to be a psychological manipulator, you should observe them and also take notes, so you know what to look out for from potential manipulators. Always carry out a case study and ensure that the manipulators are the main point of focus. It will be possible to learn a lot from them. Pay attention to how these individuals get what they want. They may also share some insight into how they manipulate people. The main issue is that you might end up being tricked, but you will gain some insight into how to manipulate people effectively, and therefore how to avoid being manipulated.

LEARN MORE ABOUT HOW TO READ PEOPLE

Each individual has a psychological and emotional makeup, and it always varies from one individual to another. When you learn about the psychological and emotional makeup of a person, it will be possible to manipulate them. Manipulative people will often learn more about the individual that they will manipulate, and in many cases, they become trusted by the person before they slowly take advantage of them. Some of the things that you may notice as you try to understand people include:

● Most people are vulnerable, and it is possible to reach out to them by evoking their emotional responses. For instance, some people may cry when watching a movie, and they may showcase high levels of sympathy and empathy. For a person to manipulate such individuals, they often joke around with their emotions while also pretending to feel sorry, and they will eventually get what they want by playing on the other person's emotions.

● Other people have a strong sense of guilt. Most of the individuals who have a guilt reflex grew up in a restrictive household, and they may have been punished for every wrong deed that they committed. Manipulators may make sure that the person feels guilty about various acts, so they are more likely to give in to a manipulator's demands at the end of it all.

● Some people usually respond to rational approaches. For example, if you have a close friend who is always logical and always keeps up with the news, thismeans that they are always after verifiable information. In such an instance, a manipulative person will make sure that they have utilized their persuasive powers accordingly when manipulating them.

PROTECTING YOURSELF FROM DARK PSYCHOLOGY AND MANIPULATION

If you want to be protected against dark psychology and manipulation, then there are a few ways that you can protect yourself. Ultimately, the best way to be defended against harm is to make sure that you just cut yourself off from those around you that are manipulative, but when that can't be done reasonably, you can fight back in other ways. When you want to protect yourself from the manipulation and harassment of dark people, the best way to do so includes the following:

REJECT THE NEED FOR APPROVAL FROM OTHERS

This is simple: if you stop letting other people define you, you can step away from needing them to constantly influence you. You can remove that need forapproval and disconnect all sorts of strings. Now, this is easier said than done, but ultimately, the best way for you to do this is to make sure that you recognize the truth: The manipulator can only manipulate you if you give him the strings to do so. Theyknow that you have that need to be needed, and theywill use it against you every single time. To do this, consider the following points as well:

RECOGNIZE THE TRUTH

See that they are just trying to manipulate you and control you. Theiraffection or attention isn't worth it.

YOU DON'T NEED TO CHANGE OTHER PEOPLE

You really can't make them change anyway. Trying to do so is futile and just a waste of your time.

DON'T DEFEND YOURSELF

You don't owe anyone an explanation most of the time. If you start getting defensive, it is time to break it off and stop trying. Forget trying to defend other people and just work with yourself instead.

PROTECT YOUR BOUNDARIES

Remember that you are allowed to say no. Telling someone no and even disappointing someone else is not off-limits. You are allowed to insist on things your way if you choose to do so, and there is no reason that you can't tell someone that you don't want to do something. You are within your rights to tell other people when they are crossing your boundaries and you deserve the respect of having them move away from you as you do so.

STOP SECOND-GUESSING YOURSELF

Make sure that when you have a gut feeling about something being a certain way, you remember to honor it. Don't tell yourself that you're overreacting if you notice something that isn't quite right. You have those gut reactions for a reason, and you owe it to yourself to honor them. Remember, you are meant to be intuitive. You know when someone is doing something cruel or unfair, and you need to honor that. If you start to doubt yourself, remind yourself that you are worthy of being trusted.

UP YOUR EMOTIONAL INTELLIGENCE

Emotional intelligence is your way of being able to understand and empathize with other people. When you are emotionally intelligent, you usually recognize your emotional reactions and tendencies and can understand them. Likewise, you start to better understand what other people are doing as well. In doing this, you develop a better understanding of what will keep yourself steady. You will be able to keep yourself calm and in control, and in doing so, you will discover that you can remain in control of many different situations. You don't have to allow manipulators to take control. You can tell yourself not to fall for it, and you can keep your emotions steady, so that is the case. Emotional intelligence is ultimately developed through self-awareness—you have to be self-aware enough to use it accordingly. If you are, you will be able to successfully navigate all sorts of situations, and you will be able to ensure that you are, ultimately, able to recognize when you are making mistakes so that you can correct them.

Chapter 12:

Techniques to Defend Yourself from Manipulation

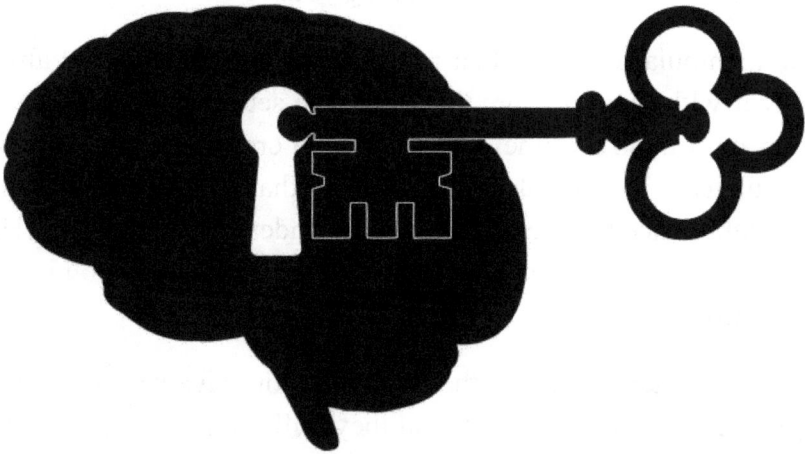

F or starters, it is good to note that it is not possible to defend yourself from a manipulative individual. The best thing that you can do in this case is to make sure that you have first identified that the individual is indeed manipulative. If they happen to showcase that they are deceptive, you should ensure that you have kept a safe distance from these individuals. If they are not deceptive, you can continue being friends. It is also good to note that some people may mislead others by spreading false information. For example, you may come across some people talking about how manipulative a certain person is, but they are the ones trying to manipulate you and your opinion of this other person.

Never issue the manipulative person a warning. If you notice early on, you should just leave and continue leading your life as usual. After leaving them, they will look for other individuals who they can manipulate into ensuring that they have heeded their demands. If a person is unwell, you should go ahead and try to find out more about their condition. Since some people do lie, you can also go ahead and seek some expert advice from a psychologist or even a psychiatrist. If the person is unwell and they do not showcase any signs of improvement, you can move on and continue living your life as usual, if they are not threatening you.

If the manipulative individual is related to you, you should always be direct with them. Ensure that you have set some boundaries and always be firm so that they cannot dare to cross the set boundaries. Manipulative individuals will realize that they will be held accountable once they tend to showcase undesirable behaviors. How such people behave toward you will also determine how you interact with them.

If they understand some of the rules that you have set, they will in some cases be okay with that, and they will not intrude in any way. Also, ensure that you have initiated a discussion with the manipulative individual, while also trying to learn more about their character and condition. Ensure that you have not lectured them in any way. Always ask questions that will help you to learn more about how they are. Never try to fix them, leave such matters to professionals such as psychiatrists or psychologists. Always ensure that you have issued them a referral to a renowned psychiatrist or any other medical practitioner who can deal with their condition accordingly. The manipulative individuals should also be issued the support that they need.

Although some of the stories issued by the manipulative individuals will appear far-fetched, you should never judge them. According to them, their story is valid, although it may appear to be made up to some extent. Ensure that you have not told them any of your stories. If anything goes wrong, they will always use the information that they have about you to fight back. Always remember that we never choose our family members; as a result, you should choose whether you will help them or ignore them. If any other people may appear to be toxic in your life, you should also avoid them. Manipulation and abuse in romantic and other close relationships can build up with "small" occurrences, and they can end with an attempt at total control of one person over another. This is very dangerous and damaging, and you must be on alert in the early stages of manipulative behavior, to be able to get free of this kind of dynamic before it becomes destructive. Always seek help if you feel you need it, to stay safe from a threatening and abusive individual, as some situations escalate to an unsafe level.

HOW TO KNOW IF YOU ARE BEING MANIPULATED AND HOW TO DEFEND YOURSELF

Psychological manipulation usually breeds some form of healthy social influence, and it usually occurs between many individuals. The relationships, in this case, usually give or take. In psychological manipulation, one person will always benefit from the other by taking advantage of them. One individual manipulating the other always does it deliberately, and they often bring about an imbalance of power since they are exploiting other people for their self-benefit.

The characteristics of manipulative individuals are;

• They know how to detect the weaknesses of other people.

• Once they identify a person's weaknesses, they will always use these weaknesses against them.

• They will always convince the victims to give up something so that they may serve their self-centered interests.

• Once a manipulative individual manages to take advantage of another person, they will always violate the other party until the exploited person ensures that the manipulation spree has come to an end.

Some of the causes of chronic manipulation are always deep-seated and complex. However, it is not easy to identify the main drive that causes a person to be manipulative psychologically. Also, when a person is being manipulated, they do encounter different challenges. The main question that arises, in this case, is how people manage such a situation. Some of the best ways to handle manipulative individuals include:

MAKE SURE YOU ARE CONVERSANT WITH YOUR HUMAN RIGHTS

When dealing with a psychologically manipulative individual, make sure that you know more about your human rights. It would be easy to recognize when any of your rights are being violated. Also, make sure that you are not harming other individuals. Every person has a right to stand up for themselves, while also defending each of their rights. If you harm other people, you may be violating each of these human rights. Some of the important rights include:

• The right to be treated with respect.

• The right to express opinions, feelings, and wants.

• The right to set your priorities.

• The right to say "no" without feeling guilty.

• The right to get anything that you pay for.

- The right to have a different opinion from that of your colleagues.

- The right to protect yourself from being mistreated mentally, physically, or emotionally.

- The right to always create your happiness while also living a healthy life.

All these human rights are meant to represent a boundary that should never be crossed by the manipulative individuals.

Our society has many people who do not respect the rights of others. Some of these psychological manipulators always want to exploit people's rights so that they may take advantage of them in every way possible. The main important thing to note is that we all have the right to declare that *we* have the power over ourselves since most people might assume that the manipulator is the one with the power. The manipulative individual does not have any power over you whatsoever.

KEEP YOUR DISTANCE

One of the most effective ways to identify a person who is a manipulator is by observing how various individuals behave when they are around you and when they are around other individuals. If the individual happens to behave differently when they are around different people, this is a character trait that symbolizes they might be manipulative. Everyone has a degree of social differentiation, and some psychological manipulators may prove to be extreme in different instances. Or they may be polite to various individuals while being extremely rude to others. They may also seem helpless, and in other instances, they will showcase some aggressiveness. When you observe such character traits regularly, you should always keep your distance. Avoid engaging such people unless you are forced to depend on the circumstances. It was mentionedearlier that it is difficult to learn more about why people tend to be psychologically manipulative. As a result, ensure that you have kept your distance since such individuals cannot be saved from their current predicaments.

AVOID SELF-BLAME AND PERSONALIZATION

In most cases, manipulative individuals tend to look for a person's weakness, and they will start exploiting them afterward. The people who are being exploited may feel inadequate, and they may also indulge in some self-blame since they may have failed to satisfy the manipulator in different ways. In some of these situations, it is good to note that although you are being manipulated, you are not the problem. The manipulator is taking advantage of you while also ensuring that you feel bad about yourself. You may surrender all your rights and power to the manipulative individuals. Always ask yourself questions such as:

- Are you being treated with the respect that you deserve?

- Are the demands of the manipulative person reasonable?

- Is the relationship beneficial to one party or both parties?

- Do you feel good about the relationship?

FOCUS ON ASKING PROBING QUESTIONS

Psychological manipulators will always issue demands to each of the individuals that they are manipulating. Some of the "offers" that they put across will seem unreasonable to some extent, but they will expect you to meet all their needs. Whenever you feel like you are being solicited unreasonably, it is good to focus on yourself by also asking the manipulator different probing questions. To look into whether each of these individuals has some self-awareness, they will recognize the inequity that is present in each of their schemes. Some of the suitable probing questions include:

- Is the relationship reasonable?

- Does what the manipulator wants to seem fair?

- Do you have a say in the relationship?

- Are you gaining anything?

- What are your expectations?

When you ask yourself some of these questions, you will be coming up with a mirror that is meant to show you the reality. The questions are meant to ensure that the manipulator can see the reality about their nature. In an instance whereby the manipulator has some form of self-awareness, they will withdraw the demands that they have been putting across, and they will back down. Some pathological manipulators can also be termed as narcissists, and they will dismiss each of the questions being directed to them. They will always insist you are getting in their way. If you ever find yourself in such a scenario, always ensure that you have applied different ideas that will ensure you have outsmarted the manipulative individuals. By being creative, you can hopefully bring an end to the manipulation spree.

UTILIZE TIME TO YOUR ADVANTAGE

Besides making some unreasonable requests, the manipulator will always ask questions and expect an immediate answer in each case. They will always exert some undue pressure while also striving to control the situation. The best example is people who are engaging in sales. Their main aim is to ensure that they have marketed different products successfully, and they may be manipulative so that people may purchase each of the products that they are selling. In such an instance, the manipulative individual will expect you to answer each of their questions immediately. They will also take advantage in different ways while also distancing themselves from the immediate influence that they have brought forth. Always exercise some sense of leadership by telling the manipulative individual that you will think about it and issue them an answer at an opportune moment.

Some of these words always prove to be powerful, and since we have used an example of sales agents, the customer, in this case, is the one who is supposed to address the salesperson and tell them that they will think about it. Always take time to think about the merits and demerits that may be present, depending on the current situation. Also, try to look into whether it is possible to come up with an equitable arrangement, or you should say no, depending on the current scenario.

ALWAYS LEARN TO SAY "NO"

It is not easy to say "no," however, you should first learn the art of communication. When you effectively learn to say "no," you will be able to stand your ground while also making sure that you have been able to maintain a workable relationship. Also, make sure that you are conversant with your human rights, most importantly the area that involves making sure that you can set your priorities without incurring any form of guilt. After all, you have the right to choose your happiness and healthy life too. Always make sure that you can resist while keeping your peace.

ALWAYS CONFRONT THE BULLIES

A psychological manipulator tends to become a bully at some point. They will always intimidate or harm their victims. The most important point to note is that the bullies will always prey on the individuals that they may perceive as weak. The manipulative individuals will go ahead with the exploitation whenever they come across an individual who is compliant and passive. When you make yourself a worthy target, the manipulative individuals will not hesitate to pounce on you. It is also evident that a majority of the people who enjoy bullying are also cowards. Whenever a person begins to showcase that they know their rights, the bullies will always back down. Various studies have also been carried out, and it is evident that most of the bullies have also been victims of violence at some point in their lives. Although the bullies have also been victimized at some point in their lives, it is not an excuse as to why they are bullying others. Such information is meant to ensure that you can view bullies from a different perspective.

When you confront a bully, you will be confident enough that you can protect yourself against various forms of danger. You may stand tall as an individual while also supporting other individuals when they are bullied.

In an instance whereby a person has been psychologically, emotionally or verbally assaulted, always make sure that you have sought the services of a counselor and also report the matters to the legal authorities, and they will take the necessary course of action. Always make sure that you can stand up to the bullies, and you may partner with some individuals who are fed up with practices such as bullying.

SET CONSEQUENCES

When an individual who thrives on manipulation insists on violating your boundaries, always make sure that you are in a position to tell them "no." Always make sure that you are in a position to assert and also identify consequences.

Possession of such knowledge can ensure that you can handle difficult people. When a bully understands the consequences that may come about as a result of their actions, always make sure that they can learn more about the value of respect.

HOW TO GET RID OF MANIPULATIVE PEOPLE?

Some people in this world only exist and flourish because they are constantly using someone to their benefit to get ahead. Manipulators can make someone else feel as if they were supposed to pay something, but often pounce on hard-working, unselfish people who are more likely to be manipulated in their job. If you're in a situation where somebody is attempting to sway you, notice - You all are your individual. Don't let anyone leave you feeling differently. At the end of the day, we are indeed human. It's precisely because of this that we get to dwell on the view of others in everything we do. We always want and love validation from others so we can subconsciously decide whether or not we will be depressed. In this millennial age, the norm has been just bragging about one'swealth onsocial media. Many of these brags are often the reality. In the end, this leads to a loose connection with reality. This kind of self-deception can dig deep into the human psyche, and one day a victim of this may wake up and realize that only in theirdreamsdoes theirperfect world exist. Depression will follow suit shortly. The first step towards protecting yourself against persuasion and manipulation is to confront the scenario and to take the position of disrupting any illusions. You won't be able to continue your normal lives. You must be careful that you regulate your own decisions. Then choose consciously to see thingsfor what they are. This agreement, which seems too good to be true, could be. . . Too good to be true. Too nice to be true. The other thing you should definitely do is trust your instincts. Sometimes you have been told a lie socompetently that you can believe it. But at a certain instinctive rate, you can feel an imbalance between what should, what is and then what is projected on you. There might be no physical sign that something is wrong, but you think that something is wrong. The next significant thing when you ask questions is to hear the answers. This can sound unbelievable because you will hear the responses. The reality is that we can deceive ourselves by choosing the responses we receive. We say that we listen, but we only care about the responses that we want to hear and not the answers that we receive. You may have broken your illusions, but some of you still hold on to the comfort of those illusions. You would not hear the real answers to your questions because of the pain of dealing with the scenario. Actual hearing needs a certain feeling of detachment, but not reality this time around. You must get rid of your feelings. Your detachment from our feelings willlead you to the next step in processing the fresh data logically. It can make situations more complicated than they have to be and make you behave irrationally. It makes it so hard for your exit strategy to allow all feelings to cool down and spring. The irrational part of you may want to let everything go to hell when you face reality. Your justified anger can encourage you to take short-term measures to calm your feelings. But in the long term, you may regret these actions. I'm not saying you ought to deny your feelings; I'm not saying you don't act on these emotions.

ADDRESSING THE ISSUE

The very first strategy for dealing with a devious person is to realize that you're being exploited, either in a job or in your private life. Such people will consider you to abandoneverything that you do when they need help and are extremely overwhelming in their requirements for help. They don't see your requirements in the least bit while they require you to do something, and they see their requirements as the highest concern. If you realize coworkers or so-called mates are putting their own needs ahead of yours, then immediately start to take measures to sabotage their efforts.

INQUIRE

Manipulators will try to even get you to do things with hardly any questions raised for them. So when you ask them a question it changes the power balance to your side so very marginally. Ask them how or why a quest would help all interested participants or whether they believe it is fair what they are looking for. If they are honest, they will have to admit they are a little irrational or nonsensical. If they choose not to be truthful, you've shifted control even further to your site, as there's no justification to do something for someone less than true to you.

RETAIN STRONG

In older people clothing manipulators just are pricks. They are preying on those they feel would not speak-up for themselves and they think they will still get whatever they want. Manipulators, however, lose power completely once their targetis standing up for their rights before them. They're so used to getting their bidding accomplished for them that they also have no clue what to do if someone disregards their requirements. They will often try and influence your decision to stand firm against such a manipulator. Don't let them do it. Only you can control yourself; compromising just once can lead to a slippery slope where aggressors are constantly victimizing you.

USE YOUR TIME TO BENEFIT

Manipulators start making demands as well as enforce time limits which cause major pressure to their perpetrators. But it's your time. If someone you know tries to take advantage of you or demands that you complete the task over a certain amount of time, inform them that you will "think about it." Doing so is as useful as completely tearing them down. In reality, going to string them along turns the table on the deceiver entirely, because they would be the ones looking for you to learn.

Of course, you do not want to be the manipulator, but allowing the aggressor a dose of their very own medicine can't harm your purpose.

SET REPERCUSSIONS

These are the demands that manipulators enforce on others - mandates which must be fulfilled in their eyes. They will be doing their utmost to make it feel that you owe something to them and have to do what they're doing. It's they who might owe you when you do such individuals this massive favor. Make that clear to those people. This works particularly if you do have other regulations that need your urgent attention. If they find that they will end up getting to do something in exchange for you, they would more than likely retract their demand. Although they will possibly try and find another target instead of finishing the work on their own, you have at least managed to get them off you.

ACT FAST

It's wonderful that you have got to grips with the truth of things. But it is so much more to defend ourselves against these dark manipulative strategies. While you try to protect yourself against the claws of these manipulators, it is often intense and exciting at first. This intensity of these feelings can slowly lead to negation. The longer you take any action, the quicker the denial will begin, and if it occurs, there is a strong likelihood that you may fall back and end up being trapped on the same web. You can avoid this by taking action as soon as you know someone is attempting to manipulate you. This can be done in the easiest way possible, as byinforming a close friend about some facts of aspecific scenario, all the events that will eventually lead you to liberty can be started. You should understand that after choosing to behave, the fabric is made of tougher material than glass. The illusion can work its way back to your core by using fragmented parts of your feelings to helpit. When a liar is caught in a lie, theymay try to hire others to implement that lying if they think they no longer hold you. A disappointed partner with whom you broke things offlately would attempt to use the other shared links in your lives to change your mind. You will need both your logic and instincts if you want to get out of this unscathed. While the reality is that when you find that you have always been lied to, you get emotionally scarred, so you are still left untouched by the scenario. However, the priority should be to follow the path that enables you to leave this toxic condition without further harm. You're mentally all over the place. Rage, rage, hurt, and disappointment are the tip of the iceberg. But you must logically believe. Keep your head above the water and warn yourself.

GET ASSISTANCE QUICKLY

When you are trapped in the manipulations of others, confusion is one of the feelings you would encounter. This enables you to obscure your rational thinking and makes you feel helpless. You could even question the truth of what you're currently facing. If you continue to have those doubts, it would lead to denial. You will likely want to say that you have the whole scenario wrong. You misunderstood certain stuff and came to the incorrect conclusion. Such thinking would lead back to the weapons of the manipulator. Developthe desire to accept a second opinion. In a health crisis, people go to another physician to get a second view. This is to clear any doubts about your first diagnosis and to confirm the best course of therapy for you. Similarly, receiving an opinion from another person can assist you to discern reality and your next steps. Just remember, it's better to go to someone who's proven to be interested in what's best for you many times. The next step is to confront the perpetrator if you have the assistance that you need. I recommend you choose the scene or place for this. Select a location that provides you the upper hand. That would involve some cautious planning on your part. If the offender exists in the cyber world, especially if you have been swindled by thisperson, you must involve the police and the authorities. Do some of your own research to find out the truth. After you face the offender and take the measures you need to get out of the scenario, the healing method must begin rapidly. The extent and severity to which you have been harmed, manipulated or abused do not matter. You have to be able to go through it and wait for your wounds to be "healed," rather than sitting on your bed and living in the past. Time willoffer you sufficient distance from your experience but it would reallybe healing for emotional scars if you learned something fromthis book. If you don't do anything, an unhealthy scab might form over the wound that makes you as vulnerable if not more than you have experienced. Speak to a consultant, take part in atreatment and actively facilitate the healing process, regardless of what you choose. It will not occur overnight, but you are sure you get nearer each day and with every phase of your treatment.

HAVE CONFIDENCE IN YOUR INSTINCTS

While your brain interprets signals based on facts, logic and experience, it operates in the opposite direction by filtering data through an emotional filter. The only thing that takes vibrations is your intestine that cannot pick up either the heart or the brain. And if you can groom up to the stage where you acknowledge your inner voice and are trained to do so, you will reduce your likelihood of becoming seduced by individuals who try to manipulate you. It's difficult to acknowledge this voice at first. This is because we have permitted voices of doubt, self-discrimination and the noisy voices of the critics within and without to drown out our true voice in our life. This voice or instinct relies on your survival. So trust that your brain cells will still be able to process stuff in your immediate area when it starts. Some individuals call it intuition, some call it instinct, and they do the same, particularly when it comes to relationships. You must acknowledge that starting to trust your instincts may not always make logical sense. If you've ever been doing something and felt like you were suddenly watched, then you understand what I mean. You have no eyes at the rear of your head, nobody else in yourspace, but you have the small shiver running down the back of your neck and you're looking at the "sudden understanding. " That is what I am talking about.. The first step in connecting with your instinct is to decode your mind with your voices. You can do this with meditation. Forget about chatting, she said. Concentrate on your middle. You're the voice that you understand. Next, be attentive to your ideas. Don't just throw away your head's eclectic monologue. Rather go with the stream of ideas.

Why do you believe in somebody somehow? How do you feel so deeply, even though you knew each other for only a few days? What's your nagging feeling about this other individual? You become more sensitive to your intuition as you explore your ideas and know when your instincts start and respond to them. You might have to learn to stop and believe if you are the type of individual who at present wants to make stimulating choices. This break provides you the chance to reflect and assess your choices. The next part is hard, and many people couldn't follow it. You can't sail or navigate this step, unfortunately. This section has to do with confidence. You need to be open to the concept of self-confidence and of trusting others to believe in your instinct. Your lack of confidence would only make you paranoid, and when you're paranoid it's not your instincts that kick. It's your fear. Every molehill tends to transform fear into a mountain. You have to let go of your fear, embrace trust, and let your fresh relationships lead. You can hear the voice better without the roadblocks of fear in your mind. Finally, your priorities must be reassessed. You may not see the past if your mind is at the forefront of money and material property. Any contact you have with individuals would be viewed as individuals who try to use you, and it will quickly become the truth if you live so often. You understand how you draw what you believe into your lives. If you always believe in material wealth, you will only attract individuals like yourself. Look at your interactions with this fresh view with this guide; the old, the new and the outlook. Don't enter into a partnership you expect to play. Be accessible to them whether it is a company relationship, a romantic relationship or even a regular acquaintance. You can receive the correct feedback from your intuition. Do not think this too, that if you encounter suspects, your gut will tell you to go in the opposite direction.

PREVENTING MANIPULATION

Manipulation normally occurs when an individual is used for the benefit of others. It is a situation where the manipulator comes up with an imbalance of power and goes ahead to exploit his victim just to serve their main agendas. Those who are manipulative are the kind of people who will disguise their desires and interests as yours. They will undertake all they can to make you believe that their own opinions are the objective facts. They will then act as if they are cornered. Manipulators will pretend to offer assistance so that you can improve your attitude, performance, and promise that they will assist you in improving your life in general. That is all that they want you to believe. The hidden truth is that the main aim of these people is to control you and not control you, as they want you to believe. They are not interested in making your life better, but just to change you. They also want to validate their lives and make sure that you don't outgrow them.

Once you have given these characters back to your life, getting rid of them will not be easy. They will appear to flip flop on issues and act so slippery when you want to hold them accountable. They also tend to promise you help that doesn't seem to be near.

People can be easily manipulated when they opt to put up with passive-aggressive behaviors. According to a recent study that was published in the Journal of Social & Personal Relationships, offensive people tend to interfere with the general performance of an individual. The study also noted that engaging withthose who are negative could do you more harm than good. When these people are ignored, the research states that their productivity and intelligence is increased. More than 100 participants were examined for this study. The participants were asked to ignore or talk with random people who had earlier been asked to either be offensive or friendly.

The participants were not aware of the kind of people they were going to meet. After interacting for about four minutes, each of the participants was offered a thought exercise that needed them to have a better concentration. The study later noted that those who ignored the negative individuals performed way much better than those who engaged the negative individuals.

The researchers then summarized that ignoring some people in a serious social interaction is one better way of conserving the mental resources of a person. The best strategy is to avoid those who are negative in their speeches and actions. But at times, that can't be enough. A negative person can also be manipulative and sneaky at times. In such situations, you will be forced to apply other strategies.

The truth is that being manipulated is not a good thing. The only possible worse thing than manipulation could just be admitting our dirty little secrets. Each time we realize that we have been manipulated, we not only feel stupid but also ashamed and weak. And all that doesn't stop there. If we continue to fall for the tricks that these people lay on us, they will leave us with an awful feeling about everything around us. Instead of being hurt for another time, the best thing to do could just be not to trust anybody.

Manipulation can only be successful if the target fails to recognize it or just decide to allow it. But regardless of all that, there exist certain things that you can do to recognize that you are under manipulative powers. They can also help you to prevent or stop a possible case of manipulation. Some of the ideas may not be desirable or possible for your situation, but that's just fine because every situation and every person is different.

KNOW ALL YOUR FUNDAMENTAL RIGHTS

One of the single most imperative guidelines, when you are in this similar situation, is to know all your fundamental rights. But that's not all, you should also recognize when any of those rights are being violated. Remember that you are at liberty to stand up for yourself and make sure no single fundamental right is being violated. You should, however, do this carefully and make sure that you do not harm others. Again, you should not forget that you might forfeit these rights if you cause harm to other people. Ensure you are conversant with some of the basic human rights such as:

- The right to be treated with dignity and respect.
- The right to express one's wants, opinions, and feelings.
- The right to give no as an answer and maintain that without any guilty feelings.
- The right to set up one's standards and priorities.
- The right to take care and safeguard yourself from being emotionally, mentally, or physically threatened.

The mentioned basic rights show the extent to which your boundaries are supposed to reach. We are living in a society where people don't represent any of these rights. The mental manipulators are particularly interested in depriving you of your rights so that they can fully control you and take advantage of you. However, you still have the moral authority and power to state that you, and not the manipulator, are fully in charge of your life.

MAINTAIN A DISTANCE WITH THESE PEOPLE

As noted, one of the surest ways of detecting a manipulator is to check if the individual acts with different faces when in front of various people and situations. Whereas all of us have mastered this art of social differentiation, the mental manipulators are masters when it comes to dwelling in extremes – where they show great humility to one person and rudeness to another. They can also feel so aggressive at one point and helpless the next minute. When you see this kind of behavior in people whom you are close to, the best thing to do is to keep a healthy distance. You should also try to avoid engaging with these people until you are forced to do that. Remember that some of the top causes of chronic psychological manipulation are deep-seated and complex; therefore, saving or changing these people cannot be your job.

STOP SELF-BLAMING & PERSONALIZATION

Given that the manipulator's agenda is to know where your weakness is and exploit it, you may even throw the blame game on yourself for not doing your best. In such situations, it is very imperative to reassure yourself that you are not part of the problem. Remember that you are just being manipulated to feel bad about your actions and surrender your rights and power in the end. It is vital to consider the kind of relationship you have with the manipulator as well. These are some of the questions that you should ask yourself:

Am I getting a respectful treatment?

Is this relationship 1-way or 2-way?

Am I satisfied being in this relationship?

The answers to these issues will offer you the most important clues about whether the problem is with the manipulator or with you.

PROBE THE MANIPULATORS

Mental manipulators will always make demands or requests from you. They do this to make you go the extra mile so that you can meet their needs. At times, it can be very important to put the focus back on the manipulator each time you hear certain solicitations. Ask them some analytical questions to check if they are fully aware of their scheme's inequity. Ask them if their actions appear reasonable to them or if what they want from you is all fair.

When you step out to ask some of these questions, you are simply placing a mirror so the manipulator is able to view the real nature of their ploy. If the manipulator happens to be a master of self-awareness, then they will withdraw and back down. Real pathological manipulators, on the other hand, will dismiss the question and insist on having things done their way. When this takes place, ensure you stand up for your fundamental rights and the manipulators will flee.

SAY NO IN A FIRM AND DIPLOMATIC WAY

Saying no firmly and diplomatically is what can be defined as real communication. When it has been articulated effectively, it will allow you to stand your ground and maintain the best working relationship. It is important to remember that one of your basic human rights is to set your standards and priorities. It is also within your rights to say no without feeling the guilt, as well as the right to pick your own healthy and happy life.

SET THE CONSEQUENCES

When a mental manipulator persists on violating the boundaries that you have made and is not hearing your "no," you will be forced to deploy the consequences. The ability to be able to point out and assert the consequences is one of the most important skills that you can deploy to resist the efforts of a manipulative person. When they are articulated effectively, consequences will stop the actions of the manipulative person and even compel them to stop the violations and respect you instead.

CONFRONT THE BULLIES IN A SAFE WAY

One fact that is not known to many is that a mental manipulator can turn into a bully when they intimidate and harm others. It is important to note that bullies only prey on those they regard as the weakest, and you can make yourself a target when you remain compliant and passive. However, the fact is that several bullies are cowards on the inside. They will often back up when their target starts to stand up for their rights. This is a common practice in office and surroundings, as well as in schoolyards.

THINK ABOUT THE LONG-TERM CONSEQUENCES OF THE ACTIONS YOU UNDERTAKE

As opposed to just doing what is easiest and fastest, do not forget about the consequences that your actions can have. Remember that psychological manipulators are the best when it comes to making their option the easiest, fastest, and also the least hurtful. They are also best at keeping the people focused on their current feelings. That explains why people do things they later regret. Instead of dealing with a consequence, later on, make sure you choose to do things that you won't be forced to rethink.

171

Chapter 13:

Stay Positive, Ignore the Predators

When it comes to dealing with the darkness in the world, you must realize that you are also part of the problem. As many dark people as there are in the world, you are not so good yourself. There are many actions that you do that display your dark side. If you wish to be a person who stays away from the dark life, you need to address the dark side in your mind.

The first question you must answer when trying to address dark psychology is "Who am I?" Do you relate to the dark side or are you on the bright side? Although most people like to think of themselves as being on the right side of life, it is clear that darkness takes root in many people. The dark side of life cannot be completely avoided. As you focus on your personality and your thoughts, you may realize that you have some dark desires lurking. The extent to which you execute your dark desires or the level at which you solve all the problems associated with darkness determines your ability to stand against them.

Through your thoughts and your ideas, you can also detect the darkness in other people. If you manage to control the voices inside your head, you will be in a position to control the darkness and how it manifests around you. However, you must first find your identity. One of the best ways to find your identity is through meditation. Meditation helps you realize the different aspects of your environment that you did not pay attention to. If you wish to realize your identity and know who you are and how you operate, you should sharpen the following skills.

SELF-AWARENESS

Self-awareness is the ability to detect and monitor your actions and emotions. In everyday life, you make choices that are guided by your emotions. Although few people pay attention to their emotions, it is a fact that emotions play an integral part in deciding who you are and whatever you do. The actions you take daily determine your personality. However, these actions are most definitely determined by your emotions. You should be able to pay attention to your emotions and how they affect your actions. A person who is emotionally aware is sensitive to all the actions they take. If you are self-aware, you strive hard to ensure that you do not give emotions room to control your life. Emotional awareness is the power that helps you know your strengths and weaknesses in every situation you go through. When you are undergoing a tough emotional situation, you can gauge your limits. You get to know how dark you are and how impulsive you get. Most people get emotional and impulsive during difficult emotional moments. It is necessary to observe your actions when you are under pressure so that you may be able to tell if you get out of control during emotional situations.

MINDFULNESS

Mindfulness is a form of meditation that allows you to focus on yourself. This is one of the best ways to try and know your identity.

In mindfulness, the person focuses on their thoughts, body or emotions. A person practicing mindfulness must focus on the emotions or thoughts that go through their mind at the time of meditation. Mindfulness is one of the most responsive ways of meditation. Mindfulness will help you know the deepest secrets that have been hiding in your subconscious mind. When you practice mindfulness, you will realize that you have some dark desires that you have never thought existed. It is important to keep in mind that such desires may make you have doubts about yourself. For this reason, mindfulness meditation is practiced under certain rules.

RULES OF MINDFULNESS MEDITATION

NO JUDGMENT

The first and the most important rule of mindful meditation is that the individual must be non-judgmental. When you focus your mind and thoughts on your personality, you will realize that you also have a dark side. The dark desires that a person has within are usually hidden in public behavior. However, a careful examination of oneself may reveal some dirty thoughts. It is important to ensure that you stick to observing yourself without being judgmental in any way. Even if you realize that you have a dark personality, you should allow yourself to enjoy your personality in the moment of meditation without raising any questions to yourself.

NO REGRET

Another important aspect of meditation is that you do not regret any of the actions or thoughts you have. If you practice mindfulness, everything you experience and observe about yourself should remain in the world in which you were observing. If you observe anything positive, you should be happy for yourself, but the positive moment must be left within the mindfulness room. The same case applies to all the negative aspects you may observe about yourself.

There is no doubt about the fact that there are many dark sides to a person. All the dark parts you observe about your feelings and desires should not be a cause for judgment. You must allow yourself to observe negativity without being regretful in any way. Even if you visualize yourself doing something dirty, you must not regret it.

ACCEPTANCE

Acceptance is another aspect of meditation that must be used if you want to enjoy the practice. The fact that you will be focusing on a detailed observation of your body and thoughts means that there are many things you may not like about yourself. You need to learn to accept the situation and move on. For instance, if you realize that you do not like the shape of your body or the look of your face, you still have to accept it and move on with life. You must never dwell in the outcome of mindful meditation in any negative way. If possible, you should only take the positives from this kind of practice.

COMMUNICATION

The other aspect that will help you understand your identity is communication. Just the same way you pay attention to the communication of others, you must also pay attention to your communication. If you observe your communication, you will realize that many factors make you different. By observing your verbal and non-verbal communication, you can draw important information from your language. You will be able to identify your dark side and determine your social aspects. All the dark personalities we have addressed above can easily be identified by observing their means of communication. The same case applies at a personal level. Although most people tend to be selfish and biased when observing their actions, you must allow yourself the chance to look at your communication objectively. Try observing your arguments and gauge your dominance in a conversation. If you realize that you always try to dominate conversations or you must always win an argument, pay close attention to your personality. You need to start watching your dark side because you have one.

THE VOICE INSIDE OUR HEAD AND HOW WE CAN OVERCOME IT FOR THE BETTER

One of the reasons why people practice dark psychology is that they listen to a voice of selfish desires. The voice within your head keeps encouraging you to go out and do something for yourself. You will find that most people listen to the dark voice that pushes them to achieve personal desires. You need to learn how to silence the negative voice that speaks to you. This voice is only interested in personal welfare and does not care about the emotions of others.

If you realize that the negative voice in your mind always gains control over your actions, chances are that you are a dark person. If you can get a genuine opinion from your close friends and family, you will learn that you are manipulative, selfish, and, to many people, arrogant. You need to learn to control all the negative voices that speak to you in every situation. You must train yourself to silence the negative voices that can lead you to take an action that you may later regret. When you realize that you constantly think negatively, you must decide in your mind to take the steps you need to help you silence those negative voices. Let's see some of the ways to overcome negative voices in your mind.

CONSIDER OTHER PEOPLE'S EMOTIONS

The only reason why manipulative people used dark psychology to achieve whatever they want is that they do not consider the emotions of others. To start considering the emotions of others, you need to train your imagination. You cannot consider another person's emotions unless you can imagine yourself being in the same situation. A person who understands and considers the emotions of others thinks about the people around them. If you have been in a certain situation, it is easy for you to relate to it. However, if you have not been in a similar situation, it becomes difficult for you to consider it. When you train your imagination, you can try to place yourself into the shoes of another person and feel the pain they are going through. Individuals who are empathetic try so much to see that, that they feel the pain of others. If you are an empathetic person, you try to put yourself in the shoes of other people. You think about the pain they go through and try hard to help in any way possible.

PRACTICE LOVE AND KINDNESS MEDITATION

Love and kindness meditation will also help you get rid of all the negative voices in your head. Love and kindness meditation is focused on doing good. When you practice this type of meditation, you visualize yourself as the center of love and kindness in the world. People who practice this type of meditation usually visualize a world where people are craving for love. As the central source of love and kindness, you visualize yourself extending your love to all the people in the world. This type of meditation is very helpful for people who have suffered abuse. If you have been abused before and the dark voice in your mind is inciting you to revenge, you need to try this type of mediation.

HOW TO PRACTICE LOVE AND KINDNESS MEDITATION

Step 1: Find the right spot, where you can enjoy calm and quietness with minimal interruptions. The meditation session should take between 15 minutes and an hour.

Step 2: Focus your mind on one person you hate so much and start thinking about them in a good way. When you focus on this person, think of yourself as the center of love. Visualize yourself extending love to that person and all the people in the world who need to be shown love. As the center of love, visualize yourself walking to a hopeless person, such as a street child, and giving them gifts. Be the person who shows people that life can be beautiful.

Step 3: Extend your love to the real world. As soon as you start realizing the peace associated with extending love to the world, you need to take your practice to the next level. Just meditating and visualizing is not good enough. Walk out and try extending love and kindness to a person who may need it. Buy someone a gift and just try to put a smile on the face of another person. Such gestures will help you start focusing on the positive aspects of life and deal with all the negative aspects of life.

LEARN EMOTIONAL CONTROL

The other way of dealing with the negative voice in your mind is learning emotional control. It is a fact that most people only get negative when they are under emotional pain. If someone said something painful to you, the chances are that you may try to get revenge. Your desire to take revenge and cause pain to another person is brought about by your dark side. To be able to silence all the negative dark voices in your mind, you need to learn to control your emotions. You need to find alternative ways of emotional release. If you realize that painful emotions make you do things that you do not want to do, you need to stop them. There are many methods of alternative emotional release. For instance, instead of getting violent when you are angry, you may choose to workout. A simple exercise might help you get all the painful emotions off your chest. This is one of the ways of dealing with negative voices. Another option is turning negative emotions into positive ones. For instance, if you are feeling angry, you may choose to engage in activities that will make you feel happy. Most people engage in activities such as listening to music, watching comedy shows, or any other activity that can make a person smile. You need to ensure that you stay in control of all your actions even when your emotions are on the edge. If you do not know how to control your emotions, people will come in and try to control your life. You must learn to control your actions and stop the bad thoughts that are associated with all the negativity in your mind.

LEARN COMMUNICATION SKILLS

Communication skills will help you learn that you do not have to always be in control. Communication skills can teach you a lot of factors related to controlling yourself and controlling your emotions. If you want to try stopping the negative voices in your mind, first learn to think before speaking. The words that come out of your mouth must be measured. You must pay keen attention to your actions and words in a communication process. The actions you take and your posture also play an important role in influencing negativity.

A person who listens more and speaks less has a greater chance of filtering their thoughts and controlling their negativity. However, if you speak more and listen less, your mind is controlled by all the negative voices. You may end up speaking anything that may show negativity. You need to learn to control your negative thoughts. You must stop all negative words before they go through your mouth by processing your thoughts properly.

YOUR INSIDE VOICE KNOWS DARK PSYCHOLOGY INSIDE OUT

Paying attention to the inside voice is the only way to stop dark psychology in your life.

You need to realize that the thoughts that go through your mind determine your actions. However, the possibility of a person controlling their thoughts is a real option. You can control yours in different ways.

INTERRUPTING NEGATIVETHOUGHTS

When you feel that the negative voice is trying to rise in your mind, find something to disrupt your thought process. You may start singing or go out jogging. Many activities can help you disrupt your mind from thinking negatively. The more you allow a bad thought to occupy your mind, the more it takes control. You should learn to say no to any negative voices before they take root in your mind.

POSITIVE BEHAVIOR

Neuroscientists say that it is possible to change the thoughts of a person by implementing positive activities. If you are a person who has negative habits, chances are that your thoughts are also negative. A person who does not have control over their actions or their daily activities is likely to have dark thoughts. However, if you can change your negative daily actions into positive ones, you may be in a position to completely change how you think. The first step to changing your behavior is developing a daily routine.

If you do not have a positive daily routine, start developing one. Your daily routine should include positive activities that will prompt your mind to think positively. For instance, if you allow one of your daily activities to be visiting orphans, you will soon start developing an emotional bond with orphans. You start realizing the hard life they face daily. A person who pays attention to orphans or other vulnerable people in society will easily develop empathy. If you pay attention, you start relating to the situations that other people have to face daily. This type of emotional awareness will help you get rid of negative voices in your mind.

DWELLING IN THE PAST

One of the reasons why people allow negative voices to speak to them is past life experiences. A person who has been through a negative life experience may put on a dark face just to protect themselves from negativity. A good example is a person who suffers from post-traumatic stress disorder. Such people are manipulative and often see evil in the world. However, their actions are not based on reality. They act based on past traumatic events. If you want to get rid of any negative voices from your life, you must stop dwelling in the past. People who dwell in the past do not live in the real world. Those who dwell in the past live in a world that is made up of lies and imagination. If you dwell in the past, your life will be characterized by worry and anxiety.

WORRY

You are always worried, thinking that the things that happened to you will happen again, eventually. Unfortunately, worry does not bring a solution to any situation. If you find yourself being worried, try to find a solution to your problem. There is no need to think so hard about a situation that you cannot solve. If you do not have a solution to a problem, then stop thinking about it.

ANXIETY

The other problem experienced by those who focus on the past is anxiety and panic attacks. You will find yourself being anxious all the time, thinking about negativity. When you allow the past to control your life, you have to live in constant fear of the unknown. You need to stay aware of those situations and try as much as possible to get rid of anxiety in your life.

HOW TO DEAL WITH A NEGATIVE PAST

Although you have been through a painful past, you should not allow the pain from the past to dictate the direction of your life. You need to take control and choose to be happy. Letting the negative voices in your mind take control only prolongs your healing process. You must allow yourself to have enough time to heal from all your negative past experiences. People who dwell in the negative past experiences never amount to anything in life. Due to fear, such people are afraid of taking risks or making investments. They are forced to stay at the same level for a very long time and, as a result, they end up living in emotional pain their whole life. You can either turn your negativity into positivity or choose forgiveness.

ACKNOWLEDGE AND TURN IT INTO POSITIVITY

If you feel that a person or a situation in your past has made it impossible for you to trust people or to trust the world, you must first acknowledge it. Most people live in denial, trying to act as if they have not suffered any type of pain. However, as soon as you choose to accept the situation and agree that you have been hurt, a big weight is lifted off your shoulders. You need to learn to accept those situations. There are some situations in life where we cannot do much more than accept things. Once you accept that you have been hurt and that you need help healing, you give yourself the freedom to move on from the painful situation. However, before you acknowledge and allow yourself the time to heal you will remain in denial, while, at the same time, you will continue suffering from the pain caused by that particular situation.

CHOOSE FORGIVENESS

After realizing that you have been hurt by someone, choose to forgive so that you may find healing. If you do not forgive, you may never heal. It is important to let go of all the pain that you hold in your heart. The first step towards complete healing is forgiveness. When you forgive, you release yourself from the emotional attachment. As a result, you release the pain and remain in peace. Those who choose forgiveness live a much happier and fulfilling life. If you do not forgive, you may never learn to trust again. Trust is an integral part of human relationships. You must give the people you work with or those you socialize with some form of trust. You should be able to show trust in people by focusing on their positive aspects. A person who holds onto the pain of past life events does not have room for other people in their life. This is a dangerous situation, given that we need people around us to succeed. As muchwealth as you may have, you still need people to enjoy life. You must love, trust and allow people to be part of your life. This is the beauty of forgiveness that you must seek. If you feel that you have been hurt and that the pain is holding your life back, you must stand up and extend a hand of forgiveness for you to live a happy life once again.

DO SOMETHING ABOUT IT

The only problem with worry and fear is that they do not bring a solution to any problem. You will find that most people who dwell in the past allow worry and fear to take root. They are afraid of the unknown to such an extent that they cannot make any progress in life. If you chose to focus your mind on the past, you might never enjoy life. Fear and worry will only continue building negative thoughts in your mind. The more you think about the negative experiences from your past, the more anxious you get.

If you are convinced that something negative may happen in your life, the best solution is to do something about it. Instead of dwelling in the past, try to do something that will help prevent any negativity from happening. If you want to live a positive life, you must train yourself to stop overthinking. You must train your mind to focus on the positives of life. Dwelling in the past does not in any way help you move in a positive direction. Dwelling in the past only makes you focus on outdated things. You only waste your time thinking about situations that may never happen again. You should be focusing on living a positive life that will stop any negative people from abusing you.

REGAIN CONTROL OF YOUR LIFE

Now, when it comes to regaining control of your life, you have a few options. You can work to protect yourself from dark psychology and manipulation just by working with yourself. Learning to set your boundaries and defend them is perhaps one of the greatest things that you can do that will allow you to regain control of your life and the sooner that you commit to doing so, the sooner that you can be free of the nonsense that will otherwise threaten to take over. If you want to make sure that you are safe from being manipulated, consider this chapter as your guide to doing exactly this. We will address first how to help yourself be protected. Then, we will consider how you can positively influence those around you.

Conclusion

I hope the knowledge you've gained by reading this will lead you forward, and that your journey will be peopled with the kind of intelligent and lively folks that will make it a thrilling tapestry of experience. Sometimes the destination is fun to think about, but if we miss the journey on the way there, we miss out on the best part.

If you have been keen, you have realized that dark psychology can affect any person. Whether you are young or old, you must equip yourself with some knowledge on the subject of dark psychology.

Dark psychology can be terrifying, and manipulators are everywhere, but you can learn to protect yourself against them.

From here, all that's left for you to do is take some time to begin learning what you can do to help yourself both use these tools for your good and make sure that you take the time to protect not just yourself, but also everyone around you. Make sure that you use the information that you got to work with those that you care about and to protect the unsuspecting. Ultimately, the tools that you have been provided in this book can be used for either good or bad purposes. You can choose to hurt or help. However, you have to be willing to deal with the consequences of what you decide to do.

As you read through this book, you should have begun to feel more confident than you have been before. You should be ready to get out there and get started with your newfound information that you have gained. Don't let yourself be taken advantage of and learn that you, too, can fight back, protect yourself and ensure that you can maintain yourself and your integrity.

We are knowingly seeing dark psychological strategies in our daily lives. The manipulators secretly strike us and we couldn't even know it. Manipulators use techniques in that matter, consciously. Some secret manipulators deliberately say and do stuff for influence and leverage to have what they want to get.

You are probably not sure how to start or where to start from in your quest to protect yourself from dark psychology. Given that the content of this book is wide, you must give yourself time to learn the protection techniques one by one. A good starting place would be an in-depth understanding of NLP. As soon as you can read the thoughts of people using NLP, you will be on track to protect yourself and any person in your family from manipulation.

Learn not to limit yourself by believing in things that are limiting themselves. An example recently read was where a person believed that birds all have feathers. It's something that limits the believer since by that premise penguins would be excluded.

It is hoped that this book has opened your mind to the possibility of taking your learning processes further on the subject of NLP. You will be very glad that you did, as the techniques briefly outlined in this book have vast potential.

BETHANY KEY

MANIPULATION AND MIND CONTROL:

The ultimate guide to learning how to recognize dark psychology techniques and use the secrets of emotional intelligence and influence to your advantage

Introduction

E very aspect of human life has two sides-positive and negative, but it depends on the human how he or she utilizes it for their good as well as for others. Consider manipulation as a part of dark psychology, and it is used greatly for the wrongdoings and harmful deeds. On the other hand, it can be utilized positively as well, but it's all in your hand how you want to utilize it. As far as persuasion is concerned, people use it in every field and part of life. For example, a salesman will always try to persuade you to buy his or her recommended product even if you do not want to. Persuasion also has two aspects of being applied. If you try to persuade a person to do something illegal or unethical, that is part of dark psychology but if you persuade someone to get out or leave a certain thing that is not beneficial in any means, let's say suicide, then you are using it for the purpose of good. Everything you do or perceive is totally in the human mind, and you are the controller of it. If you don't want to, then no one can make you do things without your will and consent. Also, it is an essential part of living life to observe your surroundings and the people who are around you. If you do not notice the small things and interpret them wisely, then you are more likely to fall prey for something negative and hazardous. Facial expressions, body language, gestures, and the words and tone used, can predict a lot about people if observed closely. If you fail to recognize such signals that are inclined towards negativity, then you will be unable to keep yourself safe from them. Dark psychology is considered to start from the point where you have no intent or motive to do things except for your self-satisfaction and pleasure, and in return, it is damaging to the other person or even the community. Every living individual has this dark side, but not all of them let that side overcome them. Once you are exposed to that side, there is no coming back. So always watch yourself and your surroundings so that you can keep yourself off of any harm. Persuasion, manipulation, and other forms of influence are ubiquitous. You can pick up on some obvious signs here and there, but there are also hidden secret ways that others control you which you might never be able to fully comprehend.

To those who aren't fully aware of manipulation and what it is all about, it is hard to see that this process takes up three steps. Most of us will just think of manipulation as one thing—there needs to be two things in addition to the act of manipulation, which will make sure that the manipulation is successful. Perhaps you are trying to sell something, maybe yourself or your brand, and you need to figure out how to get people to be more persuaded by you to help you achieve the things that you want in this life. No matter where you are or what you are trying to do, you have all the tools that you will ever need to be persuasive or influential with you already.

Before getting into this book, there are a few things that you need to know to be introduced to this topicto get into the right mindset as you read through this text. First, understand that there are no two manipulators that are alike. There are no two easily persuaded people that are the same either. Though it might seem like this sometimes, especially since you can influence a group all at once, you can't let yourself fall into a thinking pattern where you place everyone in the same category.

Don't blame yourself for not being aware of the ways that you have been manipulated in the past. Regret isn't going to do you any good in this journey, so it's best to leave those feelings of, "I wish I would have known this sooner," behind. All that you can do now is move forward, and we will help you every step of the way!

Chapter 1:

Mind Control

MIND CONTROL

Mind control is a term that is used for several psychological phenomena such as mind control, coercive control, brainwashing, coercive persuasion, malignant use of group dynamics, and a lot more. It is a psychological theory with many names. The many names given to the theory are a clear indication of the fact that there is a lack of agreement that makes room for distortion and confusion, especially in the hands of those that intend to make use of it covertly for their selfish interests.

One can, however, agree with the fact that mind control easily falls under the umbrella of influence and persuasion which deals with the way people change other people's beliefs and behaviors. While some would like to argue that all falls under manipulation, it is important to take note of the missing distinctions in this argument.

It is much better to think of influence as a continuum because at one end there are the ethical and respectful influences that make room for giving respect to an individual concerning his or her rights while at the other end there are destructive influences that rip off a person's independence, identity and his ability to come up with critical and logical thoughts.

When it comes to the darker side of the continuum, we talk about cults and sects. These are the groups of people who make use of deception and mind control skills in taking advantage of its member's strengths and weaknesses to satisfy the selfish desires of the cult leaders.

There are one-on-one cults which are intimate relationships where a person manipulates and exploits others using their influence. These are cultic relationships which are a smaller version of the larger groups that may prove to be destructive as a result of the fact that all the time and attention available are directed towards a person. These relationships may come in the form of husband/wife, pastor/worshipper, teacher/student, or therapist/client.

The best way to pin a definition to mind control is to look at it from the angle of a system of certain influences that can disrupt a person at their core and at their identity level which has to do with their preferences, beliefs, behaviors, relationships, decisions and so on.

Mind control creates a new pseudo-identity or pseudo-personality for the person and can be used in several ways to the benefit of others or that of the person himself. For example, mind control can be used for the benefit of addicts while it can also be used in bad or unethical ways.

This practice is not uncommon as it is not a mystery or dark art that is known to only a select few. It is merely a combination of words and group pressures that are packaged in a way that makes room for the manipulator to create a sense of dependence on his followers. This helps the followers make personal decisions while thinking that they are independent beings who are free to decide on their own.

When a person becomes a victim of mind control, he is unaware of the influence process as well as the changes that are taking place within him.

In discussing this topic, however, it is of utmost importance to take note of certain distinctions, as some points need to be made clear.

First, mind control is a subtle but very insidious process which means that the individual is largely unaware of the grave effects of the influence that is being imposed on them. This is the reason why they typically make little change over time with the belief that they are making decisions for themselves, when all the decisions that they are making are made for them.

It is insidious because the purpose of mind control in some cases is to entrap and cause harm to the victim.

Another distinct point to note is that it is a process that doesn't just happen in an instant. It usually takes a lot of time, which depends on factors like the skills of the manipulator, the methods that the manipulator has decided to make use of, the length of time that the victim was exposed to the techniques, and other personal factors.

However, these days manipulators do not require a whole year or several months as they have become sufficiently skilled in such a way that they can control a person's mind within a few hours.

Also, there is usually force involved in controlling the minds of others. This may not come in the form of physical force but there is certainly some form of psychological and social force/pressure.

The main aim to control the thoughts of the person you are interacting with is to achieve your desired intention. You will get many things if you can take control of the other person's mind. The approach and the techniques to use will determine whether you will be successful in achieving your goal.

You need to get hold of their unconscious to influence them. Train to be a master in controlling and at times manipulating your partner's mind and thoughts. It is attainable to take control of the intention of someone. You need to apply some techniques, and you will succeed.

POSITIVE FORMS OF MIND CONTROL

When used the right way, mind control techniques can make a substantial change in your life for the better. Mind control can teach you how to do this:

REMAIN IN CHECK

If you'd let your mind wander freely, who knows where it might lead you. One of the most distracting and dangerous thoughts is that everyone tends to be leading us down a dark and negative path.

Without mind control to compel you to take over and drive your thoughts in the direction you want them to go, the concentration you need to remain on top of your game may be difficult to sustain.

PROTECT YOURSELF

With proper mental control training, you can teach yourself how to become more resilient and protect yourself from the manipulator's willful ways. Mind control will improve and reaffirm your self-confidence by reminding you that you are a strong, positive, and capable person, and no one will ever make you doubt your abilities.

COMMON TECHNIQUES OF MIND CONTROL

There are different ways which people use to control the minds of others, below are some of these techniques:

SUBLIMINAL MESSAGING:

These are either visual or auditory messages that are sent to a receiver's brains to bypass the person's normal conscious perceptions. To do this effectively, the mind controller flashes these messages to the other person's brain without giving the person's eyes the chance to capture/see the image or by making sounds inaudible for the receiver's ears.

The messages are sent directly to the brain. The mind controller aims to influence the other person and they do that effectively with the use of this technique.

BRAINWAVE SYNCHRONIZATION:

For everything a person does or thinks, there is a league of neurons that communicate with each other in the brain. These neurons generate and transmit electrical signals between themselves, creating patterns that are in the form of waves, which are known as brainwaves. For different states of mind of a person, there are different resultant frequencies of these brainwaves.

Thus, the question becomes whether it is possible to get to a predetermined state of the mind.

NEUROLINGUISTIC PROGRAMMING (NLP):

This is a technique that has its basis in the idea that successful behavioral patterns can be made possible in either the self or other people through the modification of underlying thought patterns as well as interpersonal relationships or interactions.

COGNITIVE BEHAVIORAL THERAPY:

This is a therapeutic technique that may not be related to mind control, but it works perfectly when it comes to the underlying principle of the modification of a person's behavior, known as behavioral modification, based on corresponding thought modification.

HYPNOSIS:

This is a mind-control tool that is used by professional hypnotists to fish out a person's suggestible subconscious mind by moving past the conscious and analytical mind to create positive thoughts or replace old negative beliefs that the mind has held onto for a long time.

People in sports have used hypnosis successfully. It has also been used in other fields like education, therapy, as well as self-improvement to boost a person's self-confidence and get rid of phobias, fears, and bad habits. It is used for relaxation and stress relief too.

According to the National Institute of Health, hypnosis is an effective tool in the reduction of some kinds of pains which include the pain from cancer. Also, hypnosis has been proven to have some self-help benefits. It has been said to be a useful tool in any attempt to change the thought process of another person for things like persuasion, negotiation, or sales.

When hypnosis is used in this manner, it is known as conversational hypnosis which is based on the techniques created/developed by the American psychiatrist and medical hypnotherapist Milton H. Erickson.

SOME OF THE TRICKS TO USE FOR YOU TO CONTROL YOUR INTERLOCUTORS

PAY ATTENTION

Pay attention to your interlocutor, and they will have the confidence to express what they feel. That will make them pour out their heart to you, and you will have a base to get control of their mind in any direction that you want. When you get them to trust you, they will not keep anything from you. You will have the entire picture, and you will know how to approach them.

MAKE SURE YOU TALK ABOUT WHAT MAKES THEM HAPPY AND WHAT SEEMS TO INTEREST THEM

If you get into a topic and you may not be conversant about the issue, ask questions as a way to show that you are interested. Showing that the talk is interesting to you will earn you more trust. You should tolerate them even if the conversation is boring. That way, you will be in a position to control their minds. Being attentive is a way of showing friendliness, and that will mean pleasant conversation.

HYPNOTISM

It is a great approach to take control of someone's mind when used in the right way. When used correctly, it will help you put your interlocutor in a trance within the first few minutes of your conversation. It is a way of seducing them, and you will get them to act on your suggestions.

CONTROL THE GUARD

To make any progress in mind-controlling, you need to suppress the brain shield. It is the conscious mind that you need to deal within the first place. Use softer as well as subtle techniques to make sure that your interlocutor has relaxed.

Try and get them to be in your debt, and this will prove influential. It is okay if youperform favors for your interlocutor to make it simpler to control them. Doing them good from time to time will make them feel an obligation to do good in return. Doing all this will give you a better position in the way you relate. It is advantageous to do this regularly, and it will raise the perception of superiority. The superiority will allow you to access more things that are in the interlocutor's mind. You will have more power since the feeling of guilt in the other person's mind will turn them to your will quickly.

BE GOOD TO THEM

Be kind and offer multiple choices to them. There being overwhelming choices, their imagination will persuade them to try nearly all of them. Try and show them that following your idea would be the best thing for them to do. That will make them do what you want, and that will be an assurance that you already have control over their mind. Let what they imagine take over to leading them to see how your suggestion is powerful. Use imagination to find the best that you can acquire from a person.

REPEAT SOMETHING OVER AND OVER AGAIN

Repeating something many times makes it sturdy, and that means that what we perceive is what we believe to be real. If something happens several times, your interlocutor's mind will register that as being the real thing. Repetition is known to be a vital tool in helping people control the brain as well as the thoughts of others. To solidify a concept in someone's mind, you need to repeat it as many times as possible. Use the repetition approach to your advantage, and you will have access to someone's brain without them having a clue of it.

PRACTICE BEING POSITIVE

Make your ideas look as high as possible and demonstrate how they will end up achieving success. The positive technique makes you look supportive, even when you may not be. Engage in positive interaction, and no should not be an answer. A negative reply can act as a powerful distraction, and it will not give you the ability to control the other person's thoughts. Give yes for an answer even if you know that the results will be negative. That will make the people around you think that you are supportive as well as thoughtful. Spinning things toward the possible will lead you in achieving your desired results without the other person knowing that you are controlling their mind.

MAINTAIN A HARMONIOUS RELATIONSHIP

Going directly to the exact thing that you want them to do will trigger their curiosity and make them think critically. If they get active in thinking, your entire plan to control their mind may go into ruin. You will have lost your control over them which is not your primary aim. Use the best suitable methods to strengthen the link and make sure that your interlocutor trusts you. When they believe you, they will have no difficulty in putting their confidence in you.

SEEK TO KNOW WHAT MOTIVATES THEM

Pay full attention to what they have to say, and it will be appropriate if you watch their nonverbal response. You not only need to focus on what motivates them but look into the most powerful motivator. Their most crucial motivator will give a clue on how you need to put your point across. Manipulating this motivator will be the easiest as well as the best strategy to help you in controlling their minds. What they give the most value when it comes to decision making will be of great importance. Try and remember the steps that they have used before to make decisions and try to manipulate them.

CREATE CONFIDENCE

You must let your interlocutor view themselves as being the hero. It serves as an excellent way to convince them to do what you want without them noticing you have taken control. Demonstrate to your interlocutor their perception matters in your context. When you achieve having their confidence, you will address anything to them with a lot of ease. Tell them how important it would be for them to be directly involved in your ideas. You need to tell them that they will own the credit once the ideas become successful.

MAKE USE OF THEIR EMOTIONS

There is an approach that you can apply to how somebody feels so that you can control them. When someone has mixed feelings, they may not know that they are monitoring them. They will do what you want to be propelled by what they feel.

You can use a situation that you know has addicted your interlocutor to make them do what you desire. Anger can also be an excellent weapon to take control of someone. Use a wise way that will not alarm them of your aim to induce irritation in your interlocutor.

Chapter 2:

Types of Mind Control

F or several years now, the theory of mind control has been about. People were both fascinated and afraid of what would happen if someone could control their minds and make them do things contrary to their will. There are countless conspiracy theories about government leaders and other influential individuals who use their abilities to monitor what small groups of people do. Even some court cases were brought up using the brainwashing excuse as an explanation of why they committed the crime they are accused of. Despite the play-up of mental control depicted in the media and films, little is understood about the various forms of mental control and how each of them functions.

Although many different types of mind control can be used to control the intended victim, the most commonly thought of are five. This involves hypnosis, brainwashing, coercion, persuasion, and deceit. These are all to be discussed in the following.

BRAINWASHING

Brainwashing is the first kind of mind control to be debated. Brainwashing is essentially the process where someone would be convinced to give up convictions they had in the past and take on new principles and ideals. There are many ways this can be achieved, but not all of them are considered evil.

For instance, if you're from an African nation and then moving to America, you are always forced to change your beliefs and principles to fit in with the new community and climate in which you live. On the other hand, people in concentration camps, or when a new dictatorial regime takes over, will also go through the process of brainwashing to convince citizens to obey in peace. Many people misunderstand what brainwashing is about. Many people have more cynical ideas about the procedure, like mind-control systems that are funded by the government and thought to be quickly turned on with a remote control. On the other side of things, some skeptics don't believe brainwashing is possible at all, and whoever says it is has spread lies. The form of brainwashing will probably fall somewhere between these two theories.

During the brainwashing practice, the target can be convinced by a mixture of techniques to change their views about something. In this method, there is not just one technique that can be used, and it can be difficult to bring the practice into a tidy little package. The subject will also be disconnected from all the things they learn.

From there, they are broken down into an emotional state which makes them fragile before new concepts are implemented. As this new knowledge is absorbed by the subject, they will be rewarded for sharing ideas and thoughts that go with these new ideas. This should be used to justify the brainwashing that is taking place is rewarding.

Brainwashing is nothing new to society. For a long time, people have been using such techniques. For example, those who were prisoners of war were sometimes broken down in a historical context, before being convinced to change sides. Some of those most successful cases would result in the inmate becoming a very fervent convert to the new side. In the beginning, such activities were very new and would always be applied based on who was in command. The concept of brainwashing was developed over time, and a few more methods were added to make the practice more widespread. The newer techniques will focus on the field of psychology because many of those concepts were used to show how people, by persuasion, could change their minds.

Several steps go along with the process of brainwashing. It's not something that can happen to you just as you walk down the street and talk to someone you just met. First of all, one of the main demands that come with successful brainwashing is that the subject should be kept in isolation. If the subject is around other people and experiences, they can learn how to behave like an adult, and there will be no brainwashing at all.

They can undergo a process designed to break down their selves if the subject is isolated. They're told all the facts they know are wrong, and they're made to feel like they're wrong with everything they do. The subject will feel like they're bad after months of going through all of this and will be overwhelmed by the guilt. Once they have reached this point, the manipulator will begin to lead them to the desired new system of beliefs and identity. The subject would be led to believe that all of the new opinions are their own, and therefore, they are more likely to last. The entire brainwashing cycle can take months or even years or complete. It's not something that's going to happen in just a conversation, and it won't be able to happen outside of detention camps and a few isolated situations for the most part.

For the most part, when someone is simply trying to convince othersof a different point of view, those are people who experience brainwashing. For example, if you're in an argument with a friend, and they're telling you their ideas make sense, you've technically been through brainwashing. Sure, it may not be bad, and you might objectively think about it all, but you were also persuaded to alter previously held convictions. It is unlikely that someone undergoes real brainwashing where they would have changed their whole belief system. It will usually occur during the process of getting around to a new point of view, irrespective of whether or not the tactics used were forceful.

HYPNOSIS

The next, well-known form of mind control is hypnosis. The several meanings of what hypnosis is are different. Hypnosis is a mutual activity, according to the American Psychological Association, in which the hypnotist will provide suggestions that the patient will respond to. Many people have become familiar with hypnosis techniques thanks to popular performances in which participants are told to perform ridiculous or unusual tasks. Another form of hypnosis that is gaining in popularity is the type that uses this practice for its therapeutic and medical advantages, especially when it comes to reducing anxiety and pain. In some cases, hypnosis has been able to reduce dementia symptoms in a few patients. There are, as you can see, several different explanations that can be used for hypnosis. If the hypnotist will give solutions that may be detrimental or alter the way the client behaves in their situation, that is the point where it starts to become mind control.

When most people hear about hypnosis, they think of a person on stage who swings a watch back and forth to put the participant in a trance. If you go to a stage show for amusement, you might picture some of the absurd actions performed by the participants in your mind. Those who are going through what is considered to be real hypnosis are going through a very different process. "The individual is not hypnotized by the hypnotist. The hypnotist then acts as a sort of coach or mentor whose task is to help the person become hypnotized,"John Kihlstrom said. This means the hypnotist is trying to bring the client into a relaxed state of mind, so they are more open to suggestions offered.

Most of the hypnosis sufferers claim they are in a kind of sleeplike dream state. Notwithstanding these feelings, while the patient is in a state under hypnosis, it includes vivid hallucinations, increased suggestibility, and concentrated attention. This new condition makes them more responsive to suggestions offered by the hypnotist. The effects that hypnosis can have on subjects are difficult to describe, since the experiences can differ quite a bit for each person who undergoes it. Some participants will describe the feeling as though they are disconnected from the whole process, some will feel highly comfortable during the hypnosis, and others will even believe like their acts will take place beyond their conscious choices. On the other hand, individuals will claim to be fully aware of their surroundings and will even be able to conduct conversations during their hypnotic state.

Several studies done by Ernest Hilgard show that hypnosis can be used to alter the beliefs of the subject. Hilgard's experiment included a warning to the subject that they should not experience any pain in their head. The subject had their arm stuck in some ice water after they were told this. Those who did this experiment and did not get hypnotized had to take their arms out of the water in just a few seconds because they felt pain. Many who had been hypnotized could leave their arms in the water without experiencing any pain for a few minutes. Though more research is required, this study shows how powerful mind control can be when using the technique of hypnosis.

There are several different uses of hypnosis illustrated by studies that include:

Treatment of chronic pain like the one associated with rheumatoid arthritis. Treatment and avoidance of the suffering that comes from childbirth.

Reducing the symptoms related to dementia.

Since using hypnotherapy, some ADHD patients have reported a reduction in their symptoms.

To reduce cases of vomiting and nausea in patients going through chemotherapy.

Pain control during a dental procedure. Eliminating and reducing skin disorders, such as psoriasis and warts, alleviating symptoms linked to Irritable Bowel Syndrome.

These are only a few of the uses for which hypnosis has become popular. While many people believe that using hypnosis is used to manipulate the subject and make it perform cruel actions or reject their values, the most popular applications are those to enhance individuals' safety.

Most experts believe that hypnosis as a method of mind control is not a fact. Although it may be possible to convince the mind to make a few changes in the subject's behavior, it is impossible that the subject will change their whole belief system even by this process. Many of the people who are trained in this field would use it to assist the subject in handling self-improvement and discomfort rather than attempting to take over their minds.

MANIPULATION

Manipulation is another type of mind control which can be used in various ways to decide how the person thinks. Manipulation is referred to in this guidebook as psychological manipulation. It is a sort of social power that serves to alter other people's actions or understanding. It is done using methods that are hostile, insulting, and underhanded. This form of mind control is used, often to the detriment of others, to advance the one controlling desires. The approaches employed are also perceived as manipulative, devious, coercive, and exploitative. Most people can understand when controlled or others controlled around them, but they don't identify that as a form of mind control. It can also be a difficult form of mind control to resist as the coercion generally takes place between the subject and someone they know well. Manipulation leaves the subject feeling as if they have no choice. They would have been fed lies or half-truths outright, and they would not know the full severity of the case until it was too late. When they find out ahead of time about the situation, the manipulator would be able to threaten and use the subject to achieve the final target. By fact, the subject gets lost, and the manipulator will have worked it out in such a way that they won't fall into trouble, the subject will take the blame or get hurt when it comes to it, and the manipulator can make it to their final target.

The worst thing about this is that the manipulator is unable to sense their subject's needs or any other person's needs; they won't know whether the subject gets harmed in the process and if it's emotional or physical damage. Although the subject will be involved emotionally in the situation, the manipulator will be able to walk away (as long as they achieve their ultimate goal) without feeling any guilt or regret for what happened along the way. This can be a dangerous type of mind control because the manipulator will be an expert at it, capable of blackmailing, threatening, and doing whatever else is needed; often, they will even be able to turn it around, so the target feels like they're going insane.

PERSUASION

Persuasion is another type of mind controlthatacts to manipulate the subject's actions, emotions, thoughts, attitudes, and beliefs. There are many different reasons why persuasion could be used in everyday life, and it's often a necessary form of communication to get people on the same page with different ideas. For business, for example, the persuasion mechanism can be used to shift the attitude of a person about anything, such as, a concept, or event that is happening. During the process, either written or spoken words are used to pass reasoning, feelings, or information on to the other person. Convincing another may be used to satisfy a personal gain. This may include encouraging trials, when delivering a sales pitch, or during an election campaign. Although none of these are considered negative or bad, they are all used to convince the listener to act or think in some way. One definition of persuasion is that one uses their own personal or professional power to alter others' attitudes or behaviors. There are also many different forms of persuasion known; the process of changing beliefs or attitudes by appealing to reason and reasoning is known as systemic persuasion; the process of changing beliefs and attitudes by appealing to feelings or behaviors is known as heuristic persuasion.

Persuasion is a form of control of the mind that is used all the time in society. When you talk about politics to someone, you can try to convince them to think the same way you do. If you listen to a political advertisement, you are motivated to vote in one direction or another. If anyone wants to sell you a new product, there's a lot of persuasion going on there. This form of mind control is so widespread that most people don't even know it's happening to them. The problem will occur when someone takes the time to convince you to believe in beliefs and principles that do not suit your belief system. There are several different kinds of persuasion on sale. Maybe all of them have negative intent, but they will all try to get the target to change their minds about something. When a political candidate appears on television on election day, they try to get the subject, or the voter, to vote on the ballot a certain way. The company that produced the advertising is trying to get the audience to purchase that product when you see a commercial on television or online. These are all forms of persuasion bent on trying to get the target to change the way they think.

DECEPTION

Finally, deception is often considered a form of mind control because of its potential effect on the subject. Deception is used to spread assumptions about events and things in the subject's life which are not real, regardless of whether they are full lies or just partial lies. Deception may include several different items like hand sleight, concealment, disguise, and diversion. This kind of mind control is dangerous because the subject sometimes does not know that there is any kind of mind control at all. We are persuaded that when the complete opposite is right, one thing is real. It can become dangerous when the deception hides details that would keep the subject secure. Often during relationships, deception is seen and will usually lead to feelings of distrust and betrayal between the two partners. There has been a violation of the relationship rules when deceit happens, and it may make it impossible for the partner to trust the other for a long time. It can be particularly dangerous because most people are used to trusting those around them, especially partners and friends, and often expect them to be true to them. When they find out they're being misled by someone they're close to, they may have problems with trusting people, and they won't have the sense of security they're used to.

Deception can trigger several problems in a relationship, or the manipulator and subject. Once they find out about the deception, the subject will have a lot of issues trusting the manipulator in the future. There will be occasions where the lie is made to help the partnership out. This may involve things like not asking a partner when someone says they mean something. Other times the deception is of a more spiteful or harmful nature, such as when the manipulator hides important information from the subject or even deceives the person as to who they are. All people believe that deceit is unethical and should not be performed, no matter what form of deceit is deployed.

Chapter 3:

How to Read People

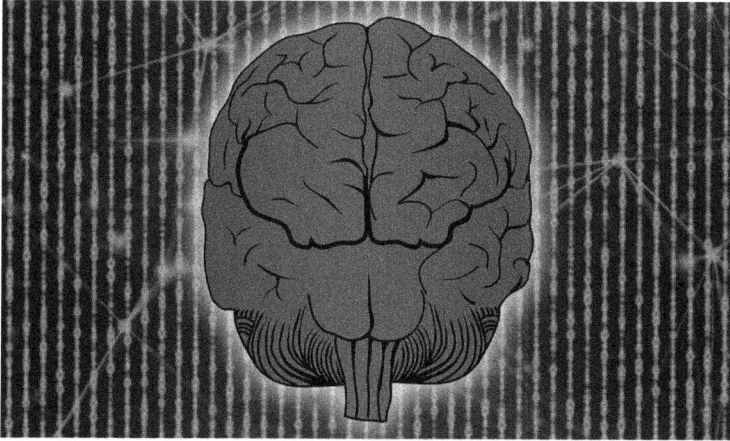

What you say communicates only half of what people hear. 40-50% of the message you send comes from your body language. Since the last century, we have made a lot of progress in understanding the thousands of non-verbal communication meanings. Here are some of the most important findings:

FACIAL EXPRESSIONS

How good are you at reading facial expressions? There are currently online tests that tell you whether you're good at reading facial expressions or not. Some tests like Reading the Mind in the Eyes Test checks to see whether you can read a person's mind simply by looking at their eyes. If you're interested in taking the test yourself, check the website: socialintelligence.labinthewild.org/mite. See how well you fare and then just come back to this book if you want. For purposes of improving communication, we're going to include all the elements that are included in reading facial expressions, which involve the eyes, eyebrows, lips, nose, and even the wrinkles around the eyes and mouth.

PUPIL

There is practically no way to fake the movement of the pupils when reading facial expressions. The pupils of the eye contract and expand without any sort of control on the part of a person. Typically, the pupils will expand when a person is interested and contract when they're not.

BLINKING MOTION

The eyes typically blink six to ten times per minute. When a person looks at something they find interesting, however, that blinking rate slows down drastically. It's therefore a great indicator when someone finds something interesting or attractive. It's often used as a sign of flirting or interest in a romantic setting. In an office or social setting, unblinking eyes could be a signal that a person is very interested in what you have to say and listening to you throughout.

RAISING THE HEAD

Raising the head from a lowered position is a sign of captured interest. Think of a student who's looking down during an exam who suddenly raises their head when they hear something important. This is the kind of movement that we are trying to describe in this situation.

HEAD TILT

A head tilt usually starts from a normal position of the head and then juts out at an angle. This is what makes it different from the motion of raising your head from a lowered position. A head tilt also indicates interest, usually towards the person or activity where it happens to be tilted too. When combined with facial expressions like a narrowing of the eyebrows, it can be a sign of confusion, curiosity, questioning, or uncertainty. A head that's tilted backward may be a sign of suspicion.

Of course, let's not forget the typical head gestures that mean practically the same for everyone. These are:

NODDING

Usually signifies agreement.

SHAKING THE HEAD

Usually signifies disagreement.

What's important about these gestures is that people are often conscious of doing this. Hence, it can be easily controlled by them, depending on the situation. Some can stop the motion entirely while others turn it into very subtle gestures so that it would be very difficult to notice.

HANDS, ARMS, AND GESTURES

SHRUG

A shrug is composed of multiple gestures which include exposed palms, hunched shoulders, and raised brows.

It's a universal sign that indicates a lack of knowledge or uncertainty over a particular activity.

It can often be translated as a sign that the other person doesn't know what you're saying or doesn't understand what you're trying to convey.

CLENCHED HANDS

Clenched hands are a sign of repression. You're trying to prevent the burst of emotions like anger or frustration. It's a self-containment mechanism often used by people who don't want to do or say something out of order. In some cases, you can read this gesture as a sign that someone has a closed mind on what you're trying to say. In the alternative, open and relaxed hands are a sign of comfort and show a positive attitude with a mind welcome to new ideas.

HAND WRINGING

This is often interpreted as a sign of anxiety or nervousness. Playing with something in your hands also has the same interpretation.

HANDSHAKE

You have to be careful with handshakes as this can tell so much about a person and vice versa. I'm sure you've managed to have presumptions of people simply because of the way they shook your hand.

The best handshake is often considered to be a firm, dry grip, that's quick but not too long. It shouldn't be too tight as to cause pain, but it should be strong enough to signify competence on the part of the person shaking their hand.

My advice is you practice your handshake with another person to help you decide on the best pressure to use when greeting someone this way. Note though—not all cultures accept handshakes as a viable way of greeting others.

For example, people in India or those who practice the Muslim faith do not approve of handshakes as a way of greeting between men and women.

COVERING THE MOUTH

Doing this is often shown as a sign of repression, like a person wanted to say something but decided against it at the last minute. Some people use this gesture as a way to show thinking or a thought process.

BODY POSTURE AND MOVEMENT

You've probably noticed that reading body language involves paying attention to different parts of the body all at once. Some gestures are centered in just one area, like the face, and therefore are slightly easier than others. Some gestures, however, are scattered all over the body, which means that different parts are moving all at once. This makes it tougher to do a reading, but you'll find that with practice, the whole thing becomes easier.

Body posture and movement is a big predictor of a person's thoughts and emotions. The general position of the chest, shoulders, legs, and so on will tell you if a person is aggressive, afraid, unsure, excited, and so on. Here are some of the typical changes in the body and what they indicate:

A PUMPED-OUT CHEST IS A SIGN OF POWER AND DOMINANCE

Typically, when the chest is spread out, the shoulders are also stretched into a straight line, pushing the chest forward and making the person appear bigger. Combined with hands placed on the hips and this can be dubbed as the "Superman" pose which makes a person appear bigger and occupy more space. This is often seen as a sign of confidence and dominance. You'll notice many animals in the wild, when protecting their territory or trying to attract a mate, tend to make their bodies appear bigger so that they'll be easily noticed. Men and women do the same thing and often for the same reasons.

TOUCHING THE CHEST CAN ALSO BE A SIGN OF SINCERITY

You'll notice how people do this when they're trying to apologize or communicate how bad they feel or their condolences to another person.

Scratching or touching the chest can also be a sign of discomfort.

BREATHING

Breathing can tell you a lot about what a person feels. You've probably noticed this already, not just in other people but also in yourself. For example, you might hold your breath when excited or take short and shallow breaths when scared. Typically, deep and even breaths are indicative of relaxation, such as when you're sleeping or when you're sitting down watching a relaxing movie. Excessive, shallow, or holding your breath, on the other hand, can be a sign of emotional turmoil. According to experts, mirroring a person's breathing pattern can also help forge a connection of mutual understanding between the two of you. Being able to match someone's breathing pattern essentially allows you to create a sense of normalcy in the situation, thereby pulling them into a sense of relaxation. Of course, this takes some skill to do, especially if the situation is nerve-wracking. At the very least, being able to identify nervous breathing patterns can help you adjust your stance to make the other person feel comfortable—all without a word said to each other.

READING LIES IN PEOPLE

One of the most valuable skills when reading people is being able to tell when they're lying. Admit it—you've always wanted to know when someone is lying to you, and that's perfectly okay. Studies show that when lying, some people have specific "tells," such as scratching their nose or brushing their hair with their fingers. People who play poker often use these "tells" to see if they should match the other person's bet and whether it would be worth the trouble.

One thing I want to remind you of is that reading lies in a person is not an exact science. People's actions when lying can vary, which is why familiarity is important. The longer you know a person, the more accurate your prediction will be about the truthfulness of what they're saying.

So, that being the case, here are the typical signs of lying according to experts.

UNDERSTANDING A BASELINE

One thing I want you to remember is that when reading body language, there's usually a "baseline" that allows you to start somewhere. A baseline is simply the "normal" way in which a person acts when around people. Hence, if a person is being truthful and confident in their surroundings, how exactly do they act? Knowing a person's baseline lets you know when they're acting out of character. Sure, you can walk into a room full of strangers and do a casual "read" of the room, but reading people close to you is often easier as you've known them for a longer period. You have a point of reference, to put it simply.

HAND MOVEMENTS

People lying tend to use gestures, but they do it after speaking. Typically, you'd find people gesturing while talking because that is a natural part of the process. Their body is working with the mind in telling a story or conveying a message. In contrast, a person who is lying is focusing too much on making up the story that the body fails to catch up. Hence, they make up the lie first and then perform the gestures to emphasize their point. Also, take note that gestures of people who are lying often involve both hands as opposed to truthful people who only use one hand. This was noted after a 2015 study about people testifying in court cases.

ITCHING AND FIDGETING

There's a popular belief that when a person lies, they tend to scratch their nose. This isn't true 100% of the time—but it does bear noting in many cases. It's fairly normal for people to have an itching sensation or fidget in their seat when they're uncomfortable; the body naturally looks for a way to distract itself. Also note that when lying, people are often nervous about what they're saying, which causes the autonomic nervous system to fluctuate, thus, creating that tingling sensation all over the body. It's a lot like the nerves you get when you sit close to someone you like during those younger days.

FACIAL EXPRESSIONS

Of course, let us not forget how the face itself can signify when someone is lying. The eyes in particular can tell you so much depending on when a person chooses to look at you and when they choose to look away. Looking too much or not looking at all can be indicative of lying. Some people prefer to meet your gaze when lying because they "think" this will impress upon you their sincerity. Non-experienced liars tend to look away when uttering a lie.

CHANGE IN COMPLEXION

This one's pretty obvious, as you read about it every day or see it as it happens every day. People blush, people become red, and people become pale depending on the circumstances. People tend to become pale when they're nervous or when they're afraid of something. When the skin turns a shade of red, however, that's indicative of anger or perhaps even excitement, like when a teenager typically blushes when sitting beside their crush.

SWEAT IN THE T ZONE

This is something you have to watch out for when wondering if a person is lying to you or not. The T Zone covers the area of the nose and across the forehead and then down to your mouth. Sweating is fairly common in this area if a person is lying, especially if they're nervous about it.

TONE OF VOICE

We're trying to focus on nonverbal communication here, but the tone of voice is still a strong indicator, even with the absence of the words themselves. High-pitched voices tend to come out of nervous people as the vocal cords tighten, making it hard to push out the particular words. There can also be a croak, a stutter, or some broken words coming out of a nervous individual. Some people clear their throat to help improve their speech, which is also indicative of nervousness. In contrast, a loud and booming voice can be a sign of confidence or anger, depending on the situation. A sudden change in the volume can also be defensive in people, especially when confronted with possible mistakes.

THE MOUTH

Playing with the lips, such as rolling them back until they almost disappear, is another good indicator. It's typically a sign of lying by omission as people physically try to hold back a word or a thought by pulling in their lips. If it goes the other way, however, it can be a sign of resistance or when a person doesn't want to talk about something.

THE WORDS THEMSELVES

Again, we're trying to focus on the nonverbal way of communicating, but I still want to cover all bases. After all, experienced liars can easily control their body language to match the situation. Hence, you still have to listen to the words themselves as they can indicate when a person is trying too hard to convince you of their truthfulness. Some common phrases used by liars include:

"Honestly…"

"Let me tell you the truth…"

"Uh…"

"Like…"

"Um…"

Chapter 4:

Users of Dark Psychology

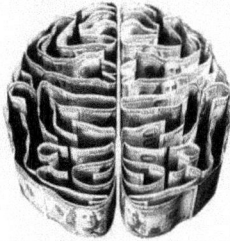

WHO USES DARK PSYCHOLOGY THESE DAYS?

ATTORNEYS

Many attorneys focus so attentively on winning their case that they turn to use techniques of dark manipulation to get the outcome they seek.

THE SELFISH PEOPLE

Someone with a secret agenda that favors itself before anyone can return to those dark, deceptive tactics if the result is a win for them.

POLITICIANS

To get the votes they need to get the people to vote in the way they want them, politicians are guilty of using dark methods of manipulation as a means of serving their purpose.

LAWYERS

Some lawyers will stop at nothing if it means winning their case, even if it means they have to resort to shady tactics.

SALESPEOPLE

Much like attorneys and politicians, specific salespeople may be so focused on doing nothing but selling that they have no shame in using deceptive techniques to convince a customer to do what they want.

LEADERS

Not every leader is there to inspire, and some rely on manipulation to get us to meet their demands.

PUBLIC SPEAKERS

Not all public speakers can be trusted, and there are some out there whowill resort to bribery if it means selling more goods to do so.

Many speakers use dark strategies to heighten the audience's emotional state of realizing it leads to more products being sold at the back of the room.

These are just a few of the many instances of people out there who would turn to the more malevolent side of the continuum of human nature, and often for the benefit of no one else but their own.

THE TRIAD OF DARK PSYCHOLOGY

Just when you felt the deceit was bad enough, an even darker side of psychology arrives here, known as the Dark Triad. The triad consists of three very distinct but interrelated forms of personality, namely narcissism, psychopathy, and Machiavellianism. Why is the Dark Triad, or the darker side of human psychology, called these three? It is because these three terms define the very tactics that some people resort to getting what they want-manipulation, persuasion, and deception. Yes, the term Dark Triad has a sinister ring to it, and it's a term that many psychologists and criminologists use as a defining predictor that signals an individual's criminal behavior. Let's look at the three personality characteristics that make up this trifecta more closely:

NARCISSISM

The word comes from the Greek mythology of Narcissus, the hunter who fell in love with his reflection when he saw it in a pool of water where he drowned. He was so consumed by himself that he could not concentrate on anything else. Those with characteristics of narcissistic personality also show signs that include being boastful, greedy, and rude, caring more for themselves and nothing else. Also, narcissistic individuals lack empathy and are highly sensitive (one may even say hypersensitive) to any sort of criticism, since they cannot bear the incomplete or false thought.

MACHIAVELLIANISM

This word comes from the famous diplomat and politician Niccolò Machiavelli who lived in Italy in the 16th century. Machiavelli became famous with the publication of his book, The Prince, in 1513. This publication has been interpreted as the recognition by Machiavelli of the deception and ruse that takes place in diplomacy. Those who tend to exhibit Machiavellianistic tendencies are often only concerned with their self-interest and are manipulative and duplicate. Some people lack both morals and conscience, so they're not into anything else but what's going to help them.

PSYCHOPATHY

Antisocial behavior, manipulative, aggressive, violent, lack of guilt, or empathy are characteristics associated with a psychopathic character. Psychopathic and being a psychopath are two very different features, the latter generally associated with or explicitly associated with crime.

THE MANIPULATOR

The term manipulative is likely to affect individuals of all social origins. The typical manipulator usually has a perverse psychological structure of the psychopathic type; he can appear as friendly or not, even as a victim. It seems that each one is more or less manipulative in the course of his life.

According to these definitions, different types of manipulators can be distinguished: those who use others without remorse, with a narcissistic goal of power, financial scam, or with malicious intent. They can rely on lies or seduction, even coercion by threat of force, or destabilize their victim by double oppression. Psychic manipulation can be one of the tools of certain forms of torture.

It can be behavior understood as deviant or perverse, a personality disorder whose causes go back to childhood or the manipulator's education, such as if his parents or educators have manipulated him. Psychologists are frequently confronted with manipulative behavior in systems such as family or socio-professional.

Mental manipulation could be a certain form of selfishness. Often the manipulator demands socially acceptable behavior from others without adapting themselves. He appropriates the ideas of another, conversely trying to make someone else take his responsibilities. The arguments of a manipulator always seem, at first glance, logical and moral. Usually, he uses pretexts such as the norm, the "good behavior" that must be observed in society or the group, knowing how to use the weaknesses of others, for example making them feel ridiculous, guilty, or hurt in their modesty, which places them in a mental situation favorable to manipulation.

A SADIST

A professional sadist can so deliberately set these conditions up that it is impossible to prove that they were involved in the guilty party. What makes it far worse is that they will never be held responsible or feel any sort of regret for the harm they caused. People can also be hesitant to assume that the sadist's charming and likable personalities are behind the chaos. A sadist will attempt to harm someone else intentionally because they believe that doing so will benefit them. They may resort to such underhanded tactics if they feel envious or threatened by others or even if they perceive someone else as weaker and less likely to retaliate against them. In some instances, it might not be obvious why the sadist opted to conduct a victim attack. We don't often think-or want to believe-that the sadist might exist within our immediate circle of connections, but they do, and they could be your parents, siblings, extended family members, spouse, friends, and the people with whom you work.

THE MANIPULATOR IN A RELATIONSHIP

One of the worst sinking feeling you might feel is knowing that all this time, your partner, the person you love and who supposedly loves you, turns out to be using you to their advantage. A partnership is supposed to be the one place we believe we can get the sincere inside support, love, dedication, and care we all yearn for. In return, to be wholeheartedly loved and respected. Sadly, there are those out there who have had their hearts broken because they know there's not just something dishonest about their partner, but they have manipulated their strings like a puppet all along.

We all have particular aspirations and romantic ideas of what we think love is due to the way in which love is portrayed in society through the films we watch, articles we read, and social media posts we scroll through almost every day. When we see on-screen jealousy, we believe it's a sign of intense love because the two people in the film are afraid to lose their loved one to another. The popular literature and Twilight movies lead us to believe that true love and relationships are about obsession. That love is an omnipresent emotion. That when there are two people in love, nothing else matters, and there are no boundaries. This romanticized notion blinds us to the fact that this isn't what life is at all, and that kind of love occurs only in movies and between the pages of books because they make for a good storyline. Such behavior is an indication of manipulation in real life. It is not love to be controlling, it is manipulation. It is not being passionate being obsessed, and it is manipulative.

On some level, we know that we should be able to recognize in a relationship the signs of an abusive partner. We know we can, but it is easier said than done. When we love, we prefer to blind ourselves to a fault with our mate. We are making excuses for the actions that should set off warning bells in our heads as we try to avoid facing the facts. We don't want our hearts to be broken that way, and we're trying to convince ourselves they aren't really like that at all. There is cause for concern when a relationship escalates from controlling to being purely abusive but being in a manipulative relationship can also be harmful and damaging.

Getting in a manipulative relationship can be as detrimental to you both physically and psychologically. Manipulative partners will try to dominate you, minimizing your freedom. They try to manipulate every decision you make, belittle you, and destroy your self-esteem so that you begin to doubt yourself and think you are the "lucky" one, and no one can possibly love you as much. They make you scared of losing this relationship and make you scared to enter into any future relationships because this experience has traumatized you from getting into another manipulative relationship. Being in a manipulative relationship will leave you with emotional wounds and scars that, if they ever do, will take a very, very long time to heal.

The more common signs you're in a manipulative relationship is when your partner continually pressures you to look or act in a way that they only approve of or decide who you can and can't spend your time with. The love and support that would come from genuine relationships is not something you will note when you're in a relationship with manipulators. Lying to try to manipulate you and the situation in their favor, when your partner is a manipulative person, is something that will be a regular occurrence in your relationship, and these are the signs to look out for:

- Lying to make you feel guilty about spending time with others—Because the manipulator needs to be in charge, they will try to cut you off as far as possible from your support network by trying to minimize the amount of time you spend with your family and friends.

- They lie and criticize— When you're with someone manipulative, every little thing you do is subject to criticism. The worst part of all this is that they lie so convincingly when they say they do it because "they love you" or "it's for your good". They'll continually criticize just about everything you're doing, the longer you remain in a relationship with them.

- You may be the most trustworthy and truthful person, but a manipulator will make you feel different. They are still individuals in their own right, as deeply in love as two people are, and all have the right to privacy.

- Manipulators may demand access to your passwords, social media accounts, and even more private information by spinning some tale about how they're "fearing" you might break their hearts by cheating on them.

- They're talking a lot about "protecting you," which, of course, is just another lie by the manipulator. They're not protecting you; they're not even thinking about it, because all they care about is their self-interest. Deep down, who wouldn't love the idea that there's somebody out there who loves them enough to protect them from the big evil world? That person exists, alas not with a manipulator. There's a natural desire to protect when you love someone and to keep them from feeling hurt.

- They provoke you with lies — Sometimes a manipulator might resort to provoking you into an argument by lying and exaggerating, blowing things out of proportion just because they know that when they do, and they push your buttons.

- Twisting lies with even more lies — Manipulators will spin lies almost as intricately as spinning their website. They will lie, twist those lies, and then twist those lies even more until you don't know what is real and what isn't. Twisting the truth and distorting them, tangling lies on top of more lies is the manipulator's favorite technique to confuse and frustrate you.

Chapter 5:

Behaviors Exhibited by Attackers

EMOTIONAL INTELLIGENCE AND MANIPULATION

The term emotional intelligence was first invented in the 1960s and has become common over the years.

However, the concept behind the term has been around for decades. In simple terms, emotional intelligence is the ability of a person to recognize and understand emotions, then using this information to make decisions.

Like any other skill, emotional intelligence is a skill we can cultivate, sharpen, and enhance. It is important to note that although emotional intelligence is a good skill, one can use it either for good or bad.

Once a person understands the power of emotions, he or she can use it ethically or unethically.

The last thing that we want is having someone manipulating our emotions, whether it is a friend, colleague, or politician.

There are some ways through which a master manipulator can use emotional intelligence against you. Please note that not everyone who has the characteristics listed below and used the said skill has selfish intentions. Some people practice them with no intended harm. Nonetheless, having an increased awareness of these behaviors will empower you to deal with manipulators strategically and sharpen your intelligence quotient in the process.

MANIPULATORS PLAY ON FEAR

The majority of manipulators will overemphasize specific points and exaggerate facts to make you scared and have you acting as they want. The way to identify this play is by looking out for statements that imply you are not strong or courageous enough or that if you miss out on a particular thing, you are a loser.

MANIPULATORS DECEIVE

Everybody values honesty and transparency, thus, will want to avoid deceivers. Manipulators understand this concept and are very cunning when lying. They twist the facts or try to show you only the side of the story that benefits them. For instance, a work colleague can spread some unconfirmed rumor to gain an upper hand.

MANIPULATORS TAKE ADVANTAGE OF YOUR HAPPINESS

Have you noticed that you are more likely to say yes to anything when you are happy or in a good mood? When we are happy, we tend to jump on opportunities that look good even before we think things through. Master manipulators have this knowledge, thus, will take advantage of the moods. To manage this emotional opportunity and avoid manipulation, work to improve awareness of your emotions, both positive and negative. strive to strike a balance between logic and emotions When making decisions.

MANIPULATORS TAKE ADVANTAGE OF RECIPROCITY

Do you know that feeling you get when you owe someone a favor especially if they helped you at one point?

That feeling of debt makes one vulnerable. It is hard to say no to a manipulator if you owe them something.

Most of the manipulators will attempt to butter and flatter you with small favors then ask for a big one in return.

As much as giving brings more joy than receiving, it is more important to know your limits.

Do not be afraid to say no, even if you owe someone a favor.

MANIPULATORS PUSH FOR A HOME-COURT ADVANTAGE

It is very easy to convince a person when you are in a familiar place. As such, a manipulator will push you towards meeting you in a place he or she is familiar with while you are not. Ownership gives power and comfort, thus, a place like home or the office will give the manipulator some authority. You will have to make requests for meeting in a neutral place where familiarity and ownership are diluted to disarm the manipulator.

THE MANIPULATOR WILL ASK A LOT OF QUESTIONS

Naturally, it is easy to talk about oneself. Master manipulators know this; thus, they take advantage to ask some probing questions.

Their agendas are hidden but they seek to discover your weaknesses or other information they can hold against you.

Of course, it would be unfair for you to assume that everyone has wrong motives because there are a few people who genuinely seek to know you better. However, it is okay to question people, especially those who reveal nothing about themselves.

THE MANIPULATOR WILL SPEAK QUICKLY

To manipulate you through your emotions, the manipulator will speak quickly and sometimes use jargon and special vocabulary.

This will give them an advantage because you will not have enough time to think. For you to counter this form of manipulation, do not feel afraid to ask for some time to process what the person said. Also, make a point of asking the person to repeat any unclear statements. To gain control of a conversation, repeat the points the other person makes in your own words, and let them sink in.

THE DISPLAY OF NEGATIVE EMOTIONS

Some manipulators will use voice tones to control your emotions. The most commonly used tone and body language by manipulators are negative.

For instance, basketball coaches (they use manipulation for positive purposes) are masters at raising their voices and using strong body language to manipulate the emotions of the players. To avoid such manipulation, you should practice pausing. It involves taking a break from the conversation orsituation and having some time to think before reacting. You may walk away for some minutes to get a grip on your own emotions.

MANIPULATORS LIMIT YOUR TIME TO ACT

Every manipulator wants to win. They may do this by ensuring that you do not have enough time to think. For instance, an individual may force you to make a serious decision in an unreasonably limited amount of time.

He or she will try to steer your thoughts to their advantage. You will not have enough time to weigh the consequences.

To avoid a situation where you give in without thought, do not be in a rush to submit. Ensure that the demand is reasonable.

Take the pause, ask for some time, and if the person does not allow you to think, walk away.

You will be happier looking for whatever you need elsewhere.

THE SILENT TREATMENT

To avoid being a victim of manipulation through silent treatment, give people deadlines, and do not allow them to intimidate you.

For instance, after attempting to communicate to a reasonable degree, let go of the matter and let the other person reach out.

Manipulators will work to increase their emotional awareness to have an upper hand on others.

A large number of people are learning how to be emotionally intelligent.

CHARACTERISTICS OF MANIPULATORS

USE OF LANGUAGE

We have shown how powerful language can bea prime tool of persuasion. There is more to the manipulative controller though, than mere words. They will use tactics that mislead and unbalance their target's inner thoughts. We now understand that through language, they will:

Use mistruths to mislead and confuse their target's normal thinking pattern.

Force their target to decide the speed, so they don't have time to analyze and think.

Overwhelmingly talk to their target, making them feel small.

Criticize their target's judgment so they begin to lose their self-esteem.

Raise the tone of their voice and not be afraid to use aggressive body language.

Ignore their target's needs, as they are only interested in getting what they want and at any cost.

INVASION OF PERSONAL SPACE

Most of us set boundaries around ourselves without realizing we are doing so. It is a kind of unspoken rule to protect our own private space, such as not sitting so close that you are touching another person, especially a stranger. A manipulative character cares nothing about overstepping such boundaries. Whether this is because they do not understand, or they do not care is unclear. Initially, they are unlikely to invade their target's personal space. They will seek to build up a good rapport first. This shows that they do understand boundaries because once they gain the confidence of their target, they will then ignore them.

FODDER FOR THOUGHT

Manipulators tend to be very egocentric, with limited social skills. Their only concern is for themselves. Everything they do in life will be concerning how it affects them, not how their actions affect others. Does this mean that they have a psychopathic disorder?

CREATING RIVALRY

Another tactic of the controlling manipulator is backstabbing. They may tell you how great a person you are to your face, making themselves look good. Behind your back, they are busy spreading malicious gossip and untruths about you. This is a classic trait of a controlling manipulator as it creates a rivalry between people. Then, they can pick sides that will make them look favorable, particularly to their target. It can act as the first stage of getting close to their target. Once bonded, they can start to build up trust, making it easier to manipulate the target in the future. If you recognize a backstabber, keep them at a distance. Their agenda is selfish, so it is better not to let them into your personal life. There is no point treating them as they treat you as revenge. It will turn out to be exhausting playing them at their own game. If they know that you are onto them, they may attempt to lure you back with praise, remember that it is false.

DOMINEERING PERSONALITY

It is unlikely that a manipulative person will outwardly show any form of weakness. An important part of their facade is to show conviction about their views. They seek to impress, believing they are right about everything. Almost to the point that if they realize they are wrong, they will still argue that they are right. On a one-to-one level, that invariably means that your position is always wrong.

PASSIVE AGGRESSIVE BEHAVIOR

A common trait of many hard-core manipulators is passive-aggressive behavior. Because they prefer to be popular, they do not wish to be seen as doing anything wrong. Not that a manipulator would ever admit to doing anything wrong. They are experts with facial expressions that are meant to dominate and intimidate. This may include; knitting eyebrows, grinding teeth, and rolling eyes. It may also include noises such as tutting and grunting sounds.

MOODY BLUES

What of the emotional stability of the manipulator? Is it that which makes them behave the way they do? Do they even know what happiness is? The answer to that is most definitely yes, at least to the latter.

Happiness is a tool used initially to help them manipulate, as a happy target is more likely to comply. This, in itself, makes the manipulator happy, or at least in a sense of what they consider happiness. But their joyfulness is a perverted model of what most others consider happiness to be. Their happiness is often built on the foundations of another's misery.

ACCUSING YOUR RIVAL OF WHAT HE IS BLAMING YOU FOR

This is often referred to as the act of pointing to another person's wrongdoing. When enduring an onslaught and experiencing difficulty regarding safeguarding themselves, manipulators tend to reverse the situation. They blame their rivals for committing the exact things that they are being blamed for. *"You state that I don't love you! I think it is you who does not cherish me!"*

APPEALING TO POWER

Numerous individuals are in wonderment of those in power or authority, or those who have status. What's more intriguing is that there are various images to which individuals experience extraordinary dedication. Remember, those who are easily manipulated admire those who are in power. Moreover, those who are in power are aware of their ability to control others by never criticizing them. Instead, they use complex misleading tactics to maneuver their thoughts and alter their decision-making process.

APPEALING TO ENCOUNTER

Nevertheless, this appeal to experience provides them with an image of someone capable; this may be used to attack their opponent's lack of experience, even though they have limited experiences. You can easily identify this manipulation tactic at times when someone is trying to distort their capabilities about a particular subject.

APPEALING TO FEAR

People have fears. The unscrupulous manipulators realize a reality that individuals will, in general, respond crudely when any of these feelings of dread are enacted.

Subsequently, they speak to themselves as being able to ensure individuals against these dangers, even when they are not capable of doing so.

This is the same for when we talked about giving the target a glimpse of how their most desired outcome is achievable, without really providing it to them.

Nonetheless, some politicians and legislators frequently utilize this methodology to ensure that individuals line up behind administrative experts and do what the legislature – that is, the government officials – need.

APPEALING TO SYMPATHY

Manipulators can depict themselves and their circumstances to the public to make them feel frustrated about their current situation.

Utilization of this ploy empowers the manipulator to gain consideration from those individuals who may be going through the same thing. Nevertheless, appealing to sympathy is a tactic that most politicians would use to redirect the attention of the public to matters that do not affect their demise.

APPEALING TO WELL-KNOWN INTERESTS

Manipulators and tricksters are always mindful as to how they introduce themselves as persons who possess the right qualities and perspectives among the group of spectators, particularly, the sacred beliefs of the crowd. Everybody has a few partialities, and a great many people feel contempt toward a person or thing. Expert manipulators tend to stir up contempt and prejudices among the crowd.

APPEALING TO CONFIDENCE

This technique is firmly identified with the past points; yet it stresses what appears to have breezed through the trial of time. Individuals are regularly oppressed by the social traditions and standards of their way of life, just as social conventions. What is conventional to most tend to appear as if it is the correct decision. It is important to note that manipulators infer how they regard sacred ideologies and beliefs that the group of spectators are familiar with. These individuals suggest that their enemy aims to obliterate the customs, as well as social conventions. Moreover, they do not stress over whether or not these conventions hurt guiltless individuals. They make the presence of being autonomous in the crowd's perspective; yet it would typically be the exact opposite. There is a realization that people are generally suspicious of the individuals

241

who conflict with present social standards and built up conventions. They realize enough to stay away from them. As a result, there is a kind of restriction on how social traditions are unwittingly and carelessly bound.

BEGGING THE INQUIRY

One simple approach to demonstrate a point is to accept it in any case. Think about this model:

"Well, what type of government do you want, a government by liberal do-gooders that can shell out your hard-earned dollars or a governmentcontrolled by business minds that know how to live within a strict budget and generate jobs that put people to work?"

One minor departure from this error has been classified as "question-begging epithets," the utilization of expressions is a prejudgment of an issue by how it is allowed. For instance, "Shall we defend freedom and democracy or cave into terrorism and tyranny?" Through the inquiry along these lines, we abstain from discussing awkward inquiries like: "Yet, would we say we are truly propelling human opportunity? Are we truly democratic or simply expanding our capacity, our control, our predominance, our access to foreign markets?" Keep in mind that these are statements individuals utilize when bringing about the truth concerning an issue. There is the regular choosing of statements that surmise the accuracy of the situation on a particular issue.

CREATING A FALSE DILEMMA

A genuine problem happens when we are compelled to pick between two similarly unsuitable choices. A false dilemma happens when we are convinced that we have just two, similarly inadmissible decisions, when we truly have multiple potential outcomes accessible to us. Think about the accompanying case:

"Either we will lose the war on terrorism, or we should surrender a portion of our traditional freedoms and rights."

Individuals are frequently prepared to acknowledge a false dilemma since few are agreeable with the complex qualifications. Clearing absolutes is a part of their manipulative tactics. There is a need to have clear and basic decisions.

HEDGING WHAT YOU STATE

Manipulators frequently hole up behind words, declining to submit themselves or give straightforward replies or answers. This enables them to withdraw in times of need. Whenever they are found forgetting data significant to the current situation, they would think of some other reason for not being able to come up with said information. At the end of the day, when forced, they may be able to give in; however, to be an excellent manipulator, you should renege on your missteps, conceal your mistakes, and gatekeep what you state at whatever point conceivable.

OVERSIMPLIFYING THE ISSUE

Since most people are uncomfortable at comprehending profound or unobtrusive contentions, some are fond of oversimplifying the issue to further their potential benefit. *"I couldn't care less what the measurements inform us concerning the purported abuse of detainees; the main problem is whether we will be tough on crime. Spare your compassion toward the criminals' victims, not for the actual criminals."* The reality being overlooked is that the maltreatment of criminals is a crime in itself. Tragically, individuals with an over-simple mindset could not care less about criminal conduct that victimizes criminals.

RAISING ONLY COMPLAINTS

Your adversary is giving valid justifications to acknowledge a contention; however, the truth of the matter is that your mind's made up and nothing can change it. Gifted manipulators would react with objection after objection. As their rivals answer one protest after another, they would proceed again to object and object. The implicit mentality of the manipulator is that *"regardless of what my rival says, I will continue to object because nothing else will convince me otherwise."*

REWRITING HISTORY

The most noticeably awful acts and outrages tend to vanish from chronicled accounts while false dreams can be made to become facts. This phenomenon is often observed with Patriotic History. The composition of a contorted type of history is supported by the adoration of the nation and is regularly defended by the charge of antagonism. The truth of the matter is that our mind is persistently attempting to re-portray occasions of the past to absolve itself and denounce its spoilers. Chronicled composing frequently goes with the same pattern, particularly in the composition of reading material for schools. In this way, in recounting an anecdote about what has happened, those who perform manipulative tactics do not hesitate to contort the past in the manners in which they accept they can pull off. As usual, the manipulator is prepared with self-justifying excuses.

SHIFTING THE BURDEN OF PROOF

This act alludes to when an individual should demonstrate some of his declarations. A good example would be the instance that happened inside a court. The examiner possesses the obligation to prove guilt past distrust. Furthermore, the defense should not claim the responsibility of having to prove innocence. Those who are capable of manipulating others do not need to assume the weight of evidence for what they attest to. Along these lines, they harness the right tool in shifting the burden of proof to their rivals.

TALKING IN VAGUE GENERALITIES AND STATEMENTS

It is difficult to refute individuals when they cannot be bound. So, as opposed to concentrating on specifics, those who are capable of manipulating others tend to speak in the most unclear phrases that they can pull off. We have already talked about how certain statements and generalities can put another person in a daze, which makes it easier for them to be manipulated. This misrepresentation is well known for politicians. For instance, *"Overlook what the cowardly liberals say. It's the right time to be tough, to be hard on criminals, to punish terrorists, and be tough on those who disparage our nation."* Manipulators ensure they do not utilize particulars that may make individuals question what they are doing in the first place.

TELLING ENORMOUS FALSEHOODS AND BIG LIES

The majority of the people are liars, even about the little things; yet there is still a reluctance to say things other than the truth. In any case, these individuals realize that if you insist on a lit long enough, numerous individuals will trust you – particularly, on the off chance that you have the tools of mass media to broadcast a particular lie.

Every gifted manipulator is centered around what you can get individuals to accept, not on what is valid or false. They realize that the human personality does not normally look for reality; it looks for solace, security, individual affirmation, and personal stake.

Individuals regularly would prefer not to know the reality, particularly, certainties that are agonizing, that uncover their logical inconsistencies and irregularities, and that uncover what they hate about themselves or even their nation.

Some so many manipulators are exceptionally gifted in telling huge lies and, in this manner, causing those lies to appear valid.

INTIMIDATION

One aspect of manipulation, often used as a last resort, is intimidation and bullying. When everything else has failed, they begin to use threats to get their way. Some though, may use intimidation from the onset. It may be a source of authority. For example, let's take the role of a manipulative boss. You have requested a day off. They don't want to allow your request but have no choice, it is your right. This type of person would want their pound of flesh first. They will set goals for you to reach so it will delay or cancel your request, such as moving project deadlines forward. This way they have their little victory over you.

THE ASSET OF LISTENING

Listening can be perhaps the most important persuasive tactic you have in your tool kit. Listening to your prospect will give you most of the information you need for a successful persuasive conversation. By listening and paying careful attention to the words and body language, your prospect is communicating and by listening carefully for the words they don't say, you'll be able to discern most of what you need.

THE FAVOR OF O SMILE

Your ability to smile is one of the most powerful tools to influence. This is true of influencing yourself or others. We've learned over thousands of years that the smile is a sign of happiness and friendship, so the smile helps to lower our defenses. When individuals smile, dozens of influential processes happen automatically.

GHOSTING YOU

Guys do this a lot, even if it is something as simple as ghosting you, because it trains you to not get used to hearing from him at certain times, and you always have to reach out to see how he is doing and checking to see if he remembers the date that he set for you. They use their profession or their education to delay you finding out the truth or make you feel like they're always the right one.

DEMONIZE YOUR REACTIONS

They tend to demonize your reactions because anytime someone that is manipulating you and they don't want you to be able to express yourself or control the situation, they will make you feel like you are the bad guy for reacting the way that you did to the situation. They will flip the script on you because you didn't agree with their actions.

You might tell him, "Hey, babe, I don't know why you just liked this girl's picture on Instagram. I thought that we agreed that you won't do this. You show me their stuff. It makes me feel embarrassed that my boy is liking the girl's photos and commenting on rubbish on Instagram, and it makes me feel insecure because you are my boyfriend".

Then he will say something like, "you are so insecure, it's just Instagram, I can't believe that you are seriously talking to me about a comment that I wrote to a girl. First of all, I don't even know her, and she looks nice.

Other guys are commenting on her photos, but why do you care because I'm with you". So, they demonize you and make you feel like the way you feel is not accounted for. They invalidate the way you feel because he doesn't know that girl, and he may even be trying to get to know her.

USING PITY

One of the greatest forms of manipulation is by using pity. Getting pity out of anybody will guilt-trip them, so because they feel bad for you,they will do what you say, hear you out and whatever trash you want to slip.

For instance, if you say, "I just realized that when we were at the get-together, you didn't want to hang out with me. You were just doing your own thing. I don't know everybody there, I felt alone, and I understand that you know everybody, but I didn't feel included." Then he will say something like, "Honey, I'm sorry that you didn't feel included. However, what do you expect me to do, all the people were people that I grew up with. So, I'm sorry that I wasn't holding your hand the entire time, but I did introduce you to some people. You know that I wouldn't do that to you. You know that I am not like that. I was just caught up. Plus, I saw one of my girlfriends from high school and we just started talking. Come on, if you know me, you know that I wouldn't do something like that. I am not like that."

IT MAKES YOU FEEL GUILTY, AND YOU DON'T KNOW WHY

A master of manipulation consistently goes to victimization. They likely have a "wild card trauma," that is, some problematic episodes in their life that they always expose as a justification for what they do incorrectly.

If, for example, you complain to them for their lack of consideration, they respond by saying something like "you get angry because I am not considerate, but I had to put up with a father who abandoned me when I was three years old." Thus, they disarm you with their traumas. Who will be so insensitive as to complain to someone who has such a past? This is their game.

IT THREATENS YOU WITH SUBTLETY

Threatening indirectly is one of the most recurrent tactics among manipulators. They have used it and continue to use it from the great leaders to the small domestic tyrants, passing through seasoned publicists. This tactic consists of anticipating the worst possible outcome as a consequence of any of your behaviors.

"If you keep eating that way, in 6 months, you will be like a whale." They don't want you to eat, and they probably have no arguments to certify what they say, they just want you not to. Maybe they are bothered by how happy you are when you eat ice cream, or they think you spend too much money on food. They do not openly tell you what they believe, but merely announce a hecatomb.

DISQUALIFY WHAT YOU DO THROUGH SARCASM

If there's one thing a master manipulator hates, it's direct communication. "They don't name you a dog, but they offer you a bone," goes the famous saying. They often use sarcasm to ridicule you or downplay the value of your thoughts, feelings, or actions. The manipulator wants others to feel insecure and inferior.

An example of this is when they send you a seemingly friendly message, but which contains quite aggressive content: "Maybe if you read a little more, you could have more select friends." Translated means: "You are an uneducated person, and that's why your friends are poor devils."

Sometimes, the manipulator's victim comes to believe that these kinds of insights are ways to help him be better. Nothing is falser. When someone wants to help another, use direct and honest communication. Also, it does not disqualify you but instead gives you a concrete contribution.

HE IS ALMOST ALWAYS CHARMING

Typical handlers know that "the horse is stroked to mount it." They usually start their job by looking cute and enjoyable. They fill you with compliments and show signs of exquisite tastes, super-entertaining conversation, and high "sensitivity" to your expectations.

SET YOURSELF THE JUDGE OF YOUR LIFE

Without knowing how suddenly the master of manipulation becomes a "spiritual guide" for your life. They are incredibly adept at telling others how they should live, even if they do not put into practice all that they proclaim.

They give you advice or expose your great philosophical sayings. They tell you what to do, bit by bit. If it doesn't work out, they blame you. He told you what to do, dare if you did not follow precisely the instructions that he so generously offered you.

Chapter 6:

The Victim

HOW MANIPULATORS AFFECT YOUR BEHAVIOR

Have you ever had that impression in one of the relationships you have that something was not, quite right? Even with a casual gathering with someone you just met. Something just didn't feel quite right, and you are left feeling far more anxious, irritated, or confused than you were when you began. That could be a sign you have been in a manipulator's presence. The reason manipulators use the tactics they do is because they are often unable to simply ask what they need or be able to express their needs in a healthy, straightforward manner. Thus, they resort to this emotionally abusive tactic to try to manipulate other people around them and compel them to bend to their will.

Manipulation comes in various forms, and it can range from abusive to just being around a bossy personality anywhere. Some deceptive habits are much easier to spot than others, and if you believe you may be a psychological bully's target, these are the tell-tale signs for which you want to keep an eye out for:

YOU SENSE FEAR, DUTY, AND GUILT

Coercive conduct comprises three factors: anxiety, responsibility, and guilt. When someone manipulates you, you're mentally coerced to do something that you usually don't want to do. You could feel afraid to do so, compelled to do so, or guilty of not doing so.

I refer to two different manipulators: "the abuser" and "the victim." An abuser makes you feel afraid and will use violence, threats, and coercion to manipulate you. The victim instills a sense of guilt in their target. Usually, the victim acts hurt, although, the fact is they're the ones who created the problem. An individual approached by a manipulator who acts as the victim always attempts to support the manipulator to avoid feeling bad. Targets of this type of manipulation frequently feel responsible for assisting the victim to stop their suffering by doing everything they can.

STRINGS ARE CONNECTED

If you don't get a favor just because, then it's not "for fun and free."If strings are applied, then it is trickery.

One manipulator form is "Mr. Nice man". This person will be supportive and offer other people plenty of favors. It's complicated, but you don't know there is anything bad. But, on the other side, there is a rope connected for any positive deed — an obligation. If you don't fulfill the standards of the manipulator, you'll be forced to feel ungrateful. One of the most common forms of trickery is to exploit the rules and standards of reciprocity.

For example, a salesman could make it appear like you would purchase the product since he or she offered you a discount. A spouse in a partnership can buy you flowers and then ask for something in return. These techniques operate as it violates societal expectations. It's normal to return the favor but we often still feel it necessary to reciprocate and comply even if someone does one insincerely.

Manipulators frequently try out one of two strategies. The first one is the strategy of foot-in-the-door, in which somebody starts with a simple yet rational request — like, do you have a moment? — Which then contributes to a bigger request — like I want 10 dollars for a taxi. That's commonly used in street frauds.

The door-in-the-face method is the opposite — it includes somebody making a large request, having it rejected, and then asking a smaller favor.

E.g., anyone doing contract work can ask you for a large amount of money upfront, and afterward, ask for a lesser proportion after you've refused. This works since, according to me, the smaller appeal appears comparatively rational after the larger demand.

YOU INTERROGATE YOURSELF

Frequently, the term "gaslighting" is used to recognize manipulation that causes people to question themselves, their actuality, consciousness, or thoughts. A dishonest individual can distort what you're saying to make it about them, hijack the discussion or make you sound like you've done something bad when you're not entirely sure you've done it.

If you're being emotionally manipulated, you may experience a false sense of shame or defensiveness — like you utterly lost or had to do something wrong when, in fact, that's not the case.

"Blame the manipulators. They are not taking responsibility for this."

THE RELATIONSHIP MAKES YOU FEEL SCARED

Here's a general tip: if a relationship is built entirely out of a foundation of fear, then you know that it might not be a good one to be in. It's normal to feel intimidated or even somewhat fearful of certain people. Perhaps, you might be meeting someone you admire and idolize. To feel somewhat intimidated by that individual is okay to a certain degree. However, when you start building a close and intimate relationship with the person and the fear still doesn't go away, then that is a bad sign.

Manipulators understand fear very well, and they know how to use it against those who don't have good control over their phobias. For instance, say you've been planning something for a while and the person always comes up with last-minute changes that give them what they want, they are utilizing your fear of losing something. In this case, the time and emotional attachment were spent making and almost executing the plan. They will utilize the fear that you have of them into making you do things that would benefit them, even if it means compromising your well-being. This is why you should always be wary of relationship environments that reek of fear and intimidation.

YOU ARE MADE TO FEEL GUILTY ABOUT EVERYTHING YOU DO

Somehow, you are made to feel guilty about everything that you do. When you are in a manipulative relationship, nothing that you ever do will be right or correct.

255

Even when you have the best intentions and you are sure about your execution, there's still always something for you to feel bad about. Generally, a manipulative individual will avoid making you feel validated for your efforts or your actions. This is because they want you to feel like you need to work harder to be worthy of their attention and approval.

This is a tactic that is designed to bully a person into thinking that they're not doing enough so that they feel pressured to become better. It's a kind of negative reinforcement that is quite common in a lot of abusive relationships all over the world. It's the same way a boss would tell a worker that their work is mediocre to get that worker to keep on trying harder out of guilt or shame.

YOU OFTEN QUESTION YOUR OWN BELIEFS

Gaslighting is another common technique that is usually employed by manipulative individuals to distort an individual's view of reality. As a victim, you are made to doubt your own beliefs and perspectives on things so that you grow reliant and dependent on another person. Essentially, you are made to distrust your senses and instincts so that you will be forced to cling onto someone else to help you stay grounded and sane.

Manipulative individuals are so good at distorting the facts and stretching the truth to the point that they make lies seem believable even when they're completely outrageous. In essence, they are just thrusting their version of "reality" down your throat.

YOU ARE MADE TO FEEL LIKE THERE ARE ALWAYS STRINGS ATTACHED

Nothing you ever do in this kind of relationship will come without any strings attached. You just get the sense that if you will be on the receiving end of some nice treatment, it's never something that you can just take at face value. You notice that there's a pattern that's emerging here whenever this person does anything that adds value to your life. You always just come to expect that there will be some kind of ulterior motives behind it. You would find it very difficult to just take a compliment or be on the receiving end of a kind gesture. You somehow get the sense that that isn't the whole story.

YOUR INSECURITIES ARE ALWAYS THRUST INTO THE LIMELIGHT

One of the grandest ways in which a manipulative person would get you to become emotionally vulnerable would be to highlight your insecurities.

Naturally, as a human being, you have your fair share of insecurities.

We all do,and the manipulative individual knows this better than anyone.

However, instead of being sensitive and empathetic toward these insecurities that you might have, they use it as ammo. They will capitalize on these insecurities to make you feel terrible about yourself, setting the brain into more reactive, survival mode.

In psychology, whenever an individual engages in self-hatred or self-loathing, they find a strong power figure to whom they can cling onto. The manipulative master knows this, and that's how they will want to present themselves in your life. They will make it seem like you need them to be there for you because of how incompetent you end up perceiving yourself to be. When you're with a manipulative person, you will constantly be bombarded with reminders of your vulnerabilities. Sparking insecurities or questioning people's identity to create "issues" people didn't know they had and then allaying these insecurities by offering the solution, is also a commonly used tactic in marketing.

YOU'RE STILL EXPECTED TO FORGET

If you don't go along with what they want, then they'll make you feel guilty. Even if you did have every right to say no. If you feel pressured continuously or compelled to do something you don't want to do, you are being manipulated. If you're afraid to say no, then you're manipulated. If you feel bothered to go along with the demands of someone else, you will be manipulated. Manipulators are experts in playing the victim card, and they will play it to make you feel as guilty as possible, as if you're doing something wrong because you've chosen to tell them no.

DOUBTING YOUR OWN JUDGMENT

You still find yourself questioning your own judgment every time you are around a particular person. Suddenly, after having a conversation with a manipulator, something you were so sure of a minute ago, fills you with doubt and makes you second guess your own decisions. Present them with an idea or an opinion, and they will somehow find a way to twist and turn it around, making you uncertain and uncomfortable. Spend enough time with them, and they will make you feel unworthy as if you were a complete failure, and nothing you could ever do is the right choice.

YOU'RE JUST BLAMING YOURSELF

Even though you've done nothing wrong, you're blaming yourself somehow. That one dishonest friend who always has an explanation for their bad conduct or poor judgment is not your friend,as they are always making you the scapegoat. This one friend is a manipulator. It's your fault; you made me believe I should, if you thought it was a bad idea, I wouldn't have done it.

A dishonest "friend's" trademark is when you're in the mix somewhere, and they are the ones who made you feel like you're wrong.

GLARING AND UNBELIEVABLE THINGS

They do glaring and unbelievable things, and then they try to convince you that what you saw wasn't true. What you saw couldn't be what you possibly think. It is because it doesn't look like you will do anything like that, and he would have to be a real idiot to do something like that to you. He wants to minimize his action and play ignorant like he has no idea what it is, and that you are tripping, because both of you are just friends. He also tries to make rude remarks in the name of humor.

WHY YOU ARE MANIPULATED

AN INABILITY TO SET BOUNDARIES OR TO SAY "NO."

Those who are easy to manipulate are generally so scared of confrontation that they are not willing to spark an argument by being resistant or by voicing their opinion. This specific trait is easy to exploit for obvious reasons—if they just cannot say no, you can burden them with favors and expectations, and anticipate no resistance in return.

HONESTY AND COMPASSION

Being honest makes you particularly manipulatable because your greatest weaknesses and loftiest aspirations are all apparent to those around you. Compassion, on the other hand, is the driving force for the first point in this list. Being overly compassionate opens you up to manipulation by those who are willing to play the victim, as master manipulators always are.

FEAR

This emotion comes in numerous structures. We, as human beings, tend to fear losing a relationship; we may fear the disapproval of other people; we dread to make somebody discontent with our actions.

We additionally dread the dangers and outcomes of the manipulator's actions. Imagine a scenario in which they prevail at doing what they threaten.

GUILT

Today, we are clouded by the idea and responsibility that we should dependably prioritize the needs and wants of other people rather than our own. At times when people would talk about the right to fulfill their own needs and wants, manipulators frequently abuse us and endeavor to allow us to feel like we are accomplishing something immoral if we do not put their needs and wants in front of our own. Those individuals who are skilled at these manipulative tactics, would tend to define love as the act of fulfilling their needs and wants as part of your obligation. Hence, if we have an opinion that goes against their beliefs, we are manipulated into thinking that we are heartless; at this point, they will make us feel very regretful of our existence and would use guilt to manipulate us.

BEING TOO NICE

We appreciate being a provider, fulfilling individuals, and dealing with the needs of other people. We discover fulfillment. Moreover, our confidence would regularly originate from doing what we can for other people. In any case, at times when there is a lack of an unmistakable feeling of these and fair limitations, skilled manipulators can detect this in people who are easy targets of this phenomenon, and will use certain tactics to further their selfish gains.

UNCONDITIONAL LOVE

Those who are the absolute easiest to manipulate are those who unconditionally love the manipulator (parents, siblings, romantic partners, friends, etc.). The reason for this is that, regardless of the kind of treatment that they are forced to endure, they continue to love the manipulator. This love is an exploitable weakness.

BEING TRUSTING

People who are easy to manipulate believe anything you tell them, this is also known as "being too trusting." Some people are simply naïve, while others perhaps only see the best in the manipulator and refuse to acknowledge the uglier side—regardless of the reason, some people are easier to deceive than others.

BEING TOO POLITE OR RESPECTFUL

Manipulators actively seek out those who will not call them out in public, and who better to target than those who are too coy to say something when they are made to feel uncomfortable? Being overly polite also makes one more likely to agree to small favors which, as discussed earlier, makes one more likely to agree to larger and larger favors as time passes.

HOW TO AVOID BEING MANIPULATED

Similarly, it is just as important to know some tactics to avoid being manipulated yourself. The author of *Are You Too Nice? How to Gain Appreciation and Respect*, Ni Preston, developed eight techniques to avoid being manipulated.

The first technique he described is by far the easiest to abide by. It simply involves practicing the art of saying "no." If you feel uncomfortable with what is being asked of you, firmly say no. You do not necessarily need to be confrontational in doing this—a simple, "Sorry, I do not have time," will likely suffice.

The second technique is to set consequences. You need to handle a manipulator a little bit like you might handle a child: he or she needs to know the rules, and when he or she breaks these rules, there needs to be a "punishment." An example of how you could use this is by telling a person, "I am uncomfortable talking with you about that. If you continue to talk about it, I will report you to human resources." Manipulators do not want to get in trouble, so when trying to avoid being manipulated, make sure that you follow through on the rules and corresponding consequences that you have set.

The third technique is remembering that your time is your own, and you are allowed to take it. Manipulators will usually demand an answer to their requests immediately, in the hope of pressuring you into complying. You can circumnavigate this manipulative technique simply by saying, "I'll think about it." You don't have to follow a manipulator's timeline, and you are certainly not obligated to answer anything straight away.

The fourth technique involves asking manipulators probing questions when they make requests of you. Next time a manipulator asks you to do something for them, consider responding with, "Are you asking me, or telling me?" or "What do I get out of this?" or "Are you really expecting me to do that?" Chances are, you will catch the manipulator off-guard and perhaps even get them to withdraw the request completely (at the very least, it will force them to pause for a second and consider whether what they are doing is right).

The fifth technique is to avoid letting the manipulator make you feel guilty. You are not obligated to do anyone any favors, and thus, you have nothing to feel guilty about. Manipulators make their targets feel guilty in the hope that they will eventually feel so bad about themselves that they will give in to the manipulator's will.

The sixth technique is to keep your distance. If you know that somebody is manipulating you (or trying to), do not give them any opportunities to do so by spending time with them. It is honestly good advice just to give a manipulator a wide berth and to avoid getting pulled into their games altogether. The seventh technique is to know your rights. Manipulators will go out of their way to violate them. Remind yourself regularly that you have the right to be treated with respect, to set your own priorities, to have a differing opinion, and to express your feelings. The eighth, and final, the technique is to confront the manipulator. Publicly. A manipulator will generally avoid the public eye, and by calling them out, you are likely to put them off trying to manipulate you ever again.

DEALING WITH A TOXIC PERSON

Other indications to keep a watch out are if the individual is constantly condescending, compulsively in desire, or unwilling to take accountability or say sorry for one's behavior.

It may be anyone who regularly takes narcotics or alcohol, lies or wants you to lie about them, regulates or demeans what you've been doing. A toxic man's life is always personally, emotionally, financially, physically, or interpersonally out of balance.

SETTING BOUNDARIES TO ELIMINATE MANIPULATORS

"If you feel unnoticed or misunderstood and feel manipulated or compelled to do stuff that is not even 'you,' then you may be affected by a negative human." Toxic individuals can make you question yourself or unconsciously do something that you wouldn't normally do—you might feel a need to be fit in or cool or get approval. Every situation is different, but by influencing people to do something, toxic individuals may have a detrimental effect on others. They try to generate turmoil by negative behaviors: to use, to lie, to steal, to control, to criticize, to bully, to manipulate, to create conflict, and so on.

EFFECT OF TOXIC PEOPLE ON YOUR LIFE

Toxic individuals can impact all aspects of people's lives, and we are always oblivious to that. We feel sympathy for them. The myths they inflict on us are accepted and rationalized. And this, in exchange, changes how we look about our values and ourselves. Toxic individuals are happy to drive happiness down from the stuff we previously enjoyed, such as jobs, relationships, interests, and even our self-love.

DEALING WITH MANIPULATORS WHO ARE A PERMANENT PART OF YOUR LIFE

If a manipulator had been in your life for a while, you might have already ceded some level of control over your life to him by now, so you have to start by regaining that control. First, you have to create and enforce boundaries in your life.

To set and enforce boundaries, you have to assess different areas of your life and set firm limits in all of those areas. You have to draw a line, and you have to make it clear to the manipulator that he or she is not allowed to cross that boundary. For example, you can set aside some "me time" and tell everyone that they are not allowed to bother you during that time.

Setting boundaries will help you reestablish the priorities in your life. If you have been a victim of manipulation, chances are the manipulator has spent months or even years establishing control over your life, so that by the point you know what's going on, he may have replaced your priorities with his own. You may find that you are using all your free time to do things he likes, and your interests have taken a back seat to his.

When you find yourself in such a situation, bouncing back can be hard, but it's going to require a lot of willpower and commitment on your part. Take control of your own life. Create a list of all your values and reexamine all of them. Look at your belief system, and question everything that you believe about yourself; did you always hold those beliefs, or did you acquire them over time as you got closer to the manipulative person?

If you notice that your time is spent doing things that don't interest you, your belief system has been infiltrated by ideas that aren't originally yours, and that your long term values no longer seem to be the driving force behind your life, you need to create new boundaries and rules for yourself to keep the manipulative person from controlling you. You need to disconnect from manipulative people, especially the ones whose machinations have caused you (or could potentially cause you) serious psychological or physical harm. One mistake most victims make is that they assume that they can change the manipulator. They convince themselves that if they spend enough time with the manipulator, he will fall in love with them, and he will be open to treating them better. However, in the end, the opposite happens. Instead of the victim changing the manipulator as she may have hoped, it's the manipulator that changes her, and not for the better. She starts accepting the emotional abuse, and little by little, she makes concessions about her values and principles, until, in the end, she is a completely different person. She becomes more subservient, and she starts making excuses for the manipulator. So, once you notice that someone is manipulating you, the best choice you have is to disconnect from them. If a clean break is possible, you should go for it. However, in situations where it's a lot more complicated (for example, where you have children together) a clean break might not be possible. Even then, spending some time away from the manipulator can help you re-enter yourself so that you can remember what your real values and priorities used to be.

Chapter 7:

What Is Manipulation? Why Manipulation Is Wrong & Why People Manipulate

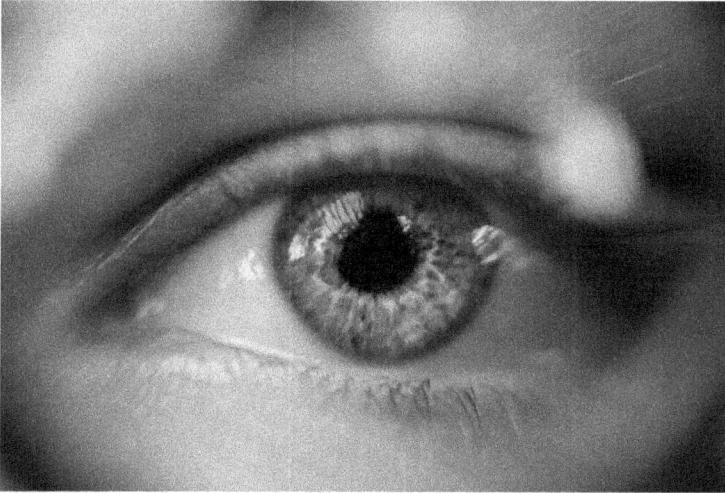

WHAT IS MANIPULATION

Manipulation is - in psychology - a method deliberately implemented to control or influence the thinking, choices, actions of an individual, via a relationship of power or influence. The methods used to distort or orient the perception of the interlocutor's reality by using, in particular, a relationship of seduction, suggestion, persuasion, involuntary or consented submission.

Manipulation is part of the daily lives of civilizations.In the modern West, power systems, conflicts of interest, power struggles are omnipresent: it develops from self-awareness, language, and the hierarchy of society which produce a large number of interactions from which everyone wants to benefit from. It is a learned skill that forms part of the culture, and which everyone knows and uses in their personal or professional life, in a positive or negative, conscious, or unconscious way. In such a civilization, any communication (body language or oral language) can, thus, be a form of influence or manipulation.

A manipulative person uses indirect means to make a person change their actions or thoughts. Some of the indirect tactics include persuasion and brainwashing. In persuasion, a person does not force you to do something, but they try to convince you to do it. A good example of persuasion in marketing. Although an advertisement is aimed directly at convincing you to purchase a certain item, you are not in any way forced to purchase it. The choice to buy it or not is in your hands. The only aspect that an advertiser works on is to ensure that you see the beauty of the item. The advertiser will only tell you about the good aspects of the item you are trying to buy without mentioning the negatives. Even those who choose to mention the negatives, also try to show them as slightly positive aspects. This is an indirect way of luring someone into making a purchase.

Manipulation is a way of socially influencing you into doing something you did not necessarily want to do. However, this does not mean that social influence in and on itself is something bad. Social influence can be used for a good cause. You can influence someone to stop taking drugs or change some unhealthy habits. When you persuade a person to do such actions, it cannot be termed as manipulation. Social influence only becomes a manipulative habit if it is aimed at benefiting the influencer. If you can persuade someone into taking another job just to benefit from their salary, you are a manipulator. Most manipulative individuals do not deem their actions harmful in any way. When a person is using manipulation tactics, they aim to benefit without directly being seen as a bad person. In most cases, a manipulative person will lure you into doing something bad and end up blaming you for it. In simple terms, a manipulative individual uses other people as puppets. You are just a tool that the manipulator uses to achieve a certain goal. A manipulative person can use you to steal money and end up putting all the blame on you.

There is a whole range of methods ranging from cunning, an action that can be legitimate, to the most degrading forms of psychic manipulation, including all kinds of lies. Manipulation as a scientific concept is mainly studied in social psychology and philosophy.

Mental manipulation induces a power relationship that results in the psychic control of a person. More precisely, it is "the modification of an individual's mental state by another to make him do something." This can be summed up in "fabricated consent."

In social psychology, the term "conditioning," is a word that appeared in the 14th century and developed following Pavlov's work. "Since then, and by extension, conditioning represents the mental or psychic conditions necessary for the performance of a behavior."

We distinguish the influence of manipulation, even if they use the same tools and psychological springs. If they are just as difficult to detect: the impact implies a transparent motivation while the manipulation includes deception without any benefit. In psychology, manipulation is defined as a secret action of a person or group of persons. The whole art of manipulation consists in depriving the manipulated of his freedom without realizing it, and that he is persuaded to be free.

The propaganda or publicity-seeking to mobilize the behavior of short-term masses, sometimes is achieved using irrational means. According to its use as a weapon of war, it is used as propaganda to manipulate public opinion. Disinformation is "probably one of the most difficult manipulations to detect and identify," and it is one of the main weak points of the information society.

The packaging is in the long-term by forming habits and playing on emotions. The indoctrination educates, also for a long time, addressing the beliefs and intelligence.

THE MANIPULATION ETHICS – COULD MANIPULATION BE GOOD AND BAD?

At the mention of the word 'manipulation,' negative connotations associated with this term is what immediately springs to mind. Manipulation means taking advantage of someone else by unscrupulous and underhanded tactics. Manipulation means theft and lying outright. Manipulation is unethical. Through the years, the word has had a poor reputation, and even the phrases used to characterize deception in play, depict an image that is quite nasty or negative. "She's got him wrapped around her little finger," "I told my boss exactly what he wanted to hear," "He's got a reputation for being a heartbreaker," "I spoke to my buddy about doing what I wanted." These traditional manipulative scenarios don't make a positive difference to the situation for the parties involved in the transaction. It makes the manipulator greedy, self-serving, deceitful, and unconcerned about manipulating someone else for their gain, and it makes the one being manipulated seem stupid, ignorant, and maybe even weak to "allow" himself to be so easily fooled.

Manipulation has always been seen as a cruel, smart, yet cunning act and always where one person ends up being manipulated. Manipulation is seen even more negatively when it is clear that the conniving person has a heartless presence, disregarding the other's feelings and placing their own selfish needs above all others. Even worse than the manipulator, he exploited the other by pretending to be his friend and then using trustfully shared information against them. There is one fact that remains in our personal or professional lives. No-one wants to learn that they were abused. Nobody. Such uncertainty associated with it is hard andit is almost painful to imagine that there is a possibility that it might be used to exploit a positive, or even that it could bring about change for the better. Manipulation isn't all evil; however, shocking it might sound. There is manipulation all around us, and often you don't have to look very far to find evidence of it. Take, for example, marketers and advertisers, with their constant messages telling us to buy this, buy that, stop doing this, and stop doing that. They all try to influence our decisions one way or the other. However, what kinds of manipulation are trying to make us change for the better?

Ads that advise us to stop smoking and eat better are trying to exploit our choices, but they're trying to do so, in this case, to promote positive change. Quitting smoking is in your own best interestsand it feeds well. Would this not make it a constructive way of manipulation, if it is for your good? Governments around the world are exploiting their people. Religion does, likewise. Yet, sometimes we choose to ignore it because it comes, so to speak, from a more "authoritative" source. Businesses are actively exploiting their customers by producing goods to raise their sales figures and then telling consumers, "without them, they cannot survive."

Whether it's utilized for "good" or "bad," manipulation is still manipulation, at the end of the day. Does any of us have any right to dictate the decisions or actions of another, even if we believe this is to their advantage? What makes the thought of manipulation so upsetting is maybe the fact that we don't like someone elsetrying to decide what we can door forcing us to do anything we wouldn't be inclined to do ourselves otherwise. Working managers try to manipulate their staff all the time, even if the good leaders do it to try and keep their staff motivated or performing their best. Active managers have mastered the art of motivational reinforcement skillfully and have turned it into an important method used to influence the success of their workers, driving them to achieve their objectives. That distinctive detail is the defining difference between what is classified as manipulation and what is called persuasion. Persuasion is a form of manipulation, but what distinguishes it from the negative image of manipulation lies in three things:

Aim.

Honesty.

What gain or positive effect the person you're trying to convince would have.

WHY ARE WE VULNERABLE TO MANIPULATION?

It is not enough to know the definition of manipulation; it is still necessary to discover the reasons for our vulnerability to manipulation. Of course, they are multiple and different from one person to another. In general, a first large group of explanations stems from motivation and its two great strengths: the avoidance of suffering and the pursuit of pleasure.

So, a manipulative person can motivate you to do whatever they want because they strike a chord with you and cause discomfort or an emotion that you don't want to feel. No one likes to suffer and feel guilt, fear, insecurity, helplessness, doubt, etc. So, in this case, you are being manipulated because you want to avoid suffering.

When your self-image is somewhat flawed; in other words, when you are unsure of yourself, of what you are, of what you want, manipulation can more easily cause you to doubt or guilt. For example, someone is sulking because you said or did something. To avoid the guilt, you say that you didn't mean it rather than endure this sulking (which is a form of passive aggression). Example number 3 above is a good illustration of this.

Besides, manipulation tactics can also touch one of your fears, such as that of being judged. No one likes to be criticized for being selfish, incompetent, ungrateful, or inhuman. It can also be the fear of hurting, not being loved, losing an advantage, losing affection, respect, a material advantage, or even your job.

The manipulative person may control your behavior by giving you the hope of some sort of gain. It will make you hope for an emotional advantage, attention, recognition, status, even love, or a material advantage such as career advancement, reaching your goals more efficiently, obtaining results, and tangible rewards.

Here you are in the other great force of motivation: the search for pleasure.

Of course, both types of motivation can coexist in each of us, depending on the context. However, you probably have one strategy that takes precedent over the other, some sort of mental program that influences your actions, no matter what decisions you have to make.

Some are more motivated by the stick or by avoidance; for others, it is the prospect of gain that motivates them to act. Recognizing this underlying tendency in you may help you understand how you come to be manipulated.

WHY DO PEOPLE USE MANIPULATION?

TO GAIN WEALTH

People use manipulation to fulfill their desires in life. If you want money, you may use any means possible to get a good job. This is a very big motivation for most people across cultures. All over the world, people use manipulation just to get wealth. Since money is a valuable asset in life, it can give you access to most of your desires and most people will do anything just to earn money. Such motivation will make most people use manipulation.

TO MAINTAIN THEIR INTEGRITY

Many people use manipulation just to keep their names clean. If a person has evil intentions but does not want the world to see them, they will use manipulation. Narcissists use manipulation and blackmail to hide their weaknesses. A narcissistic person may even ruin your name in public or lower your self-esteem just to avoid showing the world that they are weak. Most people who are striving to maintain social authenticity may go to extreme limits in their drive to maintain social standings.

TO GAIN INFLUENCE

The other reason why people use manipulation is to gain influence. Social influence gives people power. Most people enjoy it when they have power and control over others. We have talked about the example of political leaders and how they use manipulative tactics just to gain control over the masses. Politicians will do anything possible as long as they gain control. It is normal for people to employ such tactics in their search for power and influence. A person who wants power and influence will approach you with lies and trickery just to gain power over you.

To dominate relationships

Most people feel safe when they are the dominating voice in a relationship. It is normal for human beings to want to have control over a relationship. This desire to control a relationship may make a person want to manipulate others. Manipulation will help those individuals control their relationship partner and, thus, gain control of any related assets. The main reason behind that desire to have control is the fear of the unknown. If a person that is afraid of uncertainty is in a relationship and does not have clear knowledge of the future, they may use underhand methods to control the relationship.

Self-satisfaction

In some instances, people who use manipulation are just looking for a way to satisfy their ego. Many individuals suffer low self-esteem and only find satisfaction in controlling others. You may be in a manipulative relationship trying to figure out what you did that was wrong. In some cases, you may do everything right, but still become a victim of manipulation. People practice manipulation just to feel satisfied and happy. Such people have deeply rooted emotional and psychological issues that need to be addressed by an expert.

What are people's reasons for manipulating others?

Misery likes company: They do it because they gain satisfaction on an emotional level, from seeing the frustrated or negative responses of others. Certain people are so unhappy with their lives and themselves that they try to bring others down by creating problems for them.

It makes them feel powerful: Someone who is insecure and feels powerless will often try to exert power in other areas to make up for it. Getting others to do what they want gives them temporary satisfaction.

A lack of importance: Another reason why people negatively manipulate others is that they don't think that they are important. They believe that if they simply request what they wish for, they won't get it because they don't matter enough. So instead, they try to make us feel ashamed or guilty as a consequence for not doing what they want, as a preemptive measure from disappointment.

They are "too good" for some things: Other negative manipulators simply think that they are too good for certain tasks. They might see other people as below them, and therefore, expect those people to do the tasks that they don't want to do. This could be due to laziness, or simply an inflated sense of self.

Not knowing how to get things done: Some negative manipulators don't think that they are capable of gaining what they want, and instead operate under the assumption that they must convince and pressure others to do their bidding for them.

Selfishly "helping" others: Other negative manipulators convince themselves that what they are doing will help people. This is a common idea embraced by people who think that they know better than others what is best for everyone. Due to their beliefs that they have a higher intelligence or ability, they feel satisfied doing this and convince themselves that the people being manipulated are better off for it. The majority of negative manipulators are not bad people; they are simply misguided, inconsiderate, insensitive, selfish, and often, weak and insecure. Some of them believe that the people they are manipulating are not as valuable as themselves and that their desires and needs are not as important. This mistaken belief is what allows them to continue to act the way they do without considering the feelings of other people.

DIFFERENT TYPES OF NEGATIVE MANIPULATION

Turning your emotions against you: Techniques for manipulation vary widely, but usually, negative manipulators will attempt to get the feelings of others to work against them. They will try to do that by doing or saying things that are intended to stir up fear, anger, shame, guilt, or any other uncomfortable feeling. For example, they might insinuate that if we don't follow through on their suggestions or orders, something horrible will result.

Threats of future unpleasantness: They might also try to describe to you all the different types of unpleasant situations that could arise if you don't do what they want. They might imply or even overtly insist that something is our fault, responsibility, or duty, using ethics and morality to pressure us to come around to their ideas or demands. Some people will even throw every trick at us, warning us of the consequences of disappointing or letting them down.

Common phrases used: They may imply to us that we will be so happy if we do what they want us to do, or that we will make them very happy, and that they will love us so much. They may also use phrases like "You need to..." or "You must..." or "You should..." as a way to subtly pressure you into following through on what they are asking of you. They will say those phrases and others which insinuate great consequences if you don't follow the obligation they are giving to you.

What does each of the above methods and techniques share with each other? The person doing the negative manipulation doesn't offer anything of value in return for fulfilling their wishes. Instead, the victim gets exploited by a created power imbalance.

EXAMPLES OF MANIPULATION

There are many real-life examples of manipulation happening right next to you in your daily life. If you are keen enough, you may be able to notice how certain people use manipulation and blackmail to have things their way in life. It is common to spot such cases in the workplace. In family situations, manipulation comes in place when there is something valuable at stake. For instance, if a wealthy person dies without leaving a clear will, there will be many people fighting to take control of the properties of the deceased.

A real-life example of manipulation would be the case of Jonestown (Guyana). The story of Jonestown is one of the most documented cases of manipulation and brainwashing. The mastermind behind the story being Jim Jones, who was a religious/cult leader.

Jim Jones rose to fame in Northwest Guyana during the early 70s. His rise to fame was associated with supernatural affairs. Like all manipulative individuals, Jones managed to gather a small group of brainwashed individuals around himself.

One of the key characteristics of manipulative individuals is isolation, as we have already said. However, manipulators who wish to gain public influence and control large crowds of people, do not just use isolation. Most public manipulators use the inner circle approach. An inner circle is made up of people who subscribe to the ideologies of the manipulator. The ideologies are often deemed as right, and they are not seen to have anything wrong. This is an approach that most cultic sects take. When a person is introduced in the inner circle, they make them feel special, but at the same time, they are required to fulfill certain conditions. In most cases, you will find that members of the inner circle are required to pledge allegiance to the leader of the sect.

Like all sects, Jim Jones started creating a small circle of people who would later work as recruiters. The entire village of Jonestown started subscribing to the ideologies and teachings of Jones. After some time, many people subscribed to his teachings. The social pressure associated with the people joining the sect attracted even more people. The more people gathered to the sect, the more manipulative the man became. In the mid-1970s, Jim Jones pronounced himself as being a god who had come to rescue the people from their predicaments. Given that the case happened at a time when people were suffering from poor economic status, the leader took advantage of the situation. The poor villagers were drawn to him hoping that he was going to make their lives better. They gave their attention to him and allowed him to take control of all their lives.

Just like all manipulative leaders, Jim Jones did not care about the welfare of the people. He did not provide whatever he promised. Instead, he used his popularity to amass wealth from the victims. He lured the victims into giving him sexual favors and managed to control the whole village.

The story of Jim Jones climaxed with the massacre of over 900 people who followed the sect leader. The town was named after this merciless sect leader who did not bother to think about the welfare of the people. As a manipulative person, he did not mind killing 900 people just to get whatever he wanted. Although the story of Jonestown is an extreme case that looks at a person who showed sociopathic tendencies, it reveals the true character of a manipulative person. Most manipulators do not care about how you feel or what you think. They aim to gain and move on with life.

Chapter 8:

Manipulation Tactics

BEST MANIPULATION TECHNIQUES

DISTRACTION STRATEGY

This is one of the most common manipulation techniques used by governments, political parties, world leaders, politicians, and other public personalities to divert the public attention from the vital problems by introducing continuous distractions and trivial/unimportant information.

This way, the public attention remains fixated on insignificant issues, while the true political and social issues are hidden under the carpet. It gives the public the illusion of being busy with something, though that something is of little consequence in their life. They don't have the time to think about the negative impact of important issues in their lives and the inability of their leaders to resolve these issues.

CREATE PROBLEMS THAT DON'T EXIST AND OFFER SOLUTIONS

This is another classic social manipulation strategy that is widely used throughout the world. It consists of creating an imaginary or foreseen issue to stimulate a specific reaction among victims of manipulation or the public. Then, the manipulator carefully introduces a solution to become the ultimate messiah.

For example, allowing urban violence to build and thrive initially or supporting terrorist camps. This can be followed by making people aware of how their security is the government's prime concern and how leaders will go all out to intensify security measures to ensure public safety.

You introduce a problem and then offer a solution without letting the victims realize that you were directly responsible for creating the problems. This way, you become the solution provider, who can get people to act in a desired manner.

THE PAINFUL REALITY

Let us consider a scenario to understand this strategy clearly.

Your boss urges everyone at the workplace to put in additional hours of work or to work during weekends. He or she may lead you to believe that you all stand to lose your jobs and the market is tight, which means that you have to step up and go the extra mile to survive. They will inform you about how other companies who weren't able to bag big projects couldn't sustain operation costs and eventually closed down.

The managers will convince you how a few sacrifices from your side can go a long way in saving the company's fortunes. Do you see what they are doing there? They are projecting their decision as painful yet necessary. They'll tell how they don't want you to stay late at work, but there's no other option if you want to keep your job or for the company to stay afloat. A majority will resign to the idea of working late.

TO PROJECT VICTIMS AS IGNORANT OR STUPID

The easiest way to get people to do what you want them to do publicly, professionally, or socially is to make them feel how ignorant or stupid they are or how they don't understand something. For instance, if you are looking to introduce new technology that will save labor costs and increase profits, you may have a bunch of people rebelling against it for fear of losing their jobs.

By using the ignorant manipulation tactic, you inform people about how they cannot comprehend technology which is designed to make things easier. You are playing on their lack of awareness or uncertainty about a thing. You are telling them that they aren't in a position to give their view or opinion about it because they do not have the right knowledge or understanding of these systems.

Again, you are replacing revolt with guilt, by making the victims feel like they are responsible for their unfortunate situation or their lack of intelligence/capabilities. Thus, instead of rebelling, workers blame or devalue themselves, inhibiting further action.

DROWN THEM WITH FACTS, INFORMATION, AND STATISTICS

Emotional manipulation doesn't work on everyone, especially in social and professional settings. Here, people are more inclined to follow the logic and rational arguments. Drown these folks in information by quoting research, facts, figures, statistics, and more.

Have numbers ready on your fingertips for any objections and clarifications. Overwhelm people with statistics, logical arguments, and research. Be armed with the vital information to "intellectually bully" people. Present yourself as the ultimate authority or the source of knowledge in a particular field. Cleverly present research that supports your stand or point of view. Take advantage of established expertise to the fullest.

One of the best ways to manipulate people with logic is to present research, statistics, and figures in a compelling and imposing manner. Focus on areas where you believe they may not have sound knowledge and question them about it. This establishes their weakness in their own eyes. They will realize that they have little or no information about this area and that you are more experienced or knowledgeable than them.

This will automatically increase your chances of getting them to do what you want. This technique works well during business negotiations, sales, social debates, and other social or public settings.

You gain a smart subconscious edge over the other person, which makes them more defenseless and open to listening to you. It creates a sort of intellectual superiority, which makes them feel inadequate and compels them to comply with your demands.

THE VICTIM TALKS FIRST

When you are getting another party to agree to your negotiation terms or buy from you, allow them to talk first.

This allows you as a persuader, influencer, or manipulator to establish their baseline. What are their strengths and weaknesses? What are their thoughts, emotions, fears, and behavior patterns? Are they more hesitant or self-confident? Do they appear extroverted/open or introverted/closed? Are they approaching the deal or sales with an element of hesitation? Are they overwhelmed by your presence? What does their body language reveal about them?

Allowing them to communicate first, helps you set a baseline for both their strengths and weaknesses, which can be utilized to get them to act in the desired direction. You can also prepare a list of questions that you can ask them to establish a baseline. The idea is to get them thinking in the direction of acting in your favor. For instance, if you are planning to sell insurance, you ask them a list of questions that help you establish their fears and, therefore, allow you to play on these fears for getting them to sign up quickly.

TWEAK THE ENVIRONMENT TO GAIN ADVANTAGE

You can use the right environment at the right time to ask for someone to do something for you. Debunk the theory that there is a place and time for everything and make the environment work in your favor.

For instance, if you are partying with a boss or coworker on a Friday night, instead of waiting until Monday morning to ask them for a favor, use the relaxed setting of a pub or bar. They'll be less guarded, more chilled out and relaxed, and in a more positive mood. Your chances of getting them to agree to the favor may be higher in a more relaxed setting, where they don't expect you to ask for such a favor. Change the setting of where you'd normally ask something like this to increase your chances of getting people to agree.

CRITICISM

This is whereby the manipulator uses tactics such as belittling, dismissing, and ridiculing you. This keeps someone off-balance. Negative criticism is directed at a partner that makes them feel unworthy. The act of criticizing enables them to gain control over you. The manipulator creates a narrative that there is always something wrong with you and you are not good enough. This kind of narrative makes you doubt yourself, often of what you feel and know. It reaches a point where you do not trust yourself.

USING FLATTERY, KINDNESS, AND CHARM

The use of kindness, charm, and flattery is often more damaging than you realize. The generous deployment of these techniques is known as a passive-aggressive type of behavior. The manipulator uses tactics such as gifting someone items, massaging their egos with flattery, and lots of compliments. One is left to question the real reason behind the compliments, expensive gifts, and paying lots of attention to the victim. These are acts done with ulterior motives, especially when they realize you are about to catch up on the manipulative state. Bribery is also another technique of manipulating someone. It yields results when implemented. Bribery is a better technique than blackmailing an individual. You can even entice a friend with a better offer. The reward doesn't have to be of monetary value. It can be something that you would have done anyway or had already done prior. Perhaps, in the process of asking for help in your studies from a colleague, you can decide to offer her a lunch treat after studying in exchange.

LYING

Lying is normally used by con artists. Manipulators lie about everything they see, hear, or know. They create lies that are so complex that they tend to wrap people up in ways that they cannot differentiate between reality and fake life. These lies can only be disputed by checking for inconsistency in the stories. When the deal is too good, think twice before accepting an offer. Abusers use this manipulation technique as they do not have fears about it. Lying can be caught if the victim decides to do a background check on the sources of information.

285

HAVING THE HOME COURT ADVANTAGE

The process of manipulating an individual all depends on the level of control one has over the other. A manipulator will insist on meeting and having your interactions in an area he is comfortable with. This technique is used to gain an edge of control over someone by taking them out of their element. The places where you normally spend time, are usually his spots and not yours. These places include his office, house, vehicle, and hanging out joints. Such areas make the manipulator exercise his dominance. People are easy to control when he is uneasy with the environment.

This technique can be done away with when the victim makes it clear that meeting places should be where they are both comfortable. Restaurantsand events to attend should be chosen by both of you. This leads to a partnership, breeding a healthy relationship in the process.

CARESSING THE EGO

Caressing the ego is most common in personal relationships. The manipulator caresses the ego of the victim by feeding her lies. The ego grows with time and in the end, the manipulator has you on his leash.

This technique can be avoided if the victim of the act possesses humility.

MAKING UNUSUAL REQUEST BEFORE YOUR REAL REQUEST

This kind of manipulation technique is a slight "mind game" oriented. The tactic involves asking an unusual request, mostly of a higher degree. This throws the person off balance, as he wasn't expecting such a request. The manipulator knew how that person was likely to respond if he would have asked for the usual request such as money, favor, shoes. The victim was more likely to respond "no" because people's minds have been conditioned to avoid these tasks.

For instance, a salesperson knows approaching someone on the street and asking him to buy the items being sold would likely lead to no sale. The salesman would first ask the potential client to do something such as help him with directions. This will build a "relationship" with the person and makes them less likely to turn you down in your presentation.

VOICE RAISING AND IRATE OUTBURSTS

Manipulators raise their voices during arguments to intimidate someone. They believe this process of raising the voice aggressively or loudly can enable them to achieve what they wanted. In a relationship, passion can come out in different forms such as tenderness, cute smiles you give one another, laughter, and the desire to share warmth in the arms of another. Passion, however, should not be mistaken by angry unpredictable outbursts during disagreements. In marriages or couples where they tend to disagree with one another,it is not uncommon. There are various ways of handling conflict, such as, having healthy communication with your partner andnot screaming or having temper tantrums. The aggressive voice is sometimes accompanied by strong body language.

The manipulator can also start to pick quarrels about non-issues. When this starts to occur, it's a display telling you there are items that need to be ironed out.

There are forces at play. In a relationship, someone who's picking random quarrels is either cheating on the partner or looking to end the relationship.

Inspiring Fear over a Partner then Relief

This technique of manipulation tends to have a high rate of success over its victims. It normally involves making someone fear that the worst will happen by creating stories or giving out the wrong information. If the story does not happen, that person is likely to be relieved, and then he would be happy enough to grant you whatever you want. It's all about playing mind games with the victim.

Doing a Favor

When offered something, the humans feel indebted and generally try, as quickly as possible, to render a service in return to feel relieved, and thus, to let go of this feeling of obligation which they feel. This is mainly why many brands give free samples out of their products!

Consciously or not, in the human mind, incurring a debt brings about the fact of having to repay it. It is a rule which is the cement of the social bond, even in primitive human societies. However, the violation of the law of reciprocity is wrongly perceived, which makes it successful. This is why doing a service builds a bond of trust with the person and makes them more easily manipulated afterward. Angry, for owing someone something.

Another aspect of the rule of reciprocity: there is another principle, that of reciprocal concession. When an individual formulates a request that we refuse at first and reformulates his request, he makes a concession, and we, therefore, tend to respond with a reciprocal admission. To manipulate someone, ask for something rather than giving something. For example, ask for a small favor rather than rendering one. Or, ask for something you don't really want and then rephrase your request by pretending to make a concession.

USE THE PERSON'S FIRST NAME

The human brain needs to be able to name actions, things, and people. A name on a face and presto, it's no longer unknown. It is no longer "the mass." A first name, just like a word, helps make things concrete.

Besides, the first name is often the first word known and remembered by a baby. Therefore, this creates a unique connection between the baby's first name and himself—a kind of anchor. Suddenly, people who use their first name to address someone (even if they hardly know him), immediately seem more sympathetic and familiar. These are the two criteria that promote manipulation.

Have you ever heard someone say your first name without speaking to you? Yet inevitably, you turned around or at least felt concerned at that point. It was stronger than you! This is proof that there is a strong emotional anchor between your first name and you. So, the next time a stranger asks for your first name and uses it to formulate his requests, you'll know he's trying to manipulate you!

FLATTERY

Contrary to popular belief, flattery is a manipulation technique that works. However, you need to think a minimum of what you say.

If you respect this condition, then even if the person knows that you are petting them, they will be sensitive. However, be careful, this technique does not work if the person you are trying to manipulate does not think you are sincere.

Flattery is a technique of manipulation that belongs to the family of displays of love. We create a pseudo-spirit of family and belonging through embracing emotional displays, affection, and flattery. It is very beneficial because the individual immediately feels taken in by a new family.

GIVE A REASON

Our brain is hardwired to accept more of a request when it comes with a reason. Even if it's a shitty reason, "Can I go ahead of you in the queue because I have to go make photocopies afterward?"

Know that to manipulate people; you can choose to give a justification. Even if your argument is flawed, the person will be tempted to say "yes" to you. More, in any case, than if you don't bother to argue.

STEP IN THE DOOR

The foot in the door is a well-known manipulation technique. Asking someone for a small favor is a great way to build a persuasive "dynamic." Then you present your "real" request to him.

This technique is a logical continuation of that which consisted in being rendered a small service. Except that here, instead of playing on reciprocity, we are playing on commitment and consistency.

If the person answered yes to your first request or did you a little favor, you could ask for something more substantial. The person is expected to say yes because they want to justify the fact that they have already helped you and because you have built a pseudo-relationship of trust.

THE DOOR IN THE NOSE

The trick relies on the power of human guilt. It is the reverse of the foot in the door. Here you will ask for something huge or ridiculous to get a no.

When the NO answer finally comes to you, you present a second request, which is more reasonable (but genuine from the start, of course).

By the way, if by some mystery the person accedes to your first "huge" request, so much the better! But more often than not, she will accept the second instead.

THE RED SCARF

The red scarf technique involves reluctantly pretending to refuse something to have a better chance of getting a reward (which you wanted from the start).

Example to better understand is a divorce where we would insist on having the dog. At the last moment, we would reluctantly pretend to give it up in compensation for something else like a trinket (which we wanted from the start). The other party will leave it to us, thinking they've won.

THE GUILT

Guilt is a technique that can be used to manipulate someone. But be aware that, depending on who you come across, it can also irritate them and have the opposite effect.

To make someone feel guilty is to say to them, "I thought I could count on you," and that sort of thing.

Chapter 9:

How to Help Someone Being Controlled

You will encounter manipulative people in your life – there is no question about it. So, you must learn how to deal with them. There are two kinds of manipulators that you will deal with; those you can avoid (strangers, casual acquaintances, etc.) and those who are a permanent fixture in your life (family members, close friends, colleagues, etc.).

When it comes to strangers and casual accountancies, once you notice that they are manipulative, you can keep your interactions with them at a minimum. However, if it's someone close to you, dealing with them will be a lot more complicated, and it requires a lot of effort and commitment on your part.

When you encounter a manipulative person, the most important thing you can do is to keep your emotions in check and try to be as logical as possible. So, first, you need to stay calm. Manipulators know that they are more likely to get what they want when you react emotionally, so they'll do whatever they can to get a rise out of you or to emotionally destabilize you in one way or another.

So, the best thing you can do at that moment is to take a breath, calm yourself, and try to think clearly. For example, when a manipulator asks you to do something, he will keep pushing you because he wants you to say "Yes" right away. He wants you to make an instant emotional decision because he knows that if you take your time, think things over, weigh the pros and cons before making a decision; you are more likely to choose an option that isn't in your own best interest. From this point on, you should be wary of any person who tries to force you to decide the heat of the moment.

Often, manipulators will try to create a sense of urgency (a salesman may try to tell you that he is running out of stock, or your partner might give you an ultimatum). Approach every interaction with the understanding that decision making (no matter how small it may seem) is an executive function and not an emotional one, so anyone who wants you to make an emotional decision is technically a manipulator.

To help people avoid making emotional decisions in the heat of the moment, some psychologists recommend the use of grounding techniques to deal with strong emotions. For example, if you feel stressed or anxious, you can ground yourself by focusing all of your attention on what you are feeling in your body at the moment (if for instance, your heart is racing, focus your mind on your racing heart;

this will keep your mind from racing all over the place, and it will help calm you down).

Once you have your emotions in check, the next thing you need to do is learn to say a firm "no." Many of us find it difficult to turn people down outright. Even if we have every intention of saying "no," we tend to go out of our way to soften the blow for the other person, to the point that it sounds to them as though there is room for bargaining.

Manipulative people are well aware of this vulnerability, and they use it to push the envelope as far as it can go. If they detect any hint of hesitation on your part, they take it and run with it; they'll try to guilt-trip you, shame you, threaten you, and do anything else they can think of to turn your "no" into a "yes."

You can try to use diplomatic language wherever it's necessary, but when you say "no" don't leave your statement open to interpretation. For example, if you say, "I don't think I can do it" instead of "I can't do it," a manipulator will take it as a challenge to try and change your mind.

When interacting with manipulators, you also have to learn to assert yourself. Manipulators will use lots of techniques to keep you from voicing your opinion or asserting yourself because they know that if you don't clarify your position, they will be able to co-opt your view and make decisions for you. During the conversation, when you try to make a stand on an issue, the manipulator will attempt to keep you from doing so by talking over you or interrupting you. When this happens, most people will let it go, and the manipulator will get it his way.

When manipulators want you to agree with them inadvertently, they may use "we "sentences to get you to feel like they are on your side, or even to speak for you in front of others. They may also speak in incomplete sentences or ask you to confirm every assertion they make because they are trying to make you more agreeable. To counter ensure that you never let anyone speak for you. Where the manipulator is involved, always make sure that you use "I" statements (e.g., "I want" or "I disagree") to create a clear distinction between you and the manipulator.

Manipulators seek to control others to get them to do what they want. They aim to exploit people by paying with their thoughts and feelings. With this in mind, it's possible to indemnify manipulators by their words, body language, and behavior.

If you meet a person who encourages you to reveal a lot of personal details while at the same time, he is going out of his way to hide details about himself, chances are you are dealing with a manipulator.

You can also tell that you are dealing with a manipulator if the person's actions don't match his words. Manipulators want to win you over, so they'll tell you what they think you want to hear. They'll make lofty promises at first, but when it comes to following through with those promises, they'll leave you hanging. So, pay close attention to what people say and what they do, and try to see if there is a disconnection between those two things.

Manipulators will try to alter your reality and change your belief systems. So, you should watch out for people who tell you blatant lies, even if the facts are easily verifiable. For example, when you are starting to date someone, and you catch them in a lie, but they keep insisting that their version of events is the true one, you can be certain that this is just the beginning, and that over time, their lies will just get more blatant.

Manipulators undermine your grasp on reality by telling constant lies. When you hear small but incremental lies over and over, you will get to a point where you start doubting your reality. In some cases, it can turn out so badly, that you start feeling as though you are losing your mind. This is a manipulation technique that's known as "alighting," and it's more prevalent than you might think.

When you notice that someone is telling obvious lies early in a relationship, your best course of action is to terminate that relationship and to get away from that person as fast as you can.

You can also tell if you are dealing with a manipulator if he or she plays the blame game or tries to make you feel guilty about pretty much everything. Emotional manipulators understand that they can leverage guilt to make people do things for them as a way of atoning for their mistakes. While manipulators may be good at hiding their true nature during the early stages of a relationship, "guilt-tripping" and the "blame game" are two of the things that they find rather difficult to conceal. To manipulators, these techniques are useful from the outset of a relationship, so they may use them without even realizing it themselves.

If something goes wrong on your date, manipulators will try to turn it into your fault, as a matter of record. Even if you are dealing with something that is entirely out of anyone's control, they will make logical leaps to conclude that you are the one to blame. Similarly, if something goes right, they will try to take credit for it. For every small thing that they do, they'll make sure that they point it out, and that you acknowledge that they are the ones who are responsible for it.

For manipulators, the point here is to keep score. From the very beginning of the relationships, they will make sure that there is a running tally of all the good things and the bad things, and they'll make sure that they are ahead on the list of good things, and that you are ahead on the list of bad things. This way, they can always have something to hold over your head in case they want to manipulate you.

So, when you start going out with someone, pay attention to their attitude towards scorekeeping. A scorekeeper is almost always a manipulator.

Manipulators have a way of overwhelming you emotionally, even if you have only known them for a short time. If you meet someone, and you get the sense that they are just "too much too soon," chances are you are dealing with a manipulator.

Love smothering is a common manipulation technique, one that you can detect early in a relationship. Here, the manipulator will shower you with gifts and signs of affection to make you emotionally overwhelmed. When you receive an overwhelming amount of affection, you are more inclined to lead with your heart instead of stopping to think things through, so this increases the chances that you will fall for a manipulator.

Romantic gestures are great at the start of a relationship, but if you feel that they are excessive, you should consider the possibility that you are dealing with a manipulative person.

COMBATTING MANIPULATION

Fighting off manipulative tactics and advances is more than just being able to identify it. Sure, it helps to know that you are being manipulated whenever that truly is the case. That means that you aren't being naive about your situation. However, it's also just as important that you can know the common tactics in dealing with people who seek to manipulate you for their gain.

You've already been exposed to the many faces of manipulation and the kind of impact that it can have on not just one, but on a large group of people. Now, you have to learn how you would be able to spot manipulative behavior in your everyday life. In addition to that, you have to know how you will deal with it whenever you find yourself in those situations as well. It's not rare for people to find themselves in manipulative situations and not know what to do about it. This is not by accident. Manipulative people have a way of compromising their victims' inhibitions and better judgment. That's why a lot of victims of manipulation can often feel paralyzed by the situations that they find themselves in.

If you know that you are in danger of being manipulated, then you need to do something about it. The will to act is entirely up to you.

Chapter 10:

Dealing With Controlling People

HOW TO DEAL WITH A MANIPULATIVE PERSON

Psychological manipulation is always going to be a very loaded and heavy-handed issue. It can often be referred to as lying, deceiving, skewing, distorting, gaslighting, intimidating, guilting, and other such things. Manipulators can also take the form of many different people throughout your life. Sometimes, the person who is manipulating you might be a parent, sibling, boss, classmate, coworker, or romantic partner, among others. That's why manipulation is such a complex topic to handle.

It can take the form of various tactics, and it can also be employed by various agents. This is why it can be increasingly difficult for someone to be able to identify and deal with a manipulative person.

As long as you keep your eyes peeled and you make an active effort in seeking these red flags out, it shouldn't be a problem. Now, it's a matter of dealing with these people and managing their advances.

First, evaluate whether the person is more of a systematic or unconscious manipulator. The more systematic, profound manipulators are almost certainly beyond reach. They can have grand visions and don't care who they have to get by to pursue their goals, they may simply enjoy controlling others.Perhaps they have had childhood traumas and issues that lead them to exploit others for fulfillment. These types of people are more aware of it and aggressively pursue their manipulative traits. Whatever the case may be, if possible, keep your distance from these types of people. Indeed, the easy solution would be to cut this person out of your life, right? It can be so easy to just burn bridges with someone if you know that they have manipulative tendencies and that they would be so willing to advance their interests at your expense. That kind of selfishness should warrant a cutting of ties. However, it's not always going to be that simple. There will be times when the person who is manipulating you is someone you have a deep bond and connection with. There is even a chance they are not consciously aware of their behavior themselves. For instance, if your parent, partner, or friend is manipulating you, it won't be so easy to just break that relationship off entirely. This is especially true if you love your parents and you know that they love you in return. In this case, it's not just a matter of eliminating a manipulative person from your life. Rather, it becomes an issue of managing this individual.

When dealing with a manipulative person, you must tread lightly. Keep in mind that there is also a paternal kind of manipulation.

301

They might not have bad intentions, and they might take offense to the fact that you are accusing them of being manipulative. That is why you have to be extra cautious and sensitive when you broach the issue with them.

FIRST, BE SAFE

If you know that you are in danger whenever you are with this manipulative individual in your life, always make sure that there is a third-party present. You can never really know what they might do to you if the two of you are alone. So, before you confront them about your manipulation, make sure that you have someone else in the room. You need that mediator; someone who would be able to help bridge the two of you. You can always call on a mutual friend, a shared loved one, or a trusted confidante. In more serious cases, you can even seek professional help from a licensed therapist. The point here is that the confrontation process should never be conducted recklessly. Your safety is always going to be the priority here and a lot of the time, that means having someone else in the room to be with you.

TAKE A DIPLOMATIC APPROACH TO INITIATING A DIALOGUE

You can either choose to work your influence on them to lessen the negative effects, or you could just confront them. The initial confrontation doesn't have to be so hot and impassioned. The best approach to confronting this individual would be to be as calm and collected as can be. You want to make sure that you are taking emotions out of the equation here. Keep in mind that a manipulative person is always going to capitalize on the emotionality of a person. If you take that ammo away from them, then it leaves them very little to work with. In addition to that, it's more likely that they won't react in such a hostile manner if you take a more civil approach to initiating this dialogue with them. Using people's own words against them makes it harder to resist whatever it is you are asking them to do, if one claims to be selfless, then they would not partake in certain actions to begin with.

DON'T FIGHT BACK

If they will be hostile with you about it, resist the urge to fight back. You have to learn to pick your fights. Responding to them in a hostile manner is only going to result in you playing into their games. You don't want that. You want to make sure that you stay calm throughout. When they get emotional, don't invalidate these feelings. Their emotions might be very authentic regardless of whether they are based on distorted truths or not. A person can still feel angry about something that is a complete lie or fantasy. Keep that in mind.

SET CLEAR LIMITS AND BOUNDARIES

Once you have heard their side of the tale, it's now time for you to air out your grievances.

Again, you need to make sure that you keep emotions out of it. You don't want them to be invalidating what you're saying just because you're being hysterical. You want to be honest about it and be straightforward. You shouldn't be beating around the bush anymore.

Make sure that all of the skeletons come out of the closet. Be courteous, but also, don't pull any punches. No matter how uncomfortable it might be to speak honestly about your feelings, you will have to do so.

KNOW WHEN IT'S TIME TO WALK AWAY

Sometimes, you just need to be able to know when it's time to walk away. No matter how painful it is to cut yourself loose from someone who you love dearly, you still have to do so for the sake of your well-being. You should not be making any room for toxicity or manipulative behavior that causes a burden in your life, regardless of who it might be coming from. At the end of the day, the only real person who has your back is yourself. That is why you have to make it a point to protect yourself at all costs. If there is no way for you to find a peaceful means of coexisting with one another that doesn't involve any form of harmful manipulation that is taking value out of your life, then you need to be able to walk away from that.

SEEK APOLOGY FOR YOUR PART AND MOVE ON

You probably won't get an apology, but you also don't have to dwell on it. Own up to what you think you were doing, and then say nothing of the other allegations.

YOU DON'T HAVE TO BEAT THEM

There should be no two people playing this game. Instead, learn to recognize the techniques so that you can practice your responses properly.

KNOW YOUR BASIC HUMAN RIGHTS

In interacting with a psychologically manipulative individual, the most critical rule is to know your rights and understand when they are violated. You have the right to defend yourself until you harm others. On the other hand, you can forfeit those rights if you hurt others.

These are some of our basic human rights:

• You are entitled to be treated with dignity.

• You have the right to have your thoughts, views, and desires shared.

• You are entitled to set your own goals.

- You are entitled to say "no" without feeling guilty. You are entitled to get what you pay for.

- You have the freedom to have differing opinions than others.

- You have the right to care for yourself and to protect yourself against being physically, mentally, or emotionally threatened.

- You are entitled to build your own healthy and happy life.

Those basic human rights are your boundaries.

The culture is, of course, full of people who do not respect those rights. Psychological manipulators want to strip you of your freedoms, so they can take advantage of you and manipulate you. But you have the moral authority and power to announce it is you who is in charge of your life, not the manipulator.

AVOID SELF-BLAME AND PERSONALIZATION

Since the purpose of the manipulator is to try and manipulate your vulnerabilities, it is recognizable that you may feel bad, or even blame yourself for failing to satisfy the manipulator. It is important to remember that you are not the problem in these situations; you have been manipulated to feel bad about yourself so that you are more likely to surrender your power and rights.

BY PROBING QUESTIONS, YOU PUT FOCUS ON THEM

Psychological manipulators will inevitably make demands (or requests) of you. Often these "offers" make you be out of your route to satisfy their needs. When you hear an unreasonable request, it is sometimes useful to put the focus back on the manipulator by asking a few inquiring questions, to see if she or he has enough self-awareness to recognize their scheme's inequity. For instance: "Does that seem fair to you?""Sound fair what you want from me?" "Have I got a say in this?" "Are you asking me, or are you telling me?"

"So, what am I going to get out of it?" "Do you expect me to [re-establish the unjust request]?"You're putting up a mirror when you ask such questions so that the manipulator can see the true nature of his or her plan. If the manipulator has some sense of self-awareness, he or she will likely withdraw the demand and return. On the other side, genuinely pathological manipulators (such as a narcissist) will ignore your questions and convince you to get their way.

A "NO" IS A COMPLETE SENTENCE

Practicing the art of communication is to be able to say "no" diplomatically but firmly. Articulated efficiently, it lets you stand your ground while keeping a relationship. Remember that your basic human rights include the right to emphasize yourself, the right to say "no" without feeling shame, and the right to choose your own happy and healthy life.

TAKE TIME FOR YOUR ADVANTAGE

In addition to unreasonable demands, the manipulator will also often expect an immediate response from you to enhance their power and influence over you in the situation.

During these times, instead of instantly reacting to the manipulator's appeal, consider taking time to your benefit and distancing yourself from its immediate impact. You can exercise control over the situation simply by saying: "I'll think about it." Remember how powerful those few words are from a buyer to a salesperson, or from a romantic prospect to an enthusiastic pursuer, or from you to a manipulator. Take the time you need to weigh the pros and cons of a situation and decide whether you want to discuss a fairer deal, or whether you're better off by saying"no," which brings us to our next point.

CONFRONT BULLIES

The critical point to remember about bullies is that they choose those they view as weaker, so as long as you stay calm and obedient, you become a target for them. However, inside a lot of bullies are also cowards. Once their victims start showing backbone and sticking up for their rights, the bully always backs down. This is true in schoolyards, in households, and offices as well.

YOU CAN SET BOUNDARIES

• When a manipulative person becomes aware that they are losing control, their tactics can become more desperate. It is time to make some tough choices.

• If you don't need to be close to that person, consider cutting them off entirely from your life.

• If you're living with them or working closely together, you'll need to learn strategies to handle them.

• Speaking to a therapist or counselor about how to handle the situation might be helpful.

• You may also be able to recruit a trusted friend or family member to help you identify the activity and impose limits.

SET CONSEQUENCES

If a psychological manipulator persists on breaching the limits and won't take "no" for a response, the outcome will be deployed. One of the essential skills you can use to "stand up" to a stubborn person is the ability to identify and demonstrate consequence(s). Expertly formulated, the outcome gives the deceptive person a pause and compels him or her to move from abuse to respect.

Chapter 11:

Defending Yourself Against Manipulation

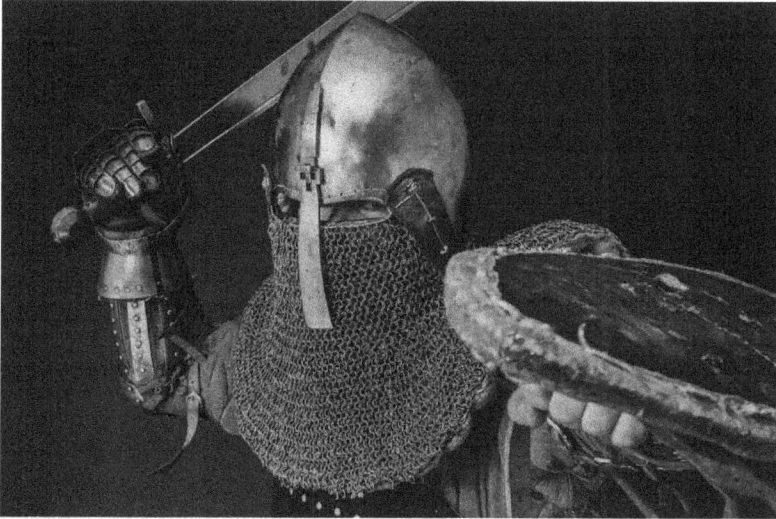

WHAT YOU NEED TO DO TO OVERCOME MANIPULATION

We have come to a point where we are here to talk about the basic skills to overcome manipulation. Moreover, manipulation will only work if you allow them to control you. Much like hypnosis, any hypnosis is self-hypnosis. What we are trying to state here is that knowledge that you are being manipulated defeats its entire purpose.

ESTABLISH A CLEAR SENSE OF SELF

There is a need to know your identity, what your needs and wants are, what your emotions are, and what you are fond of and not fond of. You must learn to accept these and not become apologetic, as these are the things that make you, you. At times, we dread that in the event of speaking up, we are viewed by others as egotistical and called out for being selfish. Nevertheless, knowing your identity or what you need in life is not at all an act of selfishness. Self-centeredness is demanding that you always get what you want or that others have always put your needs and wants first. Similarly, when another person calls you out for not following their orders or fulfilling their needs and wants, they are the ones being selfish, not you.

SAY "NO" DESPITE THE OTHER PERSON'S DISAPPROVAL

The ability to say "no" despite somebody's objection is a solid demonstration. Individuals who can do this are present in reality. Because in reality, there is no way that we can accommodate all of their needs and wants.

When this happens, they will become baffled, even disappointed.

However, keep in mind that what they are feeling is part of human nature. Most of these individuals would then forgive and forget. Sound individuals realize that getting what you want all the time is not possible, even when the desires are genuine. In any case, when we cannot endure another person's mistake or objection, it ends up hard stating "no." It winds up more diligently for us to state it or have limits. Manipulators exploit this shortcoming and use dissatisfaction and objection in extraordinary structures to get us to do what they need.

TOLERATE THE OTHER PERSON'S NEGATIVE AFFECT

We can demonstrate compassion for people's pity, hurt, or even annoyance when accommodating them without needing to back down and reverse our decision. Keep in mind, a solid relationship is described by common minding, shared genuineness, and shared regard. If you are involved with somebody who uses manipulation and unhealthy control consistently, begin to see little propensities that may not be clear to you at first.

KEEP A CONVERSATIONS JOURNAL

There are usually some kinds of signs that send hints that somebody is trying to manipulate them. Those aren't always easy to find, of course, unless you've been in the situation before or recognize coercion. One strategy that you can do if you feel you are being manipulated by someone is to keep a journal of what's said. You can write down your conversations or stuff they say to you randomly. You should even write down what they are doing at the same time. Although this may sound like an unusual thing to do, it will help you understand what is happening, since manipulators are operating on an emotional level. This is sometimes hard to notice, especially if you are already lacking in self-confidence. You may also include how the mentioned circumstance or words made you feel. You may find a connection between what is stated by the manipulator and how you feel. You might find, for example, that your self-image is starting to diminish. When you notice this, it is a sign that you have to stay away from the person or get out of the relationship as quickly as possible.

CONFRONTING MANIPULATORS ABOUT THEIR CONDUCT

With some people, that will be easier than others. For example, if your supervisor is the manipulator, and you need your job, you may not be able to confront them directly. You might also have a hard time confronting your significant other, especially if they've lowered your self-esteem. Confronting the manipulator, however, is a perfect way to let them know you understand their actions and you won't stand for it. When you are following this path, you want to be aware of the other tactics that they may be used against you. They might try to create a distraction, for example, or try to play the victim. They might also blame someone else for their behavior or tell you that you imagined it all. You need to be firm when confronting a manipulator. You need to be fully persuaded and understand that they will try and exploit you because they don't want other people to catch on to their actions. You also need to be careful, as some manipulators can become passive-aggressive or violent.

PUT THE FOCUS OF THE MANIPULATORS

You can also focus on themanipulator, in addition to confronting them. You can do this by asking a range of questions regarding their motive. You want to try and find out why they act the way they do, which is the foundation of dark psychology. Some of the questions you may ask are: "Do you feel reasonable?" "What will I get out of this?" "Is this helpful?" "That's what you want from me (state their request)." You show the manipulator what they are doing by asking questions like these. They would be remorseful or alter their request if they are not a master manipulator and did not intend to take part in that action. If they're a master manipulator, however, they'll think of other tactics to turn it back on you. They will try to act like the victim, by asking "Why are you attacking me?"or by saying "I'm just trying to help; I don't appreciate being attacked like this."

START DRIVING YOUR AGENDA

Manipulators don't want to win over other people. This puts them in a threatened position. The more you succeed, though, the more you drive a manipulator backward. Your ability to believe in and continue to succeed in yourself will depend on how long you know the manipulator and how close you are to them. For example, if you have been emotionally beaten down by the manipulator, it will be much harder to remain motivated and work hard to succeed. If you've just met them, without too much trouble you'll be able to continue pushing towards your success. Of course, having the mindset of believing that you can fulfill your dreams, and supporting people will help eliminate the manipulator through your success. And if you need to speak to someone to get better mentally and emotionally, this is what you do.

DON'T GET PHYSICALLY TIED UP

While sometimes we get trapped by a manipulator because we don't know their personality, other times we know they're manipulators, but they still need to keep in touch because they're colleagues or family. You need to protect yourself in a different way when this is the situation because you cannot simply ignore them. A lot of people also recommend you do your best not to get emotionally attached. For some people, this will be tougher than others. If you're a more emotional person, you'll be struggling to avoid becoming emotionally attached as your relationships are emotionally based.

One way to do this is to ensure that they know the boundaries. You'll also need to make sure that you stick to your limits. If you cross your boundaries, manipulators don't care, so you need to protect yourself. Tell them if you think they're jumping a fence. Don't fall back for any of their techniques and don't turn back.

DON'T FEED THE DRAMA

One of the most essential things a manipulator thrives on is suspense. For this reason, they often disagree with someone or something that will cause people to respond. So one of the best ways to stop a manipulator in their tracks is to tell them "you are right." Manipulators aren't used to having people to agree with them, and when you do, they'll be left speechless. This also creates a threat that could make them want to leave you alone. They may feel that they can't trap you with their techniques, especially if you do so right away. This is not to say that they will not try. Manipulators also aim to bring people into the network. Letting them win the argument, even if it upsets your ego a little bit, is much better than falling victim to their pitfalls.

HAVE A HEALTHY ATTITUDE

Having a healthy mindset is another way of eliminating a manipulator from your life. You want to make sure you feel confident that you can stop them from using techniques against you. You will want to make sure you feel good about your self-esteem and self-image. At the same time, you want to understand how they manipulate you. To battle them, you need to have a grasp on their techniques. You have to understand they probably won't stop with just one technique. More than likely they will use a few in hopes they can start breaking you down. The stronger you remain, the more likely the manipulator will leave you alone. If you always push them away, call them out on their behavior, and continue to believe in yourself, manipulators won't spend a lot of time trying to use different techniques.

MEDITATION

Many people don't realize how helpful meditation can be. Meditation is not just about keeping you relaxed but also about keeping you optimistic and feeling good about yourself. When you feel this way, it's easier to remove the negativity from your life, which means manipulators. Meditation is easy, so you don't have to put too much time aside. You can schedule meditation in around ten minutes out of your day. Find a time and place where you can be on your own and without interruption. You also want to keep it quiet, so you can concentrate on eliminating your body and mind from the negativity. Many people would be using relaxation exercises to help them remain focused when meditating. This is when you close your eyes and start to breathe normally. You want to concentrate on the breaths. Notice the feeling of your body on your clothes or put one hand on your chest and the other on your stomach. Feel how your hands move in and out as you breathe. Then you focus on deep breaths. Take a deep breath in, then slowly exhale. Finish the exercise until you feel soothed.

In addition to helping you eliminate manipulators who have not become a close person in your life, meditation will also help you manage your life with a manipulator. Of course, if your significant other is a manipulator for your mental health and safety, you want to leave but meditation can help give you strength. It will give you the strength to concentrate on your attitude and find ways to defend yourself against the tactics of coercion. It may give you the strength to leave as well, once you're ready.

ASEPSIS AND TOTAL AVOIDANCE

That is, do not get close to a handler, to avoid contact and contagion as much as possible. Of all the strategies, this is the most effective. It's not the most epic, but it does work the best. The first security strategy in any situation is always avoidance. The basic strategy for winning a battle with a manipulator is not to enter the battle. That is the only correct maneuver because any other way has consequences.

"A manipulator is an expert in fighting in the mud, from behind, and with low blows, he will win against us if we go down to his ground."

In bad times, both personal and business, there is a temptation to listen to more dubious clients, frequently worse companies, fall into "get rich effortlessly" or "it's always someone else's fault" schemes (so better end with them). We have to avoid that as much as possible; we have to leave them alone and put a bell of silence on the manipulator.

It is far better to miss an "opportunity" to work with a manipulator than to get bogged down with one. Nobody goes around exposing themselves to the flu just to show how strong they are. Our primary strategy with disease and with manipulation should be the same: do not enter their radius of action as far as possible.

CUT THE ROPE AT ONCE, AS SOON AS POSSIBLE

The former is the best strategy, but it is impossible to avoid 100% manipulation. Sometimes they will catch us off guard and, at other times, circumstances will drag us into a situation, whether we like it or not. There will also be times when it will be friends, family, or acquaintances who will be in a manipulative situation and we will have to get involved to help them.

"In these circumstances, and from experience, the appropriate strategy is to cut ties with the manipulator as soon as possible. We will do it quickly as if it were a clean blow of the sword. Then we take as much distance as possible."

I know it may seem suggestive to be the vigilante and believe that we will not be fooled but resist the temptation. Every minute that you spend with a manipulator, you will be draining precious energy. If we are there, the strategy is to disengage from the fight as soon as possible, "hit" only to gain distance, and then avoid further contact in the future.

If you are involved in business with a manipulator, terminate any contracts, say no to the slightest bit that you propose, seek outside support, and do not isolate yourself by listening only to the manipulator.

NEVER DIRECTLY CONFRONT A MANIPULATOR IF YOU CAN AVOID IT

If he does, he will flee by other roads, mount the number, play the victim, or use one of his hat's many tricks. We have to be smarter than them.

"If you spot a manipulator, don't go straight for it, look for an indirect angle, and strike with one of the following strategies to break away from their influence and distance yourself."

I repeat, do not go to direct war.

NEVER, NEVER, LOSE YOUR TEMPER

As the Americans say: "Business is business."This phrase alludes to a philosophy whereby there is no reason for the emotional to get in the way of business. With that mentality of separating the professional from the personal, many businesses take some huge (business) stab wounds and solve them with, "It's just business."

"The exercise to be learned is that, in business and against manipulation, you never lose your temper."

If emotion surfaces, the manipulator wins. If he fails, he begins to despair, uses more violent tactics, exposes himself, makes mistakes, discovers his game, and loses the ability to manipulate.

The manipulator seeks the brawl, and if the other loses the papers, we have to turn it around and use that strategy against him. We must know that we are winning every second that we do not lose our temper and do not get carried away by emotion.

Never get upset by a manipulator, be it in a personal or professional situation. Let's see the situation for what it is, a surgical operation to remove it from our environment, and not do more damage. It will twist, scream, and kick, getting louder and dirtier, like when little children get angry. But if we hold the guy, he loses.

LEARN TO INTERPRET THE SIGNALS.

It is vital to recognize a manipulator and be aware of our emotional state in a negotiation, sale, or discussion with one.

The four main clues that should set off the alarms because we are in front of a professional liar are:

INSULATION

Trying to isolate ourselves in a conversation, a situation, or somethingthat we do not consult or talk about with others, are signs of manipulation. Isolation is a typical manipulative tactic that is imperative, such as for cults, to make them work. Any sensible person who proposes something to us has no problem in consulting other opinions.

RUSH AND PRESSURE

When someone tries to get us to rashly buy a product, sign a contract, make any decision, or go out of business, something stinks. You have to distance yourself, consult other options, and decide calmly. "We should never make an important decision in a hurry or an upset, emotional state."

EXCESS OF EMOTIONS

Be careful when an excess of emotionality is used in the speeches, they make us or the situations they put us in, easier to manipulate. I have seen firsthand how certain unethical companies in the field of self-help act, for example. They organize weekends where attendees are isolated in a hotel or spa; they are put in an altered and highly elevated emotional state (with exercises, practices, and speeches that strike a chord). Then all this is used to sell more expensive programs and courses, of course, in a rush and pressure using a false shortage (another typical manipulation trick). "If you can put someone in a sufficiently upset emotional state, you can make them believe what you want."

EXCESS "LOVE" AND ATTENTION

One of the cults' preferred strategies for attracting followers is called the "love bomb." It is characterized because everyone accepts you unconditionally, smiles at you, and behaves like the best thing that ever happened to them, even though they hardly know you. There is no criticism; no one says no to anything, it's all gestures and acceptance smiles.

Acceptance is a harsh drug for anyone, but especially for those who have barely been able to obtain it, such as the lonely, the marginalized, or those going through a hard time. Those can all be us, and those are the scapegoats. We can all fall into the "love bomb." Likewise, the lack of seriousness, the excess confidence, the refusal to sign contracts or agreements because everyone here "are friends"... All of these are usually signs of manipulation.

IF IN DOUBT, ALSO SAY THAT YOU WANT TO GET A SECOND OPINION TO SEE THE MANIPULATOR'S REACTION.

Similar to the previous time strategy, in this case, we say we want a second opinion. Even when we are responsible for the decision to be made, we can always say that we must consult someone else: a lawyer, our spouse, a friend who is an expert on the subject.

It is about trying to get out of the isolation trap with arguments that are difficult to refute. A desperate effort on the other not to consult a superior or an expert is a sign that we are possibly being manipulated. These two strategies work as a detector for manipulators and differentiate them directly in a delicate situation.

DO NOT GIVE IN TO A MANIPULATOR OR IN THE MOST INOFFENSIVE DETAILS

If you think you are dealing with a manipulator, don't say yes to anything. No matter how innocent he seems. If we do, we are at risk of using cognitive dissonance (one of the fundamental principles of persuasion) to make us take a seemingly simple step and then gradually get more agreement from our part. When we realize it, it has pushed us to the bottom of the web.

If you know you are involved with a manipulator, never get closer than necessary, never say yes and never think you have everything under control. It must be noted that often and we are not obliged to justify this refusal, we are within our rights, and "no" is a complete sentence.

If he insists, we say the same,"no"; we do not add additional excuses that he can grab on to. Manipulators are adept at emotional blackmail and trying to get excuses to see how to turn them around.

BE VERY CLEAR ABOUT THE INITIAL OBJECTIVE YOU HAVE IN MIND

This is the first golden rule of negotiation, but it should be remembered for any situation in which we interact with a manipulator.

"If your objective in the conversation or negotiation with a manipulator is vague and diffused, you will end up at a point that the manipulator wants."

Be very clear about what you want. Never confront a manipulator without knowing precisely what you want to get out of the interaction. If you will cut the ties with the manipulator, focus everything on reducing the links and not moving from there. If you want to hear what he has to say and then reflect ahead of time, with other opinions and without pressure, keep that in mind and don't allow anything else to happen.

Listen to him, and don't let the manipulator get to anything other than the goal you have in mind. Since this is the real world, you should have an ideal target in mind and then a realistic goal, being prepared to compromise (though not quickly) from that ideal goal to the actual one. However, that is the minimum limit, do not give another step.

Know your destiny, as far as you can give in, and then be like Ulysses returning from Troy. Hold on tight to your targets and resist any manipulative siren calls.

NEVER USE THE SAME WEAPONS AS A MANIPULATOR

There is a powerful temptation to use weapons of manipulation against the manipulator. To respond with fallacies, try to isolate him, do emotional blackmail, or put on an act ourselves to increase that emotion in the situation. "Don't fall for it, because they are based on lies, which has practical consequences. I do not want to sound like a preacher, but they never come out for free."

There is a red line that delimits persuasion, and on the other side are manipulation techniques. The first few times, this line commands respect, and it is difficult to cross it. But when we've crossed it the first time and have fallen into unethical manipulation, the line is blurred even for a legitimate purpose. That way, it is much easier to transfer it again a second time.

Do it a few more times, and the line will be erased, and we will have become one of them.

But it is also that manipulation is not necessary. There is a large amount of material on ethical persuasion to learn; you can use scarcity without isolating or pressing; you can use cognitive dissonance without it being a trap to fleece a victim. Always remember to have ethics, because if there is one thing I have learned, it is that manipulators do not end up well.

ACT QUICKLY

It's great that you have come to terms with the reality of things, but defense against these dark manipulative tactics entail so much more. Attempting to defend yourself from the claws of these manipulators, is often intense and exhilarating at first.

This intensity of these emotions may cause one to slowly slide into denial. The more you delay in taking any action, that is usually what accelerates the onset of this denial, and when it happens, there are high chances that you might relapse and end up getting trapped in the same web.

This can be avoided by taking action immediately when you realize that someone is trying to manipulate you. This can present itself in the simplest of ways, like when informing a close friend of the reality of a particular situation may be all that's needed so set in motion a series of events that will eventually lead to your freedom.

You should know that the fabric of illusion is made from a tougher material than glass after choosing to act. The illusion could work its way back into your heart with your emotions in high gear by using fragments of your emotions to fix it.

When a liar is caught in a lie, he or she may attempt to recruit others to enforce that lie when they feel that they are no longer holding you.

A deceptive partner with whom you have recently broken things off, would at this point try to use the other mutual relationships in your life to change your mind.

If you want to get out of this unscathed, you will need both your logic and instincts. Although the truth of the situation is that when you discover that you've been lied to consistently, you become emotionally scarred, so the issue of leaving the situation unscathed becomes unlikely.

Priority should be given, however, to take the route that allows you to leave this toxic situation without harming yourself further. You're all over the place emotionally.

Rage, anger, hurt, and deception is the tip of the iceberg, but logically, you need to think. Keep your head above the water and warn yourself.

TRUST YOUR INSTINCTS

While your brain interprets signals based on facts, logic, and sometimes experience, your heart works in the opposite direction by screening information through an emotional filter. The only thing that picks up vibrations is your gut instinct, which neither the heart nor the brain can pick on.

If you can groom yourself to the point where you recognize your inner voice and are trained to react to it, you will lower your chances of being seduced by people trying to work on you with their manipulative will.

To begin, it's hard to recognize this voice. That's because we allowed voices of doubt, self-discrimination as well as the critics' loud voices within to be heard and without drawing out our authentic voice throughout our lives.

Your survival depends on this voice or instinct. So, trust that when it kicks in, your brain neurons can still process things in your immediate vicinity.

Some people call it intuition, and some refer to it as instinct, especially when it comes to relationships, they are undoubtedly the same thing. You must accept that it may not always make logical sense to start trusting your instincts.

If you've ever been in the middle of doing something and experienced the feeling of being watched all of a sudden, then you know what I mean. You don't have eyes at the back of your head, there's no one else with you in the room, but you get that tiny shiver running down your spine and the "sudden knowledge" that you're being watched. That's what I'm talking about.

The first step to connect with your instinct is to decode your mind with the voices you've let in. With meditation, you can do this. Forget the chatter of "he said, she said." Concentrate on your center. You are the voice you know. Next, be careful about your thoughts. Don't just throw away the eclectic monologue in your head. Rather go with the flow of thoughts.

Why do you think of a certain person in some way? How do you feel so deeply about this person, even if you only know each other for a few days? What's that nagging feeling about this other person that you have? You get more tuned to your intuition as you explore your thoughts and understand when your instincts kick in and how to react to it.

You may need to learn to take a step back to pause and think if you are the kind of person who prefers to make decisions in the spur of the moment.

This moment in which you pause, allows you to reflect on your decisions and evaluate them. The next part is hard, and it couldn't be followed by many people. Unfortunately, you can't skip or navigate around this step.

This part has to do with trust. You need to be open to the idea of trusting yourself and trusting others to be able to trust your instinct. Your failure to trust others would just make you paranoid, and it's not your instincts that kick in when you're paranoid.

It's the fear in you. Fear tends to turn every molehill into a mountain. You must let go of your fear, embrace confidence, and let that lead in your new relationships.

You are better able to hear the voice inside without the roadblocks put up by fear in your mind. Finally, your priorities need to be reevaluated.

If your mind is at the forefront of money and material possessions, you may not be able to see the past. Any interaction you have with people would be interpreted as people trying to take advantage of you, and if you dwell on that frequently enough, it will soon become your reality.

You attract into your life what you think of. If you're constantly thinking about material wealth, you're only going to attract people who think like you. Using this as a guide, look at all your relationships with this new hindsight; the old, the new, and the prospective.

Don't enter a relationship that expects to be played. Be open when you approach them, whether it's a business relationship, a romantic relationship, or even a regular acquaintance. You can get the right feedback about them from your intuition.

Do not step into this thinking, too, that your gut will tell you to run in the opposite direction when you meet suspect people.

HOW TO CONFRONT A BULLY SAFELY

Not all manipulators resort to bullying, but many of them do. Someone is being a bully when they use intimidation or harm to get what they want from you. Always remember, that a bully chooses people they see as weak to pick on, and compliance and passivity will only strengthen this. However, a lot of bullies are afraid and insecure deep down, so when their victim starts to stand up for themselves, this will often lead the bully to back off. Whether this situation is occurring in a playground or at the office, it applies, most of the time. Keep in mind that many bullies have withstood bullying and violence. Although this doesn't excuse their behaviors, it does help the victim to understand.

YOUR INFLUENCE SKILL SET

CLARITY OF PURPOSE

An important facet of the ability to influence others is your clarity. Know what you want and have a clear plan of how you will get it. Whether you're working in sales and trying to improve the team's quarterly figures or trying to encourage a student to be more diligent with study, or to set them on a career path – know what the objective is. The only way you can succeed in influencing someone to behave in a desired way is if you are clear about what you hope to achieve. You don't get in your car to drive to a destination you've never been without setting the GPS. The same goes for the application of influence toward achieving a desired effect or goal. Know where you're going.

Always be prepared in advance, with the following:

A list of prioritized objectives.

A clear picture of the final destination (what it looks like).

Preparing the environment.

If you are seeking to reach an agreement with someone, you need to make them feel comfortable. You also need to be relaxed and yourself. At the same time, for effective communication (which is important when you want to influence someone's behavior, as this book is explaining) you need to make the environment conducive to your interaction. You need to have in place a planned sequence of events at that meeting beforehand.

The best way to achieve this is to draw up a meeting agenda and circulate it to those who will attend, one day before the meeting. In this way, everyone knows what to expect and what shape the meeting will take. The agenda should make clear what the goals of the meeting are. Checking off the items on it should move you closer to the agreement, if not enable all present to reach consensus to move forward. The logical sequence of events represented by following an agenda is a function of a critically structured plan. Having a plan of such quality never fails to impress.

CONSENSUS BUILDING

In building consensus, you're making it clear you are open to suggestions (which you should always be, regardless of your single-minded focus on your ultimate goal). Hearing what people say and truly listening means you're not planning a response while they're talking. It means you're actively hearing everything they say. Subtext, word choice, and tone are all important and so are your skills at hearing what's being said. Proceeding with these skills in play can provide you with the basis for genuine and not false consensus.

False consensus is reached when people are "heard out", but not "heard". These are two entirely different animals. The first is the condescending indulgence of hearing what no longer matters because a decision has already been made and the results of that decision, imposed. Being heard means that influence on the final decision is still a possibility and that what's offered may result in concessions, if it features actual merit.

Being present to the input of others and being able to integrate their thoughts and suggestions into an existing plan is a function of leadership. Leadership is not imposed. Leadership is extended to others as a service. Consensus building is a way to bring forward the knowledge of the team and add it to your own. In the case of reaching an agreement, it's the foundation of lasting relationships that won't later be ruptured by objections to not being heard. This is extremely important. Autocratic leadership is unwelcome and will not survive for long. It is a corrosive leadership style that is not sustainable.

CREATING RAPPORT

When someone begins to enjoy your company, it becomes much easier for you to enlist their support. This makes it more likely they'll support your viewpoint in situations in which it counts. Allies are people who like and trust you. Your relationships are what will move your goals forward and create a foundation for your success and that of your allies. People, while perhaps not being entirely aware of this on an intellectual level, know this instinctively. That is why you must prioritize establishing rapport with others. It's the basis of strong allegiances.

Part of creating rapport is establishing the common interests you hold with others. Taking an interest in them and offering them information about who you are is how this is achieved. Being too veiled about yourself makes you appear cold, calculating, and detached. Establish that you're open and also, a person who can be trusted.

It's also important to establish easily with others and one way this can be done is to mirror the body language. You'll probably find (if you pay attention), that you do this anyway when you've begun to establish rapport with someone. Mirroring body language sends the unconscious signal that there is a bond already established between two people and that they're on the same team. Mirroring speech patterns is another way of doing this. Repeating keywords with enthusiasm at opportune times is another natural way we tell each other we're enjoying a conversation or agreeing with each other. Nod, smile, and respond positively when you sense a common theme emerging in conversation. This sends the message that you're accessible on the most basic, human level.

SUGGESTIONS INSTEAD OF DEMANDS

People routinely bridle at directives. In Western societies where individualism is a way of life, we like to believe in our autonomy as a value. That means it's not the best course of action to demand things from people. Much more effective is suggesting a course of action and building consensus based on the suggestion while being open to input and concessions to other points of view. This is the democratic way of achieving goals and one that is completely manageable with the application of a deft hand.

Here are examples of language that gives your listener the option to chip in and yet still leaves you the "wiggle room" to get to where you believe you need to go:

"Would you be interested in doing a-b-c?"

"Could you be interested in doing a-b-c?"

"I think we should do a-b-c. What do you think?"

"Do you think this is the best way forward, or do you have other ideas?"

Leaving space for opinion and input, while still advancing the validity of your own opinion is the stuff of which influence is made. While you're providing people with a rationale for your point of view, your willingness to entertain amendments to that point of view only increases your influential power. Imposition rarely ends in anything but resentment. By building consensus through input and exchange, you will still arrive at the goal you have in mind, but you'll do it with the support of a willing team, signed on to the plan in question. A fringe benefit? That input will undoubtedly improve on the original plan and will result in satisfaction on the part of all involved.

HEIGHTENING YOUR AWARENESS

Awareness of the responses of other people to what you're saying is key to influential action. What are their facial expressions telling you? Their body language and word choices? What about tone and pitch? All these factors are rich with information that you can draw on to temper your pitch and get people on your side. It can also cue you to back off and change lanes, while you re-group and allow others their input.

Active listening, while employing body language (head nodding, eye contact) and assenting noises ("uh-huh", "yes", "I see") is also about deeply engaging with what's being said and the complimentary messages being sent by the speaker. Your awareness in crucial situations, of all the factors that create a communicative environment, is of the utmost importance. You need to be aware, not only of what's being said but implications about what's intended, what's not being said, and the speaker's frame of mind. All these factors work together to form a more concise body of information from which you may draw to apply influential action.

WHAT TO DO IN CASE OF MANIPULATION?

You must also be aware that the manipulator will never change because he does not do it for a specific logical reason that has a right place in real life.He does it because he needs it and this need is dictated by his personality, along with his dark and problematic psychological state; in practice if he does it today then tomorrow he will start looking for reasons to go back to doing it again and again and again and again.

For this reason, a good way to escape manipulation is to remove the manipulator, be it a partner or an employer, a neighbor, or an acquaintance. When this is not possible because there is coexistence with this individual, then we must defend ourselves and a good way to do this is to be aware, as I said before, of the way the manipulator operates and to establish a virtual border between the manipulator and manipulated so that the latter does not feel responsible for all the problems that arise from this "coexistence". In other words, you have to ignore it!

To defend yourself from manipulation you also need to be able to recognize and manage your emotions and your body to understand and accept when you are being manipulated and the traumas that have been suffered. To practice advice on how to defend yourself from manipulation, you must first be able to accept it. Dark manipulation is defined so, primarily, because it is a weapon generally used by psychologically problematic subjects and believe me you can meet one more frequently than you can imagine. Secondly, it is called so because it is manipulation that has purposes that are not enough to be definedas negatives as they are subtle.

HOW TO AVOID BEING NEGATIVELY MANIPULATED BY OTHERS

Be aware of your rights: The absolute most important rule you can follow when dealing with someone who wants to manipulate you in negative ways, is to know your worth and rights. This way, you will always know when someone is attempting to violate them. So long as others are not getting harmed in the process, you should be defending yourself. Every human should have the right to have differing opinions from others, to protect yourself, to say "no" when you need to, and to decide what's important to you. You should also have the right of expressing your wants, opinions, and feelings, and always be treated with respect.

Unfortunately, the world has plenty of people who won't want to acknowledge or respect your rights, especially negative manipulators. You will also come into contact with others who generally wish to take advantage of any opportunity. However, you can proudly defy this by letting them know that you are the one who runs your life, no one else.

Maintain healthy distance: Another way to tell who is manipulative, is to pay attention to the way someone acts in varying situations and in front of various individuals. Although everyone, to a degree, puts on different faces depending on where they are, most people who are harmfully manipulative are extreme about it. They might, for example, be extremely polite and friendly to one person, and completely disrespect another, or act like a victim one second, and then act controlling immediately after.

If you notice someone acting this way regularly, it's a good sign to distance yourself from them and not engage with them unless it's an absolute necessity. Usually, the reasons behind these types of behavior are complicated, and it isn't your duty or responsibility to help or change that person. Trying to do so will often only lead to

331

suffering on your part, so it's better not to expect much when you notice these signs.

Don't blame yourself: A person who wishes to manipulate others in harmful ways searches for weaknesses to exploit, so it makes sense that someone who has been victimized by one might blame themselves or feel inadequate. But in a situation like this, you should remember that it isn't you that's the issue here; you are being pressured to feel bad by someone else who is very good at making people feel bad.

This is how they get their way. Instead, think about the relationship you have with this person and ask yourself if they are respecting you, demanding reasonable things from you, and whether you are both benefiting, or only one of you is. Ask yourself, also, if you feel good about yourself after spending time with this person, or if you would feel better being around them less. The way you answer these questions will lead to important answers about where the issue lies in the situation.

Questioning them: Eventually, this type of person will demand or request things from you. Many times, these requests or others will consider their needs, while completely ignoring yours. Next time you receive a solicitation that is completely unreasonable, turn the focus back to them by asking some questions. Ask them if their request is reasonable, or if what they are asking from you is fair. You can also try asking if you get to have an opinion in this matter or ask what benefit you will be gaining from the arrangement.

Each time you ask questions like this, you are holding a mirror up to them, allowing them to see what they are truly asking of you. If they are self-aware, they will likely retract their request or demand. But there may be some cases, such as dealing with a narcissist, who will keep insisting without even considering your questions. If that happens, follow these guidelines.

Don't answer Immediately: One way to combat manipulation is to use time as a resource. Often, the manipulator will not only ask you to fulfill an unreasonable demand, but they will want an answer immediately. When this happens, rather than answering right away, use time and distance yourself from their request and influence. This can be done by telling them that you will think about it. Although these words are simple, they give your power back to you, giving you the option to weigh the advantages and disadvantages of the situation and let you work out something better, if need be.

Teach yourself to say "no" when needed: Saying "no" is difficult for many people, since we are often taught and conditioned to be polite whenever possible. Being able to confidently but politely say "no" comes with learning communication skills. When this is articulated effectively, you can hold onto your self-respect, and also continue a healthy relationship. Keep in mind that your rights include deciding what matters to you, being able to turn down a request free from guilt and choosing health and happiness for yourself. You are responsible for your life, not the person who is making unreasonable demands of you.

Create a consequence: Next time a negative manipulator tries to violate your rights, and refuses to accept your answer, set a consequence for their behavior. Knowing how to assert and identify appropriate consequences is a crucial skill for standing down someone who is being very difficult or disrespectful. If you can articulate this clearly and thoroughly, your consequences will cause them to pause and stop violating you, shifting to a position of respect.

Chapter 12:

Protecting Yourself From Manipulation

STRATEGIES FOR PROTECTION AGAINST MANIPULATION

We all love pursuing the other sex every now and then-both men and women. It's fun and a good sport, as long as we're frank about it and bear in mind that it's all about passion. Why? For what? Since it's deceit to try and love cannot be exploited-we don't find love; love finds us. So, we should view a relationship of love as sacred ground.

Sadly, many people believe in deception – both in relationships and in industry. In my early twenties, I read something that stuck for good in my subconsciousness: if you can align yourself with the universe, it's easy to achieve success. What does this mean for this topic? It means manipulations are pointless at the end of the day. Manipulations may potentially offer a short-term benefit, but in the long run, it will eventually lead to consequences as they are opposed by the universe. But if we go with the celestial wind, we'll gravitate toward our target – more or less effortlessly. Too good to be real? Every one of us is playing a part in the cosmic game. In the grand scheme of things, we just have to know our position and let it play out. And Jesus said his cross is as light as a feather. Of course, this means giving up several wishes and aspirations that aren't part of our cameo.However, our celestial intent typically turns out to be much more grandiose than our puny, selfish ambitions.

That being said, we also need to defend ourselves from other people's childish manipulations, including those around us. Don't take this lightly; it's painful, emotional coercion and can leave deep wounds on people's psyche and soul.Once you are in a state of exploitation, it is very difficult to get out. But don't take this affair too seriously, we're doing a lot of things subconsciously, and your partner may not even know that she's manipulating you.

There will always be people trying to shake your trust - people trying to instill seeds of self-doubt inside you. Such people would do their utmost to trick you into thinking that their beliefs are objective facts. They're trying to tell you everyone in the world thinks you're rude, nuts, or not nice. Then they'll tell you how much they're worried about you, how you're living your life, spending your money, raising your children, on and on.

If you don't change the way they want you to change, then your life will be destroyed. This is what they want to believe. The truth isyou don't want to help these people. They want to get you under control. We want you to adjust, not to make your life easier, but to affirm their lives and prevent you from overgrowing them.

DON'T GET ANGRY

Manipulative people are not preoccupied with your needs. They worry about their interests. Once you allow manipulative people in your life, it can be extremely difficult to get rid of them. The trick is to have enough self-control to send the boot to dishonest people as soon as you see them. Here are a few ways to get rid of manipulative people from your life:

LISTEN TO YOUR EMOTIONS

when something is wrong, the body sends translatable signals into a sense of general malaise. It is always good to listen to these subliminal messages and try to understand what's wrong.

CHANGE YOUR POINT OF VIEW

If you happen to be in a situation where you feel the stench of manipulation, pretend to be a third person who "observes from outside" what is happening. This is because often we get involved in feelings and we don't judge things for what they are. By following this advice, you can give an objective assessment of the situation.

MAKE IT A REASON

This is easy to understand. You have to understand that manipulation is part of life, such as luck or the sun rising in the morning and setting in the evening. It is something that exists and for which you cannot do anything. On the contrary, you can try to improve and develop your positive side, this will help you a lot.

As for the tactics to be used to defend against a manipulator, having unmasked it, we can say that it will be useful to follow one or more of those listed below:

EXPRESS WHAT YOU DISAGREE WITH

This is because the manipulator criticizes everything, or almost everything, and consequently the victim tries to defend himself in every way to deny it, becoming more and more aggressive (in this case he falls completely into the trap). In this case, the victim only has to express his point of view clearly, calmly, and simply to make the manipulator understand that whatever he says, he will not be able to change his opinion in the least. This will strongly destabilize the manipulator.

ALWAYS SPEAK IN THE FIRST PERSON

Following this simple advice and pretending that the manipulator does the same is important. Many times, the manipulator speaks in third person and remains very vague in expressing his concepts and attacking someone. They never do it directly. This is because his game is to put others in a bad light so that they cannot be accused, because they don't want to "get their hands dirty".

So if you put your back against the wall with phrases like "what do you think of this person" or "what is your opinion on this situation", you are obliged to express yourself directly and take responsibility for it and maybe, feeling "hunted" will make the manipulator take a step back in their path of manipulation.

ACCEPT YOUR MISTAKES

It seems strange but actually, it is an excellent defense strategy, as the manipulator often focuses on feelings of guilt.They do so by trying to steal the victim's secrets, simple facts, or events, even if they are not necessarily serious, and makes sure that they turn against him making her "feel guilty". This applies both to things that happened in the past, to things that happen in the present, and also to things that could happen in the future.

One strategy to annihilate this type of manipulation is to be able to recognize our mistakes if there have been any. At the same time,we should be able to outline our responsibilities, because if it is true that we have made mistakes, it is also true that we cannot take the blame for everythingforever. For example, if a person blames us for our wrong behavior, we can respond by saying sentences like "yes, I made this mistake, but what you say does not concern me", in this case we assume our responsibilities but at the same time we make it clear that in addition to this we are not available to submit to anything else, which makes us appear mature and consequently, not easily manipulated.

SPEAK CALMLY

As mentioned several times in this book, the manipulator prefers emotionally fragile people because he loves to attack the victim's emotions and does not care at all about having a constructive dialogue. By virtue of this, the mistake that many make is that of counterattacking the provocations of the manipulator, which for clarity, is a normal instinctive reaction but in these cases, it is not the right one as he will continue to argueagainst the victim. It seems absurd but the manipulator is very capable of doing all this. In this case, the defense strategy to be adopted is extremely simple, one only has to recognize that his criticisms are right, never contradict him, and at the same time one must take the right distances in this regard. In practice we can say that you have to make fun of it a bit, using phrases like "I understand your point of view, but I think it's better   than   ..."
A trick that can help you can replace the term "but" with words like "despite", "nevertheless" "anyway" which according to NLP scholars, would have a "sweeter" but still effective impact.

STRONGLY DENY

When we are confident that what we say is true and we are emotionally strong people, we can also take a more impervious path to defend ourselves from a manipulator and we can deny what he is proposing to us. A dry and firm NO without the use of banal and twisted explanations, perhaps accompanied by an authoritarian body language, will be a good method to desist the manipulator.

Behavioral tone: Having a good behavioral tone is fundamental. It is very similar to a person's emotional intensity, and it is the intensity of one's actions. Don't get the wrong idea because you don't have to scare anyone, it's just about wearing a safe and decisive cover to look like a strong person. If you have or manifest this type of personality, then you will have a good chance that everyone will listen to you because, as the saying goes, actions speak louder than words. This is a good way to be both persuasive and manipulative, so it can also be used as a defense weapon to show the manipulator that you have a strong personality like him and therefore, you are difficult to manipulate.

These tips on how to defend yourself from a manipulator can be applied in multiple cases of manipulation, whether you are dealing with sellers, friends, relatives, employers, people who belong to the religious world, or partners because they are based on the reasoning principles of the manipulator itself and how it works. Keep in mind that manipulative people tend to mask their interests by pretending to help you and then force you to change.It is not to improve your life but so that they can use you, by saying that their opinions, as well as the facts, are the best and yours don't count. They will attract any form of attention and take credit in places where they don't deserve it and will do everything, they canto make sure they keep you from escaping. It is worth noting that once they are established in your life, they are difficult to eliminate. This is why I want to remind you again that the best way to defend yourself from manipulation, as many scholars and authorities in the field say, is to escape from it and the manipulator. You only have to deal with it if it is strictly necessary because dealing with a manipulator can become dangerous. In any case, whatever the decision you make, always ask an external person for help, even better if they are qualified.

DON'T FALL INTO THEIR TRAP

Most of us come across instances where others seek to manipulate our thoughts, attitudes, or actions and take advantage of them to their advantage. In one such case, you fail to understand the true motive. The person mentally dominates you, and you step into the pit. Often this emotional abuse costs you a lot when you make some critical decisions under another person's control, and you only realize when it is too late.

You have to be cautious when a relationship sounds too good to be true. They are showering you with compassion, gratitude, admiration, congratulations, and affection. You feel like you live in a dream where everything seems perfect. They don't give you a reason to worry. You simply cannot find any flaws in them. Also, if anything goes wrong, they can begin to weep or feel sorry. You can become the object of extreme intimacy and have passion for the fairy tale.

Because you began the relationship with love bombing, all of a sudden you start feeling ignored. You are receiving gratitude, presents, and recognition, but rarely. You feel like you're losing your grip or want someone else in your life. You get another gift from them, the moment you make up your mind to move on, making the decision difficult. They are trying to get leverage over you in situations like these. For most instances, amazingly, this works, and you end up going back to them

Individuals often succeed in manipulating their victims after intermittent reinforcement. We can avoid behaving in the same way while fighting back or by demanding an answer. The explanation is that they are taking complete care of you now, so there is no need for intermittent strengthening because we no longer need it. Manipulators have many different faces, and in the same manner, they can use many ways to get things done. The person may make a plan, and later deny it, so that you begin to doubt your perception. They make you feel bad when you try to make them aware of their promise. They can employ shallow sympathy and burst into crocodile tears. Eventually, you end up trusting them and even doubting whether you listened correctly.

You can't believe the smiling faces that seem confident and strong are the same manipulative people, that often have self-serving prejudices, so they think less ofother person's feelings. They have a reason to look for others who affirm them and make them even feel superior.

STEER STRAIGHT WHEREVER POSSIBLE

A manipulator's actions typically vary according to the situation they're in. For instance, a manipulator may speak rudely to one person, and act respectfully towards another the next moment. When you see these extremes frequently in a person, it would be advisable to stay away from them. And you have to communicate with this guy. That will prevent you from becoming a deceptive victim.

One way to identify a manipulator is to see how a person is behaving in different circumstances and before different people. Although we all have a sense of this sort of social distinction, some psychological manipulators seem to dwell in extremes habitually, being highly polite to one person, and gross to another - or helpless at one moment, and fiercely violent at another. If you frequently experience this form of behavior from an adult, keep a healthy distance away, and avoid interacting with the person unless you have to. As described earlier, there are nuanced and deep-seated causes for persistent psychological abuse. Saving them is not your job.

There are some circumstances in which you can't fully leave a relationship-usually when that person is a parent or an extended family member. You probably cannot go cold turkey unless the individual causes serious harm or psychological damage. Next, you need to accept this person completely for who they are and change your relationship standards accordingly. If they were someone you needed validation from before, then you would have to quit looking for their validation. Recognize that their advice is not something you need in your life. When they keep offering it, you can thank them for it, and then politely dump it. When setting these limits, be as discreet as you can, and do not tell the other person you are setting them apart. Creating this shift at your end will take some time, and when you get upset with the other person in the process, you will have to deal with their reaction on top of that.

Knowing this will drain your energy a little bit, set limits around the time you spend with that person. If you've been hanging out every Saturday with your manipulating mother-in-law, cut it down to once a month and plan something for that day so that there is a definite end time for your hangout.

CALL THEM OUT ON THEIR ACTIONS

Manipulators are always difficult to deal with, but the worst arediscreet manipulators. They will stay cool as a cucumber when confronted, and yet rigid and unbending. You may start to get frustrated when you start seeing their faulty reasoning. When you keep fighting with them, you'll find it hard not to raise your voice a bit. You will start looking like the irrational one, and they will try to take back control in remaining calm, based on their "maturity."

Defending yourself is tempting and trying to get the other person to see what is going on. But a true manipulator will not change their tune, and the more you give in to that urge to protect yourself, the more they will twist your words more. It will not be long before you get stuck in this twisted web of myths and false expectations. If you are in a situation with a true manipulator, the two goals for any conflict that is taking place should be to resolve and leave, whether that means leaving the current conversation or exiting the relationship. Avoid threats, accusations, losing patience, accusing the other person of coercion, or become excessively emotional. Stick to honest, factual, and respectful declarations when you speak.

Some things require a high degree of intelligence, flexibility, or self-discipline when dealing with a manipulative person. You might not have the self-control to react without losing your temper and making things worse. If that's the case, accept this about yourself and take extra steps to avoid a tense confrontation (invite a mediator into the conversation, for example, or send an email instead of meeting in person, so you have time to think through what you say).

For me, it can cause a bit of tension to deal with someone who loses their temper. I needed to have a friend with me to feel secure in circumstances where there were a lot of blow-up risks. However, much as I wished I could handle the conflict myself, I realized that I wasn't quite in a position to do so. I would have felt a lot of needless discomforts if I had failed to acknowledge this about myself because of my decision to act better than I was. Wouldn't you be better at handling the problem than you are? Others will be attacking the vulnerable points and trying to make it seem like the problem will be easier for you to deal with than it is. Do not equate your reaction to someone else's reaction in one case.

IGNORE WHAT THEY DO AND SAY

It is intended to ignore the dishonest men. These people flip flop over things, they're slippery when you try to keep them accountable, they promise support that never comes, they're always making you feel guiltyeverything you don't want in person. The greatest mistake you can make when dealing with a dishonest person is trying to correct him or her. You sink deeper into their pit, by correcting them. Humans will use anger and misunderstanding to lure you into a confrontation. We want to make you feel nervous so that they can see how you tick. When they learn the triggering factors, you will use them to affect your actions. A smarter approach is to ignore them entirely. Only erase them from your life if you can't delete them instantly-even if they're a supervisor, coworker, or member of the family and then carry on doing your own thing anyway.

TOUCH THEIR CENTRE OF GRAVITY

Manipulative people actively take advantage of their tactics against you. Through your enemies, they will become enemies, and turn them against you. They will dangle some small reward in front of you and make you chase it relentlessly-they're going to take it away any time you get close to it. You will forever keep past acts up against you and on and on. Avoid letting those who exploit you, by using their tactics against you. Switch the tables instead. Build your plan and hit them where it hurts. When you are forced to deal with a dishonest person who, no matter how hard you try to avoid them, tries to make your life miserable, your only choice is to find their center of gravity and destroy it. This center may be associates, followers, or subordinates to the deceptive individual. It may be a high-level talent or advanced knowledge of a particular area. They can manage it as a particular resource.

Figure out what their center of gravity is and make it yours anyway. Creating alliances with those close to them, hiring people to replace them with their skill sets and knowledge base, or siphoning away their precious assets. This will throw them off balance and push them to concentrate on managing their life, not yours.

BELIEVE IN YOUR DECISION

You know better than anyone else what is best for your future. Many people are going around asking for the views of other people on anything. "What do I want to do with my life?""What am I fantastic at?""Where am I, then?", avoid searching for other people's validationand describe it yourself. Define yourself. Believe in yourself. What distinguishes winners from losers is not the ability to listen to other people's opinions; it's the ability to listen to one's own opinions. You prevent dishonest people from influencing your life by setting up your values and keeping them tightly onto them. This will serve as a firewall to your convictions, keeping manipulators ostracized and out of your way.

TRY NOT TO FIT RIGHT IN

Keep reinventing yourself. One myth is the belief that continuity is somehow admirable or related to achievement. Manipulative people want you to be consistent so that they can count on you to advance their agendas. They want you to show up at 9 am every day and work at minimum wage for them. We want you to come home on time and make them feel good about themselves and clean the house. Consistent assembly lines. The prison is uniform. Consistency is how they trap you in a shell. It's their way of manipulating you. The only way to stop being exploited is by consciously going against all the barriers other people seek to create for you. Let go of trying to blend in. Instead, lookto stand out. Act different in some way, and never remain the same for too long. By design, personal growth needs a lack of consistency. Constant change is expected to achieve constant reinvention.

AVOID CONCESSION

Guilt is an emotion of no use, but this is a powerful tool. Guilt is one of those weapons that would be used against you by dishonest men. They will make you feel bad for past defeats and small mistakes, or they will make you feel guilty for being overconfident and prideful. They'll use it against you if you spend time feeling happy or sure of yourself. One will never feel too good about themselves; they would claim. Another tool that is being used against you by manipulators is doubt. They will work to instill within you a sense of self-doubt-doubts about your ability and your worth. Their ultimate goal is to take you off balance and make you second guess yourself. Within this state of confusion, manipulators gain control. Their power is getting greater and they are twice as likely to convince you to compromise on your principles, ambitions, and yourself.

Simple solution-avoid feeling guilty. When it comes to your own life, you owe nothing to anyone. You deserve to feel good about yourself and to be stunned by your achievements. You deserve to have a good sense of confidence and self-belief in what you do. It is neither moral nor enlightened to compromise on either of these issues. This is then the path to self-destruction.

NEVER ASK FOR PERMISSION

Asking for forgiveness is better than asking for permission. The problem is that we have been conditioned to ask for permission constantly. As a boy, we had to ask for everything we wanted — to be fed, changed, and burped. We had to ask permission to go to the bathroom, and we had to wait to eat lunch at a designated time and wait for our turn to play with toys. As a result, most people expect to seek permission.

Employees around the world are waiting for a promotion and waiting for their turn to talk. Most are so used to being chosen that they sit in meetings in silence, afraid to talk out of turn or even lift their hands. It's a different way of living.

What if you did it what you wanted to, whenever you want? And what if you quit being too worried about politeness and feel relaxed with others? What if, instead, you live your life exactly the way you want to live it? These are all things you can do whenever you want.

Manipulative people want you to feel constrained by some abstract law or principle that says you can't behave freely without consulting an authority figure or a party. The reality is that at any given moment, you can miss this feeling of confinement. You will continue living a completely different life today than you lived yesterday. Your decision is yours.

BUILD A GREATER SENSE OF MISSION

Destiny driven people aren't easily fooled. The reason manipulators in this world tend to prosper is that so many people lead a purposeless life. If there is no reason in your life, you cannot believe anything. They will do anything. Because, somehow, nothing matters. People who lack intent waste time. There is no rhyme or explanation behind how they live their lives. We don't know where to go, or why they are here. They remain busy to avoid the desperate feeling of emptiness growing inside them. This profession and loneliness empower deceptive individuals. Every minute, a sucker is born. When you are constantly distracted, consuming pointless stuff, trying to stay busy-you are the sucker. By peddling meaningless knowledge and events, manipulators manipulate purposeless people. The only way to escape this, is by cultivating a sense of destiny. Destiny is doing away with distraction. The manipulators can't hurt you because you think for yourself. They cannot confuse you or lead you astray.

TAKE NEW OPPORTUNITIES

The universe wants to put your eggs in one bowl. People all around you ask you to lock yourself in on decisions such as a mortgage, a car payment, a secure relationship, a single position at the office. They want you staked down to a single choice for the rest of your life. Nowadays, it is also looked down upon for being optimistic. Staying hungry is also seen as a sign of weakness. Why can't you just be happy with what you have? Why should you be so greedy? If you show a desire for more, this is what dishonest people would ask you. They will call you vain, greedy, prideful. They'll make you feel cold and uncomfortable like you're heartless and inhumane. The reality is that they want to keep you in your place. They want you to stay at the same job and spend the rest of your life living in the same place. They want you and the structures they control to remain dependent upon them.

The only way to stay autonomous is to look for new possibilities and build new ones actively. Continue applying for new jobs, continue to start at new companies, developing new partnerships, and seeking new experiences.

AVOID BEING AN INFANT

When you get fooled by someone, shame on them. When you're fooled by someone ten times, you're an idiot. Avoid letting manipulators walk all over you. Nobody feels sorry for you, and you're always being humiliated. Have enough self-consciousness and reverence for yourself to say no to dishonest men.

You cannot just walk around life, blaming the troubles on others. You cannot simply walk away from the people trying to control you, either. Yes, some people are negative and manipulative. And yes, these people will try to use you. Yet, that doesn't mean that you have a free pass to make mistakes. Without your permission, no-one can control you. You are to blame for your achievements and defeats. If others outstrip you, it's your fault, not theirs, so be smart. Learn from your wrongs. You don't want to fall victim to the same slippery person again and again. Slice them free. Remove them from your life. Commit to connecting yourself with like-minded people who will not be exploiting you.

BETTING ON YOURSELF

Take a gamble on the one thing in life that you can control yourself. Too many people restrict themselves to considering only external factors when making difficult decisions. They consider the financial consequences of a situation and its relationships. Yet they fail to acknowledge the impact on their satisfaction and sense of self-worth their choice would have. As a result, when they should be taking chances on themselves, they take chances on other people. Then, they wonder why they are unhappy.

If you just take chances on strangers and things, you put yourself at the mercy of those people and things. It makes you weak and ready to be exploited. You should take chances on yourself instead. In any tough situation you find yourself facing, don't ask questions like, "Who's the right one to side with?" or "What choice would be more likely to succeed?" rather, say, "What am I most likely to do?" so go out and do that. For example, if you face an opportunity to start your own company or keep working at the same dead-end job, don't keep the job just because the pay is stable. Don't just leave because the relationships are slightly unpleasant. You are betting on external factors when you do so, which is a mistake. Betting on yourself is a safer plan. You would never regret making a bet on yourself. You will, of course, have to take full responsibility for any mistakes that you make. Sure, you need to stick to a higher standard. Yet you, too, must be solely responsible for your victories. You will continue to rise and achieve greater and higher rates of success.

STOP GETTING EMOTIONALLY ATTACHED TO THEM

All you do with a manipulator is fake. Every fight you have been through is your fault. Manipulation will wreak havoc on your feelings. You go from crying to being furious in a short period of time, then to feeling guilty and indignant. Then you feelsorry you did not stick up for yourself. You are ashamed to let them do that to you again, and your emotions are more stable once you've left a manipulator. Life is a journey into an adventure. On the way, many people come to give us company at various times, for a certain amount of time and leave after they play their part in our lives. There is no problem with the people coming and going, but the difficulties occur when you are emotionally attached to the people and feel powerless, tense, and worried when the relationship ends, especially with an emotional manipulator. Therefore, if you want to stay healthy and make progress in life, you need to resolve the emotional connection as soon as possible. There is no doubt that some individuals will become the driving force for you to move towards the path you have chosen but when being separated from them, you should be careful not to get distracted. You need to make judicious use of the relationships. Be attached to individuals with a detached approach and take care of them to create a confident atmosphere. However, when you push them out of your life for being a manipulator with another relationship waiting for you, do not be dependent on that person for your growth by stopping your life. You need to re-focus on your journey, leaving behind memories. Handling emotional connection measures the degree of sophistication of one's journey down the desired direction, and its gravity. Treat yourself to the moments you share with friends. Learn from them, love them, and look after them, but don't make them your walking sticks. Much of the time, people are usually afraid to lose anyone because of their incapacity to go on in life alone. So, if you dare walk alone on the chosen path, you no longer have to be dependent on emotional connections.

INSPIRING THEM

Using all the experience you've acquired to become your best self, help others to become their best. If you are having trouble improving their behavior, work with a counselor. It can be very difficult to change their behavior, and you may not be able to do it on your own. A psychologist or therapist may help him recognize habits that need to be altered and discuss the feelings that are behind him. These will also help him develop new, healthy behaviors.

TELL THEM "YOU'RE OK."

This begins with you not responding to their techniques anymore. If you don't want to something, you say "no," or you speak your mind even though they don't like it. Work on feeling okay with how negatively they may react. When they're not yours, don't pick them up.

You can only keep your act under control. That's crucial because you won't be able to alter a manipulator's behavior, however, you can avoid being their victim. That happens when you start saying, "no." The first step in breaking the cycle is to recognize that they manipulate us because we allow it and do not refuse to be manipulated. Manipulators are good at what they do, so watch out for their reaction. You would probably say or do things that tug at the heartstrings. Stand firm in saying "no," realizing we are taking the first step to free ourselves from their power.

LET GO OF NASTY RELATIONSHIPS

Toxic partnerships can be hard to let go of. Many people find themselves caught in a cycle of returning to relationships that are not good for them. This just creates a cycle of hurt and grief. Toxic relationships can be let go of. Psychologists have worked with people who have had this issue to be able to write a whole handbook about it. The very first step to getting out of a toxic relationship is admitting to yourself that the relationship isn't perfect. You can try and note down explanations of the sign indicating a toxic relationship. It's called 'cognitive dissonance' if you notice that uncomfortable feeling in the back of your mind, and it's your brain trying to protect you from what you know is true. Take note of the things that make you feel this way in a relationship. The first step is to recognize that your relationship is toxic. You have to be conscious of all the things that affect you before you can truly be free.

Relationships are a side lane. Two people are involved in the relationship, meaning that two people are involved in all the disagreements, arguments, and behavior. You cannot fully take the blame yourself. If you blame yourself for all of the relationship problems, you'll find yourself going back to trying to fix them. Recognize that both parties are sometimes at fault for a dysfunctional relationship. Recognize your responsibilities, but your responsibilities alone. Within a toxic relationship, you don't need to be concernedwith anyone else's issues. There's no need to hoist it on yourself because you aren't to blame.

Some of the best things you can do while trying to let go of a controlling partner is to cut off communication. Keeping in touch would just make letting go harder. This involves seeking outtoxic people that are no longer in your life by scrolling through their social media or questioning how they are doing through mutual friends. You should still follow your intuition when it comes to cutting people out of your life, according to Sarah Newman, M.A. Although it may sound drastic, Newman advises loosening the bonds when it comes to a toxic relationship. You need to be in a position to move on, where you can feel optimistic about the lack of touch, rather than pain.

Mariana Bockarova, Ph.D., says that closure is one of the best things to move on from a manipulative and broken relationship. Bockarova understands that closure will help people reconstruct their whole lives safely and positively. Thus, one way to help you let go of a toxic relationship is to find closure. Healing comes from inside for many people by considering all the ways the relationship went wrong in the first place. Writing one more letter or making the other party recognize the toxicity will provide closure for some. Whatever it is, the closure might help you move on.

The most important thing in quitting and letting go of an abusive relationship is having someone there to catch you if you fall. It can be unsettling to let go, especially if it is a long-term one. Keep in contact with friends and relatives who will support you through the more stressful moments. This will also help to keep you accountable when it comes to not reaching out those you've cut off. Aid networks are essential in allowing dysfunctional partnerships to go away. Don't fear reaching out to people who love you the most.

DEVELOP A STRONG MINDSET

Although one toxic person may use coercion and lies, another may have recourse to intimidation and incivility. If you're not careful, it can take a serious toll on your life because of people like this. Nevertheless, mentally healthy people deal skillfully with manipulative people. They refuse to give away their strength, and no matter who surrounds them, they continue to be their best self.

Putting a label on emotions reduces their intensity. So, whether you feel sad, nervous, frustrated, or afraid, confess it — at least to yourself. Pay attention also to how those emotions can affect your choices. You can be less likely to take chances when you are feeling nervous. You may get more impulsive when you're excited. Increasing the understanding of the feelings will reduce the risk that you will make emotionally driven, unreasonable decisions.

Listing your emotions is just part of the fight — you need skills to control your emotions as well. Think of your current abilities to cope. Should you eat something when you're nervous? Should you drink to keep yourself calm? When you're mad, will you show it to your friends? If you're anxious, will you stay at home? These conventional strategies can make you feel better right now, but they will make you feel worse in the long run. Search for long-term coping strategies that are perfect for you. Keep in mind that what works for one person doesn't always work for another, and you need to figure out what's best for you to manage your emotions. Experimenting with various coping mechanisms to figure out what works for you, deep breathing, exercising, meditating, reading, painting, and spending time in nature are only a few techniques that could help.

The way you think has an impact on how you feel and how you behave. You are deprived of intellectual energy by saying things like, "I can't take this," or "I'm such an idiot." Pay attention to what you think. You'll probably note recurring trends and themes. Maybe you're telling yourself things you feel uncomfortable about doing. Or maybe you're telling yourself you're not in control of your life.

Respond with something more constructive to the unproductive and unreasonable feelings. Instead of saying, "I'm going to screw this up," think, "This is my chance to shine, and I'm going to do my best." Changing the interactions you're having with yourself can be the most instrumental thing you can do to improve your existence. Changing your attitude is the only way to teach your brain to think differently. Do tough things — and keep doing them even though you don't think you should. You will be demonstrating to yourself that you are stronger than you think. Set up healthy daily habits too. Practice appreciation, exercise, get plenty of sleep and follow a balanced diet for the brain and body to be at its best. Seek out individuals who inspire you to be your best and create an atmosphere that helps you develop a balanced lifestyle.

Many positive habits won't work if you practice them alongside your bad habits. It is like eating donuts on a treadmill while you're running. Pay attention to your bad habits (we all have them) that rob you of the mental strength. Whether you feel bad for yourself or envy the success of other people, it takes only one or two to keep you stuck in life. Once you realize your bad habits, spend your energy replacing them with healthier alternatives. You will then be able to step out of the hamster wheel and actively work towards your goals.

Just as it takes time and practice to become physically strong, it takes dedication to build mental strength. The key to feeling your best and reaching your most significant potential is to build mental muscle.

GIVE YOURSELF CONSTRUCTIVE SELF-APPRAISAL ALL DAY LONG

An emotional manipulator will tarnish your mood, so make sure you restore yourself during the day with uplifting self-talks. Each of us has a set of messages that keep playing in our minds over and over. Our responses to life and its circumstances are represented by this internal dialog or personal commentary. One way to recognize, encourage, and maintain optimism, hope, and happiness is to fill our minds with optimistic self-talking consciously. Far too often, because of our manipulative partner, the self-talk pattern that we have formed is negative. We recall the derogatory things our friends, parents, siblings, or teachers told us as children. We remember other children's adverse reactions, which undermined the way we felt about ourselves. Such messages have been playing in our minds over the years, strengthening our feelings of rage, fear, guilt, and hopelessness.

Some of the most important approaches used in dealing with those suffering from depression are to determine the root of these messages and to work with the individual to "overwrite" them deliberately. If a person learned he was worthless as a child, we'd show him how special he is. If a person has learned to expect disasters and catastrophic events while growing up, we will teach her a better way to predict the future. Check the exercise below. Within your head, write down some of the negative thoughts that hinder your desire to resolve your circumstance. Whenever possible, be precise, and include everyone you know who contributed to it. Now, take a moment to consciously combat the negative messages in your life with constructive truths. Don't give up when you're not quick to find them, because thereare always truths for every negative message which will help override them. So keep looking until you find them. You can get a negative message replaying in your mind if you make a mistake. You might have been told as a child, "You're never going to amount to anything," or "You can't do anything right." When you make a mistake, and you will because we all do - you can choose to overwrite that message with a positive one, such as "I choose to accept and grow from my mistake" or "As I learn from my mistakes, I become a better person." Good self-conversation isn't self-deception. It's not looking at circumstances through rose tinted glasses, instead, it is about acknowledging the truth in situations and within you. One of the fundamental truths is that you will be making mistakes. It is unfair to expect perfection in yourself or someone else. It's also unrealistic to expect no difficulties in life, whether by your actions or by pure circumstances.

When adverse events or mistakes occur, positive self-talk is aimed at bringing the positive out of the negative to help you do better, go further, or simply move forward. The practice of constructive self-talk is also the mechanism that helps you to discover in any given situation the hidden happiness, hope, and joy.

STAY OBSERVANT

If you know that you are a target, you must be observant at all times. In other words, we all need to stay observant. Everybody is a prime target of manipulation. People will come to you to take advantage of your situation. Staying observant means that you can look at people and read their intentions. As we have observed, NLP professionals will use their extraction techniques to try and gauge our thoughts and beliefs. If you wish to stop those individuals from controlling your life and thinking process, you must stay aware. Always try to remember that there is someone out there who may be looking to take control of your thoughts.

BE SECRETIVE

Do not be a person who gives out your information to everyone. A manipulative person can only control you if they know something about you. If the manipulator does not have any information about you, they may not have any valid reasons to control your life. If you want to stay on your feet and stop all the people who come to your life to control you, you must learn to stop them by blocking their quest to gain knowledge about your life.

LEARN TO CONTROL YOUR EMOTIONS

NLP experts do not need you to speak for them to gather information. NLP experts rely more on the emotional clues that you send out during conversations. You must learn how to control your expressive and physiological aspects of emotions. The physiological aspects of emotion include the bodily changes that take place when you are emotional. For instance, the sweating of hands when you are anxious or afraid. Such physiological changes may sell you out to the person who wants to get more information to manipulate you. The expressive aspect of emotions includes bodily actions that you display when you are emotional. A good example would be running away when you are afraid. Although you may choose to stay, the actions of running away or choosing to fight are an expressive part of your emotions that NLP experts may use to gather more information about your past.

AVOID ISOLATION

Try as much as possible to ensure that you do not allow a manipulative person to isolate you. When you are isolated, you are weak and vulnerable. Most manipulative people gain control during moments of weakness, such as isolation.

Conclusion

There has been lots of discussion about dark psychology, how and in which situations it is practiced most commonly and what the factors hidden behind it are. This is also considered to be a dark side of human nature, which is seldom exposed. Every human being, no matter how nice and positive they are, are always going to be evil in someone else's eyes. For the person whom you made suffer, you are evil, even if you deny it. Every person must evaluate him or herself and see if any of the hazardous or negative elements are found in them. You have to keep fighting your dark side so that it does not take control over you completely. Once you know to keep off that side, you will be able to identify it in others as well and can prevent yourself from falling prey to it. One must be aware of its indications and related signs so that people who have the qualities of dark psychology can be avoided. If you have fallen prey to dark psychology, then there is a chance for you to regain normality by assessing and evaluating yourself or by seeking medical advice.

Remember that deception is not always practiced on other people. We can often self-deceive to preserve our self-esteem. Telling ourselves that we can achieve certain goals when all the evidence points to the fact that we can't, is a healthy form of deception, but self-deception can lead to serious delusions.

Whatever happens in the novice stages of your path to becoming a master of manipulation and persuasion, you must remember your end goal. Ask yourself in the beginning why you want to do this and keep coming back to that when it gets hard. Never give up; you are to master these skills.

I hope that through this book, you have realized that brainwashing, manipulation, and persuasion depends greatly on an authoritative command of words. You might be able to list twenty manipulation techniques from memory; you may be able to get someone with little psychic resistance to go with your ideas.

You may have gotten to the end of the book — and you may have all the knowledge necessary to manipulate people — but you are just beginning when it comes to putting this all into practice.

Also, remember manipulation is classified into positive and negative (Egocentric and Malicious). The study shows how toavoid negative manipulators and try as hard as possible to stay in your lane. Work on the positive aspect of manipulation to help yourself and help others — best of luck!

www.ingramcontent.com/pod-product-compliance
Lightning Source LLC
Chambersburg PA
CBHW060306030426
42336CB00011B/958